Money
and
American
Society

By The Same Author

THE TOLERANT POPULISTS: KANSAS POPULISM AND
NATIVISM (1963)

CREATIVE HISTORY: AN INTRODUCTION TO
HISTORICAL STUDY (1967)

THE MONEY QUESTION DURING RECONSTRUCTION
(1967)

Walter T. K. Nugent

Money
and
American
Society

1865-1880

[FP] The Free Press, *New York*
Collier-Macmillan Limited, *London*

To Kack, again

ACKNOWLEDGMENTS

I am deeply grateful to many friends who helped, knowingly or unknowingly, in the writing of this book. I hope my use of their generously given insights or suggestions will not disappoint them totally. Special thanks must go to Allen Weinstein, who kindly shared with me some of the findings of his own study of the Republican party and the silver question; to J. R. Hollingsworth, for intriguing discussions of the interest-group approach; and to Walter Johnson, James T. Patterson, Martin Ridge, and Bernard Weisberger, for critical readings which saved me from myself at innumerable points. I am grateful for support and encouragement of many kinds from Daniel J. Boorstin, Robert F. Byrnes, Martin B. Duberman, Charlotte Erickson, Robert H. Ferrell, Arthur S. Link, Albert U. Romasco, Mr. and Mrs. V. L. Seyd, David E. Smith, Leo F. Solt, Robert M. Thornton, and C. Vann Woodward; and to Congressman William G.

Bray and the Hon. Ralph R. Roberts, Clerk of the U. S. House of Representatives, who kindly secured me access to House papers in the U. S. Archives. Others whom I have not named I thank also.

Among the many librarians and archivists who have been most courteous and helpful, I must mention particularly the staffs of the British Museum, the Institute of Historical Research in London, and the Archives of the United States.

I enjoyed grants, especially for travel, from Kansas State University and later from the Indiana University Graduate School. Finally, to the John Simon Guggenheim Memorial Foundation for a Fellowship, and to the Indiana University Foundation and Chancellor Herman B. Wells, go my thanks for their very generous support.

WALTER T. K. NUGENT

Contents

[ix]

Part II: Groups and Rhetoric in the Tranquility Period, 1865-1873   21

Part III: Narratives, 1865-1873: The Spread of the Gold Standard and the Rhetoric of Harmony   65

Part IV: Groups and Rhetoric in the Period of Stress, 1873-1879   173

Part V: Narratives, 1873-1879: The Return of Silver and the Rhetorics of Social Combat

Part VI: Postscript   261

Abbreviations

NA LB	National Archives, Washington, Legislative Branch
NA RG 56	National Archives, Washington, Diplomatic, Legal, and Fiscal Branch, Record Group 56 (Office of the Secretary of the Treasury)
NA RG 104	National Archives, Washington, Diplomatic, Legal, and Fiscal Branch, Record Group 104 (Philadelphia Mint)
GCM	General Correspondence of the Mint
to ST	Letters to the Secretary of the Treasury
HED	House Executive Document
HMD	House Miscellaneous Document
SED	Senate Executive Document
SMD	Senate Miscellaneous Document

Sessions of the United States Congress are abbreviated thus: e.g., 43:2 = Second Session of the Forty-third Congress.

International Chronology

	U.S.A.	Great Britain	France	Germany
1865	April: end of Civil War	Death of Palmerstone	Latin Union Treaty, Dec.	
1866	McCulloch starts contraction policy; metric bill, spring	Metric agitation; Overend, Gurney Panic		Norddeutsche Bund formed
1867	Sen. Sherman formulates gold standard bill	Second Reform Bill	Paris Universal Exposition; International Monetary Conference, June; Silver, long higher, falls below 1:15½	Adolph Soetbeer announces start of silver price decline
1868	Gold bill tabled; Contraction ends	Gladstone P.M. Royal Monetary Commission	Enquete Monétaire	Handelstag supports gold; metric act
1869	Public Credit Act in March; Coinage bill, to drop silver dollar, introduced, December	"Gold Coinage Controversy"	Enquete Monétaire	
1870	Currency Act, and Funding Act, July	Coinage Act of 1870	End of Second Empire; war with Germany; specie payments suspended; report to Enquete	Franco-Prussian War

	U.S.A.	Great Britain	France	Germany
1871	Coinage bill in Senate		Paris Commune; Third Republic begins; Germany exacts gold indemnity	German Empire founded; first gold coinage act
1872	Coinage bill in House		Indemnity paid; Thiers denounces Cobden-Chevalier Treaty	Gold standard act; financial panic
1873	"Crime of '73"; Jay Cooke failure; panic; Comstock silver strike			
1874	"Inflation" bill; Free Banking Act	Depression starts; Indian exchanges fall	Latin Union agrees to limit or suspend silver coinage	
1875	Specie Resumption Act, January			Banks of Issue Act
1876	Monetary Commission; Kelley and Bland free-silver bills introduced	Silver at low point; talk of "imperial bimetallism"	suspension of five-franc silver coinage	Delbrück dismissed; silver sales suspended
1877	Great Strike, July		Suspension renewed	
1878	Bland-Allison Act		International Monetary Conference, Paris, August	Tariff protection resumed
1879	Specie payments resumed; depression over	Depression ends	Depression ends	Depression ends

PART ONE

Scaffolding

Monetary symbolism is the "simple," the "god-term,"
in terms of which all this great complexity attains a
unity transcending distinctions of climate, class, nation, cultural traditions, etc.

KENNETH BURKE, *A Grammar of Motives*

1

THE MONEY QUESTION

AS A

SOCIAL AND MORAL EVENT

The subject of this book is the response of groups in American society to changing social conditions in the years immediately following the Civil War. However we define the term "group," and I mean by it something more than just economic interest groups, we cannot argue with the assertion that groups in American society changed their attitudes toward public questions and toward each other during the fifteen postwar years. Most importantly, they changed in their views of what American society ought to be like, then and in the future. The changes made American society in 1880 begin to resemble clearly the industrial society that was taking shape as the society of the future, while the society of 1865 entertained views reflecting the more bucolic past.

In order to sketch these group changes in as black-and-white a form as possible, I will relate them here to a question of public policy that was also an economic issue, and a moral issue. This was, in contemporary language, the "money question." While the money question, on the level of legislative or administrative policy, was a generic term—it included the problems of how to resume specie payments, stabilize the greenback currency, put the Civil War floating debt on a funded basis, and keep a lid on silver coinage—it amounted fundamentally to the question of what the proper standard of money ought to be. For various reasons, to be described, this was very close to saying what the proper moral standard ought to be.

To delineate group attitudes, self-images, and coalitions, I could have chosen some problem other than money as a key. Race attitudes and Reconstruction in the South was a possibility. But these problems inflamed Americans only briefly; within three years after Appomattox there was not much argument about them (though most people today would agree that there should have been). Tariff policy was another possibility, since the tariff, along with money, was one of the hardy perennials of late nineteenth-century political argumentation. But the tariff, although it would be a superb device for exploring the intricacies of economic groups, never carried the moral overtones and ideological superstructure that the money question did. The money question, moreover, was a major preoccupation of the public and policy-makers not only during the "Reconstruction" period, or a little longer (1865–1879), but it was also the battleground upon which was fought the critical group conflict of the 1890's, which has sometimes been called the last battle of agrarian America (though William Jennings Bryan thought 1896 was the first battle).

This, then, is a social-intellectual history of the money question during the first of its two late nineteenth-century phases, the late sixties and the seventies. I am not going to deal with legislation or finance except as they demonstrate group attitudes and group interaction—there are very good histories, some very recent, of the money question as a political-economic or social-political problem (especially Robert P. Sharkey's *Money, Class, and Party* and Irwin Unger's *The Greenback Era*.)[1] There is no point duplicating these excellent efforts. Inevitably this book will overlap with them at a few points, but its focus is different. Because I am interested in group self-images as the money question brought them into the open, I will discuss at considerable length the postures of various kinds of groups, the ways in which they expressed their postures verbally and in print, and how a group position affected national policy. This is a book about the governing influences on those who governed.

Another point of difference between this book and the other literature on the money question is the present study's emphasis on the international context. Not only were there many parallels between the American money question and monetary developments in Europe but also the actual course of political, economic, and ideological events in America intertwined at many points with events in Europe. America did not exist in a vacuum, and we can understand what happened in the United States much more clearly if we take some account of what happened elsewhere.

The work of other writers, especially Unger and Sharkey, published in the past few years, is fascinating in itself—excellent analytical history of American monetary policy, using an interest-group approach. But there are some questions they did not focus upon directly: What were the international parallels and connections? What deep changes took place in the self-images—the moral wish-patterns, so to speak—of important groups? How did it happen, as I will contend, that the first part of the period, until about 1873, was relatively tranquil and marked by intergroup harmony, while the succeeding years were a time of stress, conflict, and fragmentation? What values, in the sense of convictions about what American society ought to look like in the future, did Americans share, and what values did they not share? How finally, did the values and interests of groups converge to shape public policy on the money question—and why was the whole enrapturement of Americans with the money question a blunder? For a blunder it was, so it seems to me; so much so that I have been tempted to call this book something like "Futility and Filthy Lucre, a Failure in the West."

But that is getting into the story. Suffice it to say that the changes in American society in the post-Civil War years were changes that reverberated through the rest of the nineteenth century and even down to our own day. The seventies were a watershed of the future, and the money question reveals why.

2

A SKETCH OF

THE

ECONOMIC BACKGROUND

The American Civil War, among its many effects, played hob with cherished economic and financial practices. It not only upset the business cycle by producing a galloping inflation but also it required such extraordinary expenses and strained the economy so greatly, that it forced rearrangements in the very economic and financial machinery itself. Tradition bent to the breaking point in four respects especially: the monetary standard, the currency in circulation, the national debt, and the banking system.

The money standard did not change legally during the Civil War, but it drifted dismayingly far from the currency that was in day-to-day use. The United States was one of several countries (France was another) that was legally on a bimetallic monetary standard; that is, she gave equal legal status to both gold and silver, and had done so since 1792. Silver dollars and gold dollars

[6]

both embodied "the standard and unit of money," and they had equal standing as legal tenders in the payment of any debts. As was customary in countries with bimetallic standards, the law directed the Mint as to how much gold should go into a gold dollar (25.8 grains 900 fine—i.e., nine-tenths pure), and how much silver should go into a silver dollar (412½ grains 900 fine). The arithmetic ratio between gold and silver thus came to just about one to sixteen; one grain of gold was worth about sixteen grains of silver at the Mint. The ratio varied from country to country; in France it was one to fifteen-and-a-half. But whatever the ratio, it was supposed to keep the two monetary metals circulating concurrently and in some kind of rough balance with each other. It had not worked out that way in America for a long time. During the Jackson Administration, when the one-to-sixteen ratio was written willy-nilly into law, silver was just scarce enough that the price of it was a little higher than that. One grain of gold would not buy sixteen grains of silver. Silver, in other words, was slightly undervalued, gold slightly overvalued.

Gold and silver were commodities as well as monetary metals; mints were not their only consumers, and if a holder of silver could sell it commercially for more than he could get at the Mint, he would sell it somewhere else than the Mint. If someone held a considerable number of silver dollars, he could turn a profit by melting down the silver dollars and selling them on the open market in exchange for gold or other currency; his gold dollars would be just as good legally as his silver ones had been, but he would have more of them. Because of this dual nature of gold and silver as commodities as well as monetary metals, because they could be sold to domestic or foreign private buyers or to foreign mints that had a lower coinage ratio than one to sixteen, silver dollars would disappear from circulation and silver would cease to be brought to the U.S. Mint for coinage if the mint ratio gave silver less value than it had in the open market. Under the one-to-sixteen ratio, this was exactly the case. Silver dollars rather quickly disappeared after the one-to-sixteen ratio became law in the 1830's, and when great heaps of gold came into world markets after the Californian and Australian discoveries of the late 1840's and early fifties, silver was more undervalued and farther from the one-to-sixteen ratio than ever. In the fifties, it was even more valuable than indicated in the French ratio of one to fifteen-and-a-half, and it began disappearing in Europe as well as America.

The upshot of all this was that a whole generation of Americans grew up between the 1830's and the Civil War scarcely realizing that silver dollars existed. What is even more important, they quite forgot that silver was a standard monetary metal. This was understandable, since silver dollars were almost never seen. It was even more understandable for two more reasons. A coinage law of 1853 kept some silver in the coinage system by using it for "minor coins," such as halves, quarters, and dimes, through the simple expedient of debasing it. The silver content of these coins was sufficiently beneath the appropriate fraction of 412½ grains that the coins were not worth melting down. But this meant that such experience as Americans had with silver coins was with debased, nonstandard ones.

The other reason which helped Americans forget that silver was a monetary standard was the coinage practice of America's major partner in foreign trade, Great Britain. Britain was one of the very few countries in the world which was gold monometallist —her monetary standard consisted solely of gold, her monetary unit the gold pound sterling, or "sovereign." But Britain was the leading trading, financial, and manufacturing country in the world. If people, including Americans, bought British goods or services, they paid in gold. Many Britons attributed their country's material preeminence to the gold standard that it had had since 1816, and many Americans believed them. In any case, American foreign trade and finance was virtually on the gold standard.

For all of these reasons, Americans in 1860 had almost completely forgotten about silver as a monetary standard. They firmly, if innocently, believed that the United States was legally on the gold standard. Gold they saw and used; silver they did not.

Gold dollars, of course, were not the only currency circulating before the Civil War. Paper dollars, in the form of bank notes, were used very widely. But the paper was never considered to be a money in its own right, but only a convenient substitute for "real money," i.e., gold. It was a test of the solvency of a bank, and of the United States Treasury, to be able to take paper currency to a bank or the Treasury and have it exchanged for gold dollars, no questions asked, on demand. This practice was called "specie payments." It was the rule in the United States, in Britain, and in other "enlightened" countries.

The first great casualty that the Civil War brought to the monetary system of the United States was its forcing a suspension of specie payments. Demands on the banks from public and private sources were so heavy and sudden that there was simply not enough gold to meet them in 1861. Specie payments were gone for the duration, and perhaps longer. But no one seriously doubted that postwar normality, whenever it came, would include the resumption of specie payments on the single standard of gold.

The other three ways in which the Civil War forced a departure from traditional arrangements were products of the shortage of funds that faced the Lincoln Administration as it undertook to pacify the South. Money had to come from somewhere. Congress levied new taxes, but some currency had to exist in which to pay them. Congress authorized bond sales, but something had to exist with which people could buy them. Reluctantly, and as a temporary wartime expedient only, Congress authorized the Treasury to issue paper currency that did not have a specie backing. This currency, the famous "greenbacks," had full legal tender powers and could buy a government bond or pay a tax (except customs duties). The greenbacks were a *sine qua non* of victory. But, so most people believed, they were like a mud-clogged road to a troop convoy: a necessary evil, to be drained of water at the first peacetime opportunity. During the later stages of the War, the greenbacks inflated so badly that upwards of three greenback dollars had to be plunked down to buy one dollar in gold. Such monetary abundance worked to the benefit of certain people, such as borrowers, and of course it had been created by the biggest borrower of all, the government. But others, such as foreign traders who had to pay British and other creditors in gold just as they always had, prayed for deliverance from the greenbacks and the "gold premium," the extra dollars and cents the inflated greenbacks cost them to buy a gold dollar.

One thing that greenbacks could buy very cheaply indeed were the interest-bearing bonds issued by the government to raise cash for the war effort. The laws enabling the Treasury to sell these bonds were numerous, and several of them were vague about whether the principal, or the interest, or both, were ultimately to be paid in "lawful money" (the greenbacks or other paper) or in gold. But many buyers were given to understand by the government's bond-selling agent, Jay Cooke & Co., that the government would pay in gold. By the close of the Civil War, the interest-bearing debt had reached the colossal total of more than two billion dollars. Many of the bonds would begin to come due within five years. The government was faced with the distinct possibility that it would be unable to meet these obligations, unless the debt was refunded into long-term issues. In order to induce bondholders to exchange the new bonds for the old, however, the government was going to have to promise its creditors to pay them, principal and interest, in gold, rather than in possibly less valuable paper currency. This was fine for bondholders, but not so fine for others. But the government had no alternative.

The Civil War emergency engendered one other change in the banking and currency system, this one permanent: federally chartered national banks. The national banks were a clever way of alleviating two aspects of the financial emergency of the War. First, they provided the government with an additional market for its bonds, since one of the conditions for obtaining a charter was that the banking corporation had to deposit part of its capital, in gold, with the Treasury in return for bonds. Second, the banks were empowered to issue currency, called national bank notes, on the security of their bonds. This "national currency," together with the government's own paper currency, the greenbacks, quickly became the main circulating medium of the country during and after the War. The government did what it could to make national banking attractive and thus enhance the banks' bond-buying and currency-issuing purposes. It placed a tax of ten per cent on the notes of state and private banks, virtually taxing them out of existence in favor of national bank notes. It also issued the bulk of the available charters and thus distributed the bulk of the bank-note currency—Congress had put a firm upper limit on the total amount—to the Northeast. This was fine for that section, but not so fine for others. But the government's banking policy, like its funding policy, seemed to allow no alternatives, especially during the War emergency.

In four ways, then, the Civil War seriously modified the monetary system of the country. Appomattox ended the armed conflict, but it left the government with a set of financial conundrums: how to stabilize the bank note currency, especially to make all sections and groups happy? How to reduce the disparity between a greenback dollar and a gold dollar? How to refund the bonds equitably? And above all, how to resume specie payments?

Within a very few years, another question faced policy-makers, and it outlasted all the others: how to prevent silver from pushing gold out of circulation?

These problems were the raw stuff of the money question in the fifteen years that followed the Civil War in the United States. Every one of them was "solved" during that period by some combination of legislation and administrative action. The national banks and their note issues were stabilized in the Currency Act of July, 1870, and the Specie Resumption Act of January, 1875. The gold premium on greenbacks jerked and slid downward through the whole period until it finally disappeared in the closing days of 1878; but government policy was only one factor among several in bringing this about. As for the bonds, Congress declared in the Public Credit Act of March, 1869, that the bonds were payable, principal and interest, in coin (and not greenbacks) unless they specifically stated otherwise; then in the Funding Act of July, 1870, Congress gave the Treasury the authority to replace the floating short-term high-interest bonds with funded longer-term lower-interest ones. The resumption of specie payments proved very elusive, but Congress finally declared in the Specie Resumption Act of 1875 that resumption should occur four years later, and left it to the Treasury to work out a method. When the long-time undervaluation of silver ended, and silver began to threaten to push gold out of circulation, Congress simply discontinued the silver dollar and thus got rid of silver as a standard, in the Coinage Act of 1873. This assured that specie resumption, whenever it came, and the repayment of the bonds, would take place on the gold standard.

All of this says nothing about the ways in which the financial problems left by the Civil War were solved, or about how satisfactory the solutions were. It states only the raw problems and the raw results in a very simple way. But every one of these problems and every one of the results depended on the actions of people. The agreements and disagreements of these people, as individuals or as bearers of ideas or as representatives of sectional, economic, partisan, or national interests, were profound and extremely complicated. Monetary policy was not discussable or enforceable without some people being pleased, others distressed, some helped, and still others hurt. Banks and bonds may seem dull, gold and greenbacks may seem dead, and bimetallism versus monometallism may seem positively desiccated. For the post-Civil War years, however, they were smoky battlegrounds of social conflict, and for the present day, therefore, they are excellent indices of social change and social tension.

Several aspects of the American money question intertwined closely with events and policies that developed in other countries. The chief reason for this, to mention no others yet, is because the major nations of the world all looked upon gold and silver as the ultimate form of money, and all used one or both of those metals as monetary standards. Gold and silver, however, either in the form of bullion (refined metal) or specie (coined gold or silver), knew no national boundaries. Because they were commodities as well as money, they were saleable in more than one country. Paper money, such as the greenbacks, were literally worth no more than the paper they were printed on, *except* in the country that issued them, because the government of that country said they were worth something and backed up its word with the force of law. There could be as few or as many paper notes as their creator desired. With gold and silver, of course, it was decidedly otherwise; there was only so much of it available in the world at any given time. What one nation did would affect others, particularly those who attempted to maintain a bimetallic standard of gold and silver, with the two metals at some official ratio or other. In 1865, the United States and France were both officially on bimetallic standards, Britain's standard was gold alone, and the yet-to-be-united Germanies were on the single standard of silver. Ten years later, Germany and the United States had gone over to gold monometallism, and France was hanging on to silver by the sheerest of legal threads. The intervening decade had brought what was in fact the first great swing toward a worldwide gold standard. It was a story not without conflicts and sequels.

One more piece of background may be useful. The curve of economic activity fluctuated almost spastically from 1865 to 1880, and the fluctuations in each of the major countries paralleled each other closely. Leaving aside some "local" disturbances, one can generalize that the years before 1873 were relatively prosperous, and the years from 1873 to 1879 relatively depressed. There was a postwar recession in the United States in 1866–67, a sharp but short depression in Britain in 1866–67 following the failure of the financial house of Overend, Gurney; a brief recession in Germany in 1867 following the Seven Weeks' War with Austria; and panic and depression in France at the time of the Franco-Prussian War in 1870–71. But these were, broadly speaking, exceptions to the rule. The early seventies, especially, were rosy years, marked by a surge of railroad building and capital investment in the major countries as well as in their economic dependencies such as British India. In 1873–74 all this changed drastically. Panics in Germany, Austria, and the United States heralded depressions that lasted until almost the end of the decade; the British economy plummeted gloomily downward from late 1873 and stayed there until late 1879; France felt the strain least, but even she was undeniably depressed in 1877 and 1878. The sun began to shine again everywhere in 1879. But the worldwide depression, meanwhile, had triggered policy revisions and group conflicts that had not been imagined before the depression began.

3

DEFINING "GROUP,"

"RHETORIC,"

"IDEOLOGY," AND "INTEREST"

The terms *group, rhetoric, ideology,* and *interest* will reappear frequently in the following pages. They will be employed in particular ways and hence require definition.

A group, in its simplest sense, is a number of people, more than one person but less than all, who share some characteristic that other people do not share. The characteristic may be physical (height, race, location, etc.) or social (occupation, belief, participation in an event, etc.). Membership in a group may be voluntary or it may not: a person chooses whether to join such groups as vegetarians, golfers, or Republicans, but his membership in the blue-eyed or Negro or forty-three-year-old groups is beyond his control. Membership in a group may or may not be conscious: a person may be paranoid or highly educated or upper middle class without realizing it, though his membership in one of those groups may be perfectly apparent to an observer. Even

[14]

if the person knows such groups exist, he may be oblivious to his own possession of the indices that place him in them. The person's image of himself as a member of society may have distortions or blind spots.

Any kind of group membership can interest a sociologist, because unconscious group memberships may be just as significant in the structure of society as conscious ones. To a political scientist, however, unconscious group memberships will probably not be as important as conscious ones, particularly conscious voluntary ones, because a person unaware of his own membership in a group will not be taking political action in that group's behalf. In other words, a group can conceivably play a social role without being aware of itself, but it cannot easily play a political role without knowing who it is and what it wants. Consequently, the definition of a group given above (a collection of people who have some characteristic others do not have) may be true, but it is not politically operational. An operational definition would state that the collection of people, to qualify as a group, must seek power in order to influence public policy in the direction of something they want or believe in.[1]

The discussion in the present book will use *group* in a sense somewhere between the sociological and the political-scientific. My use of *group* partakes of the sociological because some of the groups involved in the story were only limitedly conscious of themselves as groups, at least a large part of the time. Gold monometallists, for example, were an identifiable group, but did not think of themselves as such, and certainly never came close to forming an organized association. Agrarians, to cite a quite different kind of example, had very little group consciousness before 1873 or 1874, and likewise were not united in a large power-seeking organization, except the Grange, which by no means included all agrarians. But after 1873 or 1874, agrarians developed a very intense group consciousness and attempted vigorously to shape policy. But both of these groups, as well as some others, lacked self-consciousness (to say nothing of formal organization) sufficiently to disqualify them from a normal political-scientific definition of group and allow them to be classified as sociological.

Nevertheless, since I will isolate, describe, and relate every one of the groups that appear below according to their position on the money question, which in its concrete sense was a matter of public policy, my use of group shares a great deal with the operational political-scientific definition. The money question obviously comprised a set of public laws and administrative decisions, but it also had the quality of evoking moral pronouncements and utopian value-judgments from people. It triggered them into making known what they thought the future of America ought to be like. Some groups did no more than attitudinize, while others were so well organized that chairmen of congressional committees rewrote legislation to satisfy them. But both types, and those in between, were groups as I intend to use the term.

The possible groupings within American society in the late nineteenth century are theoretically numberless. Those used here all meet three criteria: they are few and large enough to afford broad comparisons of large numbers of people, without gross overgeneralizing on the one hand, or getting lost in an atomistic jungle on the other. They are represented by verbal (nonquantitative) sources still extant. They were those who had something to say about money or in some way shaped monetary policy.

These criteria exclude certain kinds of groups. The first criterion forbids looking through a microscope at successively smaller but increasingly more homogeneous groups: from economic groups in general, to manufacturers, to woolen manufacturers, to woolen manufacturers with copious water power, *ad infinitum*. The second criterion puts aside the consideration of certain important types of social groupings, such as the analysis of society according to structures of class or status, since these would require data and methods we do not now have; or according to social-psychological syndromes, since these would demand classifications based on recondite and shifting clinical categories. The third criterion excludes groups that are identifiable in the historical sources and are often important in political or social history, such as ethnicity or religious affiliation, but which did not divide people very clearly on the money question.

The criteria do retain, however, five major types of groups

—ideological, economic, sectional, political, and national—each type including several groups. Ideological groups included those who believed that gold should be the sole monetary standard (gold monometallists), those who believed silver should be the sole monetary standard (silver monometallists), those who advocated the use of both metals, a double standard (bimetallists), and those who advocated paper money not convertible into specie (the American greenbackers). Economic groups included farmers, laborites, bankers, commercial people, transporters, and manufacturers. Sectional groups were Northeastern, Southern, Midwestern, and Far Western. Political groups were chiefly Republicans or Democrats. National groups mean simply the American, British, French, and German popular or policy positions on the money question.

These groups, of course, overlapped. The same man could be an American Northeastern Republican gold-monometallist merchant. But the next man could be four of these five things but something very different in the fifth category. The ways in which the groups overlapped, coalesced, and divided on the money question suggest a great deal about why people acted and thought as they did.

The groups were the ways in which society divided; the boundaries of groups were the fissures in society. But America was hardly made up solely of groups and divisive forces, even on the money question. Many things bound society together. Some of these were obvious and concrete, such as political unity, a national economy, a common language. American and Western Europe were also bound together by such tangibles as common levels of technology, business cycles, and bullion supplies. Another force, however, bound groups together within the United States, and also bound together America and Western Europe. This force was *rhetoric*.

Rhetoric has many definitions. As it will be used here, it means a collection of terms and ideas that cut across group lines and served to represent the common elements in the ideologies and rationalized interests of many groups. For a group, rhetoric was something the group had in common with others; rhetoric was the general theme, the group position a variation on it. For an individual, rhetoric was a set of terms and ideas, a verbal currency, which served to express and communicate his internal thought-patterns or world-views about society. It created for a person a set of fixed and related pegs, assuring him who he was, making his society comprehensible, telling him where he fit into it, showing him where he and his society were heading. Rhetoric connected a man's internal concerns with public issues, and made it possible for him and his society to understand and communicate with each other. Rhetoric was more than ideology; gold monometallism and greenbackism, for example, came to almost polar conclusions on policy, but both of these ideologies shared contemporary rhetorical elements such as belief in natural laws, the desirability of social harmony, and certain liberal-utilitarian values.

During the 1867–1873 period, rhetoric performed this centripetal function very well. It was an agent of social cohesion, and at the same time the product of such cohesion. The more it was believed, the more it was believable. From 1873 onward, however, it served these functions less and less well. Under the conditions of social and economic stress that prevailed during the depression years of the seventies, the rhetorical terms and ideas that were formerly the common property of a number of groups became increasingly appropriated by particular groups to serve their several ends. Rhetoric proved too fragile to survive strong social stress; it fragmented; and it then became virtually indistinguishable from the ideological aims and wish-systems of separate groups.

With the fragmenting of rhetoric and the ending of the relative tranquillity of the pre-1873 period, the money question became a matter which American society could neither solve nor ignore. This change in the function of rhetoric, a change which upset the dynamic equilibrium of the value systems of groups, was one of the major changes in American society between the Civil War and 1880—or, for that matter, for the rest of the nineteenth century and beyond. But that is better described later.

Because of rhetoric and because of the group structure involved with it, the money question was something at once shared and not shared, agreed and disagreed about, by the members of society. This ambivalence prevailed in several conspicuous ways, and the degrees and ways of sharing and not sharing formed a complex and shifting configuration of interests and beliefs.

A final note. "Interest groups" have often been interpreted, especially by American historians, to mean economic interest groups. Here, however, ideological and economic groups will have equal status. It remains to be proved that economic interests are primary in human actions, even actions like the formulation of public policy on money. As the foregoing definition of group implies, this book is not going to be an economic interpretation. One of the things it will reveal, in fact, is that group or personal ideologies far more often coincided with economic interest than contradicted it. The implied accusation in economic interpretation, that actions flow from economic interest rather than from some "nobler" motive, and would somehow be purer if they followed the latter, is not borne out. This is only logical: There is no more reason, *a priori*, to assume that ideology and economic interest should conflict than to assume that they should match. And match, it seems, they did, at least on the money question in trans-Atlantic society as the Late Victorian Age began.

If the sources of human motivation in history are ever discovered and systematized, I should suspect that their relative importance will be found to have shifted in time as much as the very issues and actions that manifest them. There is one very plausible reason for this. The distinction often made between ideology and economic interest may be a distinction without much of a difference. Could it be that the identifications a man makes for himself with various groups simply represent different channellings of his loyalty? Whatever the loyalty, whether to pocketbook, party, section, nation, ideas, or even rhetoric, perhaps the psychological mechanisms of self-identification are roughly the same. Assuming an antinomy between ideology and economic interest not only assumes historical and psychological principles that are unproven, but it must rest on some kind of metaphysics that separates the ideal from the material and endows only the latter with reality. Despite the comfortableness of such an antinomy, it is probably false. In the case of the money question the distinction is particularly muddy. Ideology itself became a kind of interest, and interests, whether economic, political, sectional, or national, frequently evoked the loyalty usually attributed to ideology.

The mechanisms by which people identified themselves into ideological, economic, or other kinds of groups are unclear. The ways by which rhetoric united people across group lines are unclear too. But unite them it did. In fact the very rhetoric itself became an object of loyalty, especially as the period drew to a close and rhetoric became less and less distinguishable from particular group viewpoints. By that time, rhetoric no longer bound, but separated, groups; it became part of, at most a function of, competing group positions. The servant became master.

PART TWO

Groups and Rhetoric

in the

Tranquility Period

1865–1873

What is known as Utilitarianism, or Philosophical Radicalism, can be defined as nothing but an attempt to apply the principles of Newton to the affairs of politics and of morals.

ELIE HALÉVY, *The Growth of Philosophic Radicalism*

4

THINGS SHARED:

RHETORIC

Anyone reconnoitering through the historical sources on the money question in the 1860's and seventies will find certain terms and ideas reappearing almost ubiquitously. Civilization, law, a set of economic principles, the belief that society was harmonious, and that producers were good people—such were the standard impedimenta of monetary pundits of all persuasions. Although this rhetoric was defined and employed somewhat differently by different groups, it provided a common stratum of meaning and thus linked the groups together. Or so it did, at any rate, until after 1873.

In 1865–66, whether one stood in Paris, London, New York, or San Francisco, or in Brisbane, Simla, or Cape Town, the term *civilization* immediately suggested "the fine things we have done in this enlightened nineteenth century." *Science* and *reason* were civilization's causes and noblest effects. *Progress* was its proof. In the effusions of statesmen and writers of the age, one of these terms seldom appeared without one or more of the others.

The close connection between money and the catchwords of civilization, progress, science, and reason was felt most strongly by the large majority that believed that real money had to exist in the form of gold and silver. Monometallists and bimetallists both made the connection. Both groups recalled, they felt with crushing effect, that Isaac Newton had been Master of the Royal Mint; what greater exponent of science than he? Louis Wolowski, the leader of the bimetallic theorists in France, considered the monetary opinions of the late-medieval astronomers Nicholas Oresme and Copernicus useful documentation for his own views, not least because as astronomers they had pioneered in a field whose methods and results seemed impregnably precise and eternal. In a similar vein, Wolowski once stated his confident belief that the Cartesian spirit of scientific skepticism was the weapon that would ultimately undo monometallism.

Good monometallists, in their turn, identified science and progress with gold standard. One of their favorite arguments was that silver was too bulky and inconvenient for the massive transactions of modern civilized peoples; civilization and progress had left silver behind. Michel Chevalier, the leading French monometallic theorist, damned the practice of charging a fee for coining gold as a holdover from monarchical despotism, and the abolishing of such fees as a plain duty of modern liberalism.[1]

Even nonbullionists connected civilization with money, and tied to it science, reason, and progress. But they did these things differently from the bullionists. Probably the outstanding exponent of permanent inconvertible paper money in any of the major countries was the American political economist, Henry C. Carey. Carey and his followers saw civilization and progress as the ultimate ends of economic activity. Everyday financial policy was a means to a much greater end: the harmonious association of mankind in society. That was civilization, and it was attainable by rational means. The Careyites' advocacy of paper money prevented them from accepting the civilization-progress-science-reason rhetoric in quite the same way that bullionists did, but these same terms were used and responded to by both groups. Though the monometallists' claims to these terms were the loudest, others appropriated them too. Nobody openly yearned for barbarism.

Law was another common rhetorical peg, often accompanied by *order, nature, harmony,* and *equilibrium.* Like science, law was supposed to be rationally discoverable, immutable, and (so many people thought) even of divine origin. Nobody could doubt the law of gravity; nobody should doubt "the laws of political economy." The sixties and seventies often affirmed their faith in "natural law," and law to them was not evolutionary, but mechanistic, like Newton's physical universe.

Belief in law and its associated terms, like belief in civilization, was shared by monometallists and bimetallists on both sides of the Atlantic. Louis Wolowski considered bimetallism the surest route to the unfettered operation of natural economic laws, and he was fond of terms and phrases such as "equilibrium," "balance," "the nature of things." American monometallists believed that "the laws of finance . . . like those of other sciences, are universal and invariable in their operation," and that, moreover, "the economical laws of human nature (i.e., the principles of Political Economy), through their general effects upon the well-being of society, manifest the contrivance, the wisdom and beneficence, of the Deity, just as clearly as do the marvellous arrangements of the material universe."

In America, Amasa Walker entitled his treatise on political economy *The Science of Wealth,* and in Britain in 1872 Walter Bagehot's *Physics and Politics* appeared, with the subtitle, "Thoughts on the application of the principles of 'natural selection' and 'inheritance' to political society." At the same time, at quite the opposite pole of monetary thought. Henry C. Carey published *The Unity of Law; as Exhibited in the Relations of Physical, Social, Mental and Moral Science.* As Edward Kirkland has made clear in a remarkable essay, American leaders of the day as different as Charles Francis Adams, Jr., Edwin Godkin, and Andrew Carnegie, assumed the existence of overarching natural laws of business and social operations. Equilibrium and balance in monetary exchange was an element in the rhetorical air, part of the natural order, for these men and many others in America and in Europe.

In many areas, but especially money and political economy, late nineteenth-century man seldom found it possible to escape the idea that the universe consisted of an intricate arrangement of balance scales. To add force or mass, physical or economic, on one side of the scales meant to take it away from the other. This was the scheme of Newtonian mechanics and of classical economics, part and parcel of the mechanistic world-view that gripped many men in that age and touched virtually everyone to some degree. It contrasts profoundly with today's ideas of an expanding universe and the economics of growth. In the light of that contrast, it is all the more surprising that the late nineteenth century accomplished so much despite such confining views. Yet the notions of "gold up, prices down," or "One man's loss is another man's gain," seemed as inescapable as the laws of motion. The "law of supply and demand," in a very stark form, was the most tenaciously held economic axiom of the time.

Logically this belief in equilibrium does not square very well with the equally common belief in "progress," but the potentially dismal connotations of the equilibrium notion were squelched by the frequent coupling of it with the term "harmony." Amasa Walker and many other economic thinkers of the time admired Frédéric Bastiat's *Harmonies Economiques;* in their opinion, America was the greatest proof of Bastiat's idea that *laissez faire* was the policy key to social harmony. Nearly every monetary rhetorician, bullionist or nonbullionist, claimed that his monetary system was the one most firmly grounded in economic law, nature, and order; that it most clearly discerned the principles of economic equilibrium; that it was best equipped to achieve the social harmony that everyone desired. Anarchy was no more favored than was barbarism.[2]

Another "thing shared" by people who were allies and enemies on the policy level of the money question was a collection of economic principles. The commonest of these principles was the law of supply and demand; a man would no more disagree with that law than state publicly that the earth was flat. Lessening the supply increased the demand (and price), increasing the supply lessened the demand (and price). Gold and silver were subject to it just as much as were other commodities. As another evidence of the equilibria of nature, the law of supply and demand was, ideally, to be kept free from frictions and "artificial" (governmental) interferences.

Belief that labor was the sole source of wealth, one of Adam Smith's basic principles that was reaffirmed by Utilitarians and other nineteenth-century political economists, was also shared by groups whose policy views diverged. Their applications of the idea differed wildly. Another hoary principle on which there was slight disagreement anywhere was the defining of money not only as a medium of exchange but as a measure of wealth; wealth produced by labor had to have some yardstick, so it was thought; that yardstick was money. Closely related to this was the belief that money was also a store of wealth, a notion not stressed much by greenbackers, whose favorite money was not obviously the product of much labor. But nearly everyone agreed that money, as medium, measure, or store, had to be unvarying in value—worth the same at one time as at another—or as nearly so as possible. This notion was derived from Adam Smith and Ricardo, and those luminaries were often appealed to by all sides.

A wide spectrum of groups also believed that the quantity of the money stock mattered a great deal. Changes in the money supply would affect different economic interests in different ways, again according to an equilibrium: an increase in money would bring higher prices; reduction of the money supply would deflate prices. Through the 1867–69 period, in America and often in other Western countries, the "quantity theory of money" was accepted in a crude form both by people who wanted the quantity kept limited because they wanted to avoid any increase in fixed assets they already possessed, and by people who thought the money supply should be increased in order to reflect accurately the new wealth that they felt their labor was producing. Again a common principle, but a diverging application. I have found only one writer through the whole period who recognized that monetary inflationists and contractionists alike were "firm believers in the doctrine that the volume of the currency regulates prices, or, in other words, determines the degree of its purchasing power." That writer's insight was rare; even rarer was the fact that he thought the doctrine was "wholly untenable."[3]

Producer (and its inflectional forms) was another rhetorical term common to the age. Of the several clusters of terms and ideas described here as "things shared," it was the most provincial: only Americans used it, and even some American groups used it infrequently. But for those who did use it, it was the rhetorical device with the loosest content and the deepest resonance. This is because its users thought of "producers" as encompassing almost all of society. Producers were not just another group, but the social norm.

Producerism was simply an interpretation of society that attributed the supreme economic function to producers—not for what they produced, but because they did produce. Nonproducers, who only exchanged or "manipulated" goods or wealth already produced, were secondary and often suspect. Producerism may seem very materialistic, but it actually involved an idealism no less high than the idealisms of civilization or progress. Producerism was rhetorically resonant because although it divided people according to economic function, it was really a view of the good society morally considered.

Flabby in its economics and diverse in its roots, producerism was so common a rhetorical theme in America during the later two-thirds of the nineteenth century that its significance as a guidepost to the American mind of that time cannot be questioned. On the other hand, its usefulness, if indeed it ever had any, as a device for understanding the structure of American society, had largely disappeared by 1865. But nineteenth-century Americans thought it helped them understand themselves and their society. If, like many shibboleths, it lived too long and died too hard, it was nevertheless believable to those who embraced it. To understand those people, one must understand their belief.

Producerism has been linked most closely to farmers when it has been discussed, and understandably so. Farmers in various sections of the country tried to have it refer only to themselves, and it was not until the eighties that agrarian spokesmen fully realized its potential as a means of creating a farmer-labor coalition. Before this happened, nonfarmers sometimes took farm voices at their word and used the term "producers" to refer to farmers and planters exclusively.[4]

Yet there were many variants of it, and it must be understood that its usage was by no means restricted to farmers, or even to farmers together with workers. Knights of Labor and Populists sometimes attempted to give it such a restriction after the mid-eighties, but even then, when it was probably confined more narrowly than at any previous time, its rubbery limits not only stretched to allow farmers to constitute a sizable segment of the Knights of Labor, but to surround also many nonfarmers and nonworkers. This explains in part the presence of bankers, loan agents, railroaders and implement dealers in the Populist party.

Thus the philosophy of producerism was much more than a rhetorical glorification of agricultural production alone. Labor editorialists and speakers, for example, sometimes widened it to include anyone who did anything at all. One of them, Samuel F. Cary, included in it

> not those only who open up and cultivate farms, build cities, construct railroads, and toil in workshops, but those also, who, by intellectual labor, extract the principles of science from the great arcana of nature, and give them practical form of art and direct the hand of industry. In short, EVERY HUMAN BEING, who, by physical or intellectual labor, contributes to the substantial wealth of the nation. . . .

To the Labor Reform party leader, Alexander Campbell, producers included

> all who are employed in mining, agriculture, the mechanic arts, manufacturing, or in the distribution of the products of industry and enterprise, as well as in the useful callings and professions—in a word, all who, by the labor of the head or hand, restore to society an equivalent for what they receive from it,

and who wished to "unite with us in common effort to restore the government to its original design and primitive purity." William

Sylvis, of the National Labor Union, specifically counted manufacturers among producers. A leading agrarian journal took a similar line by identifying the "industrial classes" as including members of Granges, "Farmers' Clubs, Cheap Transportation Associations, Boards of Trade, Chambers of Commerce, Merchants' and Workingmens' Associations"—anyone desiring to "secur[e] to the cause of Labor and Enterprise their legitimate rewards."[5]

Farmers and labor spokesmen, with their wide-open definition of producerism, were not its only votaries. The curious thing is the identity of other self-styled producerites. They were groups that have normally been thought of, ever since the late seventies, as socioeconomic enemies of farmers and laborites. But before 1873, manufacturers saw themselves as producerites, with more in common with farmers and laborites than with capitalists who were "nonproducing." The statements of Henry C. Carey, the prophet of burgeoning manufacturing, closely resembled in philosophy and policy the views of the *Workingman's Advocate*, the organ of the National Labor Union, as Professors Sharkey and Unger pointed out. Andrew Carnegie, Professor Kirkland has shown, had little respect for speculators and considered producers and sellers of tangible goods, like himself, to be the honorable and virtuous men of business. Secretary of the Treasury Hugh McCulloch, a banker and even for his day a man of exceptionally rigorous monetary views, stated that increased production was "alone" the route to specie resumption. The nation's leading banking journal worried that speculation was a peculiar temptation for bankers and condemned it no less vigorously than Grangers did, "because it is a nonproductive business [and] diverts wealth from productive business." Simon Newcomb, the Harvard astronomer and mathematician whose competence in exact sciences seemed to qualify him as a political economist, and Amasa Walker, author of the *Science of Wealth* (both of them bullionists, by the way), included among "producers" practically everyone: users of capital such as farmers, merchants, manufacturers; nonusers of capital such as professionals and laborers; and lenders. Even Henry Varnum Poor, who argued the extreme gold-monometallist case perhaps more violently than any other man of the time and who thought Grangers were Communists, made a case for the superiority of national bank notes over greenbacks on the ground that the bank notes supposedly rested on the accumulated results of "production and trade."[6]

Obviously producerism could be extremely inclusive. Indeed it was far too inclusive to serve effectively as social explanation. Producerism, vague as it was, quite lacked the tough consistency that a social rhetoric had to have if it was to help create orderly and useful change. In spite of its optimism, in spite of its view of society as a happy harmony of interests, it stood in the way of progress. Even after 1873, when its inclusiveness suddenly dwindled, it still failed as rhetoric or social explanation because of its wholly undiscriminating economic vocabulary. On the money question, its conceptions of capital, labor, and money were of the crudest; its adherents generally agreed that while labor was the basis of wealth, capital was simply accumulated labor, and money, paper or metallic, was a form of capital. This was as far as it went. Since it operated on definitions no subtler than this, it was easy for the producer advocates to look upon money as a spur to production, and therefore upon those who objected to increases in the money supply as enemies of production and enterprise, millstones about the national neck. Rather more wisely than the rigorous bullionists, who in many cases believed wealth to rest in precious metals above anything else, the producerites thought of the productive process as economically and socially prior to money. But they squandered this insight. In the absence of further refinement, their argument on the policy level became little more than a plea for inflation.

Tactically as well as theoretically, this was unwise. Such vagueness worked well enough in the period of tranquillity before the latter part of 1873, when producers, whether farmers, laborites, manufacturers, or otherwise, were willing to believe that American society actually consisted of a harmony of interests. But with the crisis of late 1873 and the ensuing period of stress, the coalition began to crumble. Western farmer-labor spokesmen suddenly found they had less in common with eastern merchants and manufacturers than they had thought. Henry C. Carey still assumed the existence of farmer-labor-manufacturer solidarity when the depression became gloomiest, but by then even he placed "traders, transporters, and money-lenders" outside the pale and condemned Treasury Secretary Hugh McCulloch's policies of the previous decade for bringing about "the ruin of the producing classes."[7]

During the 1865–73 period, however, all of these rhetorical terms and ideas muted social antagonisms and assuaged social-moral concerns. When different people saw the money question differently because their group affiliations varied, these things shared modified the centrifugal forces that group variations engendered. They made possible a certain productive tension by giving people with differing interests a common language. Harmony involves communication, but so does war. It was when these terms and ideas lost all flexibility under post-1873 social and economic stress that they ceased representing thought and became merely slogans. Even then they made communication possible, but in such circumstances that the communication could only be hostile.

5

THINGS NOT SHARED:

IDEOLOGICAL GROUPS

As rhetoric united people, ideology divided them. Ideologies were supposed to say what money was, what its functions were, what its physical form should be. The answers varied.

Bimetallism was the legal monetary standard in the United States until 1873. Ironically, it had far more defenders after that time than before it. The idea that money should consist of gold *and silver* gained great support in the middle and late seventies and remained an ideological salient into the days of McKinley and Bryan in the nineties. There were good reasons for this. As a type of bullionism, bimetallism could claim validity on many of the same grounds that supported the more orthodox ideology of gold monometallism; but since it employed two metals, which were much more plentiful than only one, it gained allegiance from many people who leaned toward greenbackism for "inflationist" reasons. Before 1873, however, bimetallism hardly existed as an ideology in America. During the 1865-73 period, it was more an atavistic slip of the pens of bullionist writers than a full-blown monetary ideology. Bullionists singing the praises of the gold standard would occasionally, in fits of absentmindedness, dredge up the telltale phrase, "and silver," from the debris of bullionist ideology. In the Germanies, in Britain, and above all in bimetallic France, the theory of bimetallism was hotly argued during those years. But not in America. The almost total absence of bimetallic advocacy in the United States before 1873 proves, if anything, the later contention of gold monometallists that the vast majority of Americans did not even know they had a bimetallic standard before it was legislated out of existence in 1873.

Gold monometallism was the prevailing orthodoxy. In America and Britain, the term was practically equivalent to bullionism. Gold was the sole standard in Britain and had been since 1816; it became the standard of the newly created German Empire in 1871; a strong party in France wanted to replace bimetallism with it; the smaller European countries followed the leads of the larger ones; Americans thought they were already on the gold standard. Many people, in fact, believed it to be the only conceivable civilized monetary standard. More confidently than any other group, the gold monometallists claimed exclusive rights to the rhetoric of civilization, law, and their satellite terms. Britain's industrial leadership, London's preeminence as a money market, seemed significantly (if mysteriously) tied to Britain's gold standard. Certainly there was a practical side to this: to a debtor-buyer country like the United States, British demands for payment in gold and her ability to set the price of anything, including silver, in gold, was inescapable. Not surprisingly, the most redoubtable monometallists were people who were most conscious of America's position internationally, either as theorists *au courant* with European ideas, statesmen anxious to protect the country's credit rating abroad, or businessmen involved in foreign trade. These people tended to be Northeasterners of fairly high status. But regardless of their social and economic affiliations, they upheld gold monometallism with an elaborateness and fervor that could only come from true believers.

American gold monometallists longed for the day when the United States would resume specie payments in gold. Anything that postponed that day struck them as a "relic of barbarism." Ultraconservative they seem today, because their policies most benefited people of entrenched capital and high status, and left untouched the crying social devastations that were the offal of industrialization. By their own lights, however, they were neither conservative nor anti-social, nor consciously dedicated to preserving an invidious status system. They believed deeply in reform and enlightenment, progress and law, civilization and reason. As moderns, utilitarians, liberals, they would be shocked to know how shocking much of what they did would be to a later age.

The leading monometallists were the opinion-leaders of their time. Linked frequently by personal friendships, they shared a prevalent trans-Atlantic liberalism. National boundaries and legislative interference were holdovers from a moribund and unenlightened past that was ignorant of the natural laws of political economy. Free trade, an internationally constant standard of value, free passage of people and goods among nations, governmental abstention from the machinery of the social universe: these were the evidences of a better world. When monometallists justified the universal adoption of the gold standard, they often gave practical reasons for it, such as the simplification of exchange, the convenience of travellers, and the stabilizing of values. But the practicality and the idealism were but two sides of the same ideological coin.[1]

The gold monometallists viewed the world fundamentally as a mechanistic cosmogony of universally operative natural laws. Society as well as the stars were subject to these laws: the monometallists were social Newtonians *par excellence*. The worldview of these nineteenth-century liberals had been avant-garde in the eighteenth century and are today associated with the Enlightenment. But their broad popular acceptance came in the nineteenth century, especially when such seeming miracles as steam power and the codifications of political economists apparently realized and proved Enlightenment dreams. The monometallists may seem reactionary now, but in their own day they felt themselves to be in the vanguard of civilized progress, the hoplites of liberalism.[2]

Free trade, unfettered exchange, and fixed value embodied in gold were basic policy tenets derived by the monometallists from their mechanistic, natural-law convictions. Government, as the American writer Amasa Walker said, cannot determine the value of money and has no business trying to do so; in operating a mint, it "simply certifies to the weight and purity of the coin." Other monometallists agreed.[3] Hugh McCulloch, Secretary of the Treasury in the late sixties, put it succinctly in one of his annual reports to Congress. "Coin," he said,

> being the circulating medium of the world, flows from one country to another in obedience to the law of trade, which prevents it from becoming anywhere, for any considerable period, excessive in amount; when this law is not interfered with by legislation, the evils of an excessive currency are corrected by the law itself. An increase of money beyond what is needed for the purposes above named, according to all experience, not only inflates prices, but diminishes labor.

To McCulloch, to Congressman Samuel Hooper of Massachusetts, and to other monometallists who had had wide practical experience in banking or commerce, these were not theories but facts. Amasa Walker claimed that "as man's being and nature's laws are found in experience, political economy is to be regarded as a positive science. Nothing in its fundamental principles is hypothetical or problematic."[4]

Value could not change; otherwise supply and demand might not balance, and all equations had to balance. The monometallists' version of the "quantity theory of money" differed from the greenbackers' in one crucial way: The monometallists insisted that money had to have "intrinsic value," a quality dependably provided solely by precious metals, particularly gold. Paper money was not money, and was not even a money substitute, unless it was redeemable in coin. Great increases in the total world supply of precious metals would theoretically change their prices; as Francis Bowen stated in his widely used textbook, "If gold were but one fourth as plentiful as it is now, one grain of it

would be quadrupled in value." But because gold and silver had
been used as money for so long, and the world supply was so
large, sharp changes in the available amount were not likely.
The metals were "comparatively of an unvarying value," Samuel
Hooper claimed, and monometallists usually shared the view of the
Harvard astronomer Simon Newcomb that "The fact that prices
in general do not fluctuate in exact correspondence with gold,
no more disproves these general propositions than the existence
of mountains disproves the rotundity of the earth." When
pressed, monometallists admitted that nothing, not even gold,
provided a standard of value that absolutely did not vary a jot.
But gold, of all materials, most closely approached this ideal
invariance and was thus the ideal monetary standard. For the
same reasons, it was the ideal standard of deferred payments, a
measurement of something borrowed to be paid back later. Loan
gold today, receive it back in ten years, and the sums will be the
same in value. Because gold had all these properties, Newcomb
observed, it "will be the standard of value in this and every other
civilized country, in spite of any thing any Government may do
to prevent it."[5]

Monometallism, moreover, benefited everybody, not just those
who had some gold or held bonds that might be repaid in gold.
Payment of the public debt in any other way was unthinkable:
Senator John Sherman of Ohio, Chairman of the Senate Finance
Committee, stated that "The public faith holds the scales between
[the bondholder] and the United States . . ., and the penalties
for a breach of this faith are far more severe and disastrous to
the nation than courts, constables, and sheriffs can be to the
private creditor." Infringing public contracts by paying them in
anything but gold meant "public dishonor" and "the sure and
speedy decline of national honor and prestige."[6] Monometallism,
so its advocates claimed, helped all groups, not just bondholders,
in a positive way. Hugh McCulloch, for example, in his wide correspondence with financial leaders, assured everyone that his
rigorous gold-resumption policies would be best for everyone.
Amasa Walker told McCulloch that it was "depreciated paper"
(i.e., the greenbacks) that severely depressed the laborers, agriculturists, and "manufacturing interest" of the country, while New-

comb assured laborers that sound money, not strikes, was the real solution to their problems. It would be ridiculous to doubt their sincerity.[7]

The only monetary ideology that maintained so much as a beachhead against gold monometallism in America before 1873 was greenbackism, the theory and policy of paper currency not convertible into specie. The greenbackers and the gold mono-metallists split completely on policy, but they both believed and used the rhetoric of civilization, law, prevailing monetary principles, and producerism. They ranked the rhetoric differently, however. The first two sets of terms were the crucial and common ones for the monometallists, producerism the mainstay of the greenbackers. Central to the thinking of both were monetary notions such as supply and demand, the economic necessity of both capital and labor (the greenbackers were not anti-capitalist but would not abide the monometallists' version of capitalism), the natural harmony of the economic interests constituting society, and the importance of money in all economic and social processes. Both groups claimed Adam Smith, Jean-Baptiste Say, and various of the Utilitarians, as ideological ancestors.

But while monometallists and greenbackers both thought society operated according to natural laws, their interpretations of these laws differed. The natural laws of society were to the bullionists akin to physical or astronomical natural laws; nature and society were harmonious, but mechanistically so. For the green-backers, natural social laws found a closer analogy in the laws governing living organisms. Nature and society were indeed harmonious, but in the manner of living, growing, happy social bodies. Another difference was the bullionists' habit of thinking in universal terms, with laws governing the whole world across time, while the greenbackers' society was fairly congruent with national boundaries. The greenbackers were no xenophobes—they were quite ecumenical—but neither were they overburdened with a logic that demanded universal applicability of their concepts. Instead of the monometallists' ennobling vision of universal peace and liberalism, with goods flowing freely and the same gold currency passing current all over the world, the greenbackers had a different but equally noble vision of their own: harmonious cooperation and mutual achievement and progress by people associated together in the same society. *Association* was the operative word. What promoted it was good. Protective tariffs and paper money did promote it, and so they ought to be the law of the land. Universal association was a fine idea, but it could wait.

The chief ideologue of inconvertible paper, and practically the only greenback advocate who pushed his system through to what with the greatest generosity might be called a metaphysical level, was the Philadelphia political economist, Henry C. Carey. Carey stood to the paper-money men as Bowen, Newcomb, or Amasa Walker stood to the monometallists. He not only talked and scribbled on behalf of paper money and protectionism before businessmen and politicians, but he was a theoretician who provided others with the means for linking their social world-views to issues. For Carey himself, principles remained consistent while he switched from free trade to protection in the 1840's and from bullionism to greenbackism around the time of the Civil War. The one great principle which he held throughout the long span of his active life was his idea of association. Political and economic life existed to emphasize "the distinctive qualities of man —facilitating the growth of association, and promoting the development of individuality."

Carey made that statement in 1857, and at that time he added that gold and silver coin were "the indispensable instruments of society, or commerce." But even then he insisted that quasi-money such as checks or bank notes were a social good, because they also stimulated production and exchange, and hence the harmonious association of individuals. From that position to greenback advocacy a decade later was an easy step. After the Civil War, Carey was unequivocal. Money was important because it supplied "the machinery of circulation" and promoted "facility of combination." The more money there was in circulation, and the more rapidly it circulated, "the more instant become the exchanges of society, the greater is the economy of mental and physical force, and the greater the power to produce commodities to be given in exchange for further supplies of these great instruments of association and combination." Money was no end in itself. It certainly did not need to have "intrinsic value," nor should it be limited to coin: the function was important, not the form. Money, whatever its shape, was good because it helped people associate productively and harmoniously.

Carey maintained these views in his major works, the *Principles of Political Economy* (1837–40), the *Principles of Social Science* (1858–59), and *The Unity of Law* (1872). The last, written during the greenback period when Carey was actively supporting greenbacks and protective tariffs, presented social science as a branch of moral and natural philosophy, attached to morals and nature by the same "power of association" that had been the linch-pin of his thought for decades.[8]

Carey had considerable direct influence, through his ponderous tomes, periodical articles (some of them in the *Bulletin* of the American Iron and Steel Association), and his devoted followers. His more prominent American disciples included the manufacturers Stephen Colwell and Joseph Wharton, the economists Condy Raguet and E. Peshine Smith, several academics, his nephew and ideological executor Henry Carey Baird, and Congressman William Darrah Kelley (who earned the nickname "Pig-Iron" for the stentoriousness of his Careyite advocacy of protective tariffs). In Europe, Carey was almost certainly the most respected American economist of the century. Frédéric Bastiat's *Harmonies Economiques* owed much to Carey (even to the point of plagiarism, according to some Careyites); Eugen Dühring, chiefly remembered today because Friedrich Engels attacked him in the *Anti-Dühring*, respected Carey and exchanged ideas with him. Several other European economists, particularly Germans who were forerunners or founders of the historical school of economics, regarded Carey as a progenitor and kindred spirit.[9]

The rhetoric of harmony, progress, and producerism, in the form in which Carey explicated it, helped make greenbackism congenial to several clearly separable economic groups. Farmer and labor interests, especially Western ones, though their greenbackism had several sources, got the message in part from Alexander Campbell, a manufacturer with many ideas similar to Carey's, and used it as a call to organize. Eastern manufacturers, especially Pennsylvanians, heard it from Kelley, Baird, their colleagues Wharton and Colwell, and of course from Carey himself. Greenbacks, so it seemed to Kelley, Alexander Campbell, and their audiences, were the means by which the combined efforts of labor and capital could be shared more harmoniously. Metallic money was too scarce; bank notes were too prone to speculation and monopoly. Greenbacks, said Campbell and Kelley, were the safe road to the realization of Carey's principle of association. In 1867, Campbell was telling this to the national convention of the National Labor Union, while Kelley was similarly exhorting his Radical Republican colleagues in the U.S. House of Representatives.[10]

Greenbackers and gold monometallists were remarkably agreed on most important points of rhetoric, but abominated each others' policy conclusions derived from that rhetoric. The standard of value should be stable from year to year, both sides insisted. But the greenbackers wanted no return to specie payments, certainly no rapid return, on the grounds that it would inhibit association, interfere with existing values by deflating them severely, paralyze producers, and benefit those undeserving few whose labor was past and over with and accumulated in the form of capital assets. To repay the Civil War bonds in gold would be a crime against society. It would give creditors a tremendous windfall, since they would get back far more than they invested. Nobody should receive on any investment a rate of interest higher than the normal increase in society's total productivity (three to four per cent a year). Monometallists, on the other hand, insisted that "depreciated paper" was the destroyer of the stability of values. Paper money, they said, had no intrinsic value; its only source was the capricious fiat of legislators, and thus the very existence of the greenbacks led to an uncertainty which played havoc with contracts. America's Civil War greenbacks were inexcusable except on grounds of vital national necessity. Samuel Hooper, who had been one of the drafters of the law creating the greenbacks, called them "the greatest mischief"; Secretary McCulloch warned that "an irredeemable currency is a financial disease which retards growth instead of encouraging it; which stimulates speculation, but diminishes labor." Paper cur-

rency not redeemable in gold, and "depreciated" below its face
value, was nothing more than a "broken promise" by the government, an unmitigated evil.[11]

Both sides insisted that speculation and monopoly were bad.
But to the greenbackers, the speculator and monopolist was the
man who bought bonds or lent money in greenbacks, and then
demanded payment in gold. He gouged the producer, he received
a return on his capital that he did not earn. To the monometallists it was the reverse: Hugh McCulloch was sure that if the
greenbacks came down to the specie level, prices would stop fluctuating wildly, Wall Street rings would disappear, and the
country could settle down to normal, quiet production. Amasa
Walker lamented that opting during the Civil War for inconvertible paper currency had been a "terrible alternative" that
"completed the work of financial demoralization, which the
States had previously begun, inaugurated a system of unparalleled
injustice, and transferred, with great rapidity, the wealth of the
producing many into the hands of the nonproducing few." The
bullionism and concern for the welfare of the "producing classes"
that had been hallmarks of the Jacksonians of thirty years earlier
found its last refuge among "conservative" monometallists of the
post-Civil War years. It was no accident that Hugh McCulloch,
who longed for the old hard-money days of his Jacksonian-
Democratic youth, was among them.[12]

Greenbackers and monometallists generally split not only over
currency and the monetary standard but also over national banks,
debt policy, and tariffs. Greenbackers (and, interestingly, the most
rigorous monometallists) viewed the national banks as pernicious,
unnatural, government-created monopolies. They were nonpublic
bodies usurping the exclusively public right to create money (the
national bank notes), and they drew double interest, once on the
lending of their own notes and again on the bonds they were
required to own as a note reserve. But all except the most extreme monometallists thought the national banks and their note
issues were a convenience and a positive good, so long as the total
note issue was strictly limited, adequately backed by specie, and
convertible into "lawful money" as the law provided.[13] Natural-
law liberalism led monometallists toward free trade, but the desire

to benefit producers led a great many greenbackers toward vocal support of tariff protection.[14] Monometallists, stoutly demanding that the Civil War debt be paid in gold, believed they were only upholding the public credit in simple honesty; to greenbackers, it was just as obvious that a bond bought in greenbacks should be paid in greenbacks.

Despite all of its doctrine and its often well-founded disagreements with monometallism, greenbackism never really had a chance. During the years between the end of the Civil War and 1873, it was never more than a minority position, far from the arena of power, fighting a frustrating guerrilla battle against an overwhelming orthodoxy. The gold-monometallist orthodoxy embraced many variants; its most rigorous sectaries wanted no paper currency of any kind and a return to specie payments immediately, while others, including most policy-makers, had resigned themselves at least by 1870 to "living with" some inconvertible paper until specie resumption could be had without severely deflating the economy and upsetting values. But whatever their stripe, the gold monometallists viewed greenbackism as a wild aberration. Gold-silver bimetallism, which seemed to them to involve a built-in fluctuation and instability, was simply incomprehensible, and in any case, bimetallism was not a practical possibility in America.

6

THINGS NOT SHARED:

ECONOMIC GROUPS

Thanks to some excellent research published in recent years, so much is now known about economic interest groups in America in the 1865–1880 period that aside from summarizing that research, only one task remains.[1] But this task is important, and it involves groups with rhetoric in three respects. The first is to show how each major economic group devised a rhetoric to represent verbally its own monetary needs; second, how these several rhetorics were special adaptations of the general rhetoric (civilization, law, producerism, and economic principles); third, how these several rhetorics, having points in common with each other and with the general rhetoric, thereby created both bridges and gulfs among economic groups.

Everyone assumes that bankers were a thoroughly hard-money group, no doubt in part because so much agrarian rhetoric in the Jacksonian and Populist periods was anti-banker. In the 1865–73 period, however, the banking community was so divided on many financial questions that hard-money does not adequately describe it. Large metropolitan commercial banks, even ones with national-bank charters, needed and liked national bank notes less than smaller commercial banks. Demand deposits, clearing house certificates, and other forms of money suited the big banks amply, but bank notes greatly augmented the reserve and general business requirements of the smaller banks. Many commercial bankers disliked national bank notes and greenbacks equally, because both were depreciated in terms of gold. Investment and commercial bankers alike wanted the public debt paid in specie, which to them meant gold.[2]

Most bankers, at least in the late sixties, felt that the resumption of specie payments was urgent. Secretary of the Treasury Hugh McCulloch, a one-time state banker, agreed. From early 1866 until Congress stopped him in 1868, he set about resuming by the direct if drastic means of taking greenbacks out of circulation as they arrived at the Treasury. This policy, called "contraction," was obviously deflationary. But it suited the economic interests of some bankers, and the moral attitudes of nearly all of them. Speedy resumption and speedy refunding of the public debt were thoroughly desirable policies in the minds of men who had high regard for honest labor, hated speculation and prodigality, and saw it as their duty to treat their workers and customers in a moral and Christian manner. "Every greenback withdrawn from circulation is a fresh nail in the coffin of the speculator, the forestaller, and the stock-gambler," admonished the *Banker's Magazine.* An officer of the City Bank of New York assured McCulloch that the only enemies of his contraction policy were "stock speculators" and "Gold Gamblers," and a Massachusetts country banker blamed the "inflationists," not the Secretary, for "radical error" in financial thinking. Strong ethical views particularly marked the New York financial community, where mutual trust and high personal probity was essential to normal business (and at the same time made the occasional Fisk or Gould into repugnant outcasts).[3]

Banker opposition to greenbacks followed monometallist ideology fairly straighforwardly. As the New York banker George

Coe put it, "they represent no real value." Unlike theoreticians such as Bowen or Newcomb, however, banker monometallists exempted their own paper, national bank notes, from such opprobrium, the crucial distinction being that the bank notes were "secured" and rested on productive value. "A bank-note is payable in legal tenders or coin," asserted the *Banker's Magazine,*

> and if the government reduces its currency and thereby increases its power to resume, it brings nearer the day of resumption by the banks. A bank-note represents property in existence pledged to the bank for the payment of the note, but a legal tender represents a war debt, arms, clothing and powder wasted, or wages paid, and is only good, not in itself, but because its issuer—that is, the government—is not in good credit. A legal-tender note is a confession of weakness on the part of the government, while a National bank-note is a legitimate medium of exchange, called into existence by the demands of trade. So that the substitution of a bank-note for legal tender is a conservative move, and in every way desirable and beneficial to the country.

Jay Cooke, the investment banker who had managed the sale of hundreds of millions in government bonds during and after the Civil War, had promised buyers that the bonds would be paid in gold, and to Cooke, "repudiation"—payment of the bonds in anything else—was unthinkable.

Yet even Cooke, although he sympathized with McCulloch, disagreed with the Secretary's contraction policy because it depressed business badly. Many other bankers agreed. Threat of depression, together with fear that the currency rigidities of the national banking system would exacerbate financial panics, caused them to "look with anxiety on all movements tending toward a resumption of specie payments," and to "make all possible efforts to prolong and perpetuate the existing state of inflation, by which they profit so enormously." A few bankers, in fact, found greenbacks useful as reserves; if greenback circulation was properly limited, said one, it would be a very practical currency, helping to curb speculation and regulate prices "by supply and demand, and not by the Bulls and Bears in Wall street, as now."[4]

With these few exceptions, however, the banking interest in general looked forward longingly to America's return to the gold standard. Greenbacks and enormous public indebtedness were in the last analysis temporary residues of the Civil War. Though many bankers saw utility in various forms of inflation, particularly national bank note issues, the underlying ideological orientation of the group was gold monometallist.

The mercantile or commercial group shared many of the bankers' viewpoints, and like them, looked upon specie resumption as the chief, nearly the sole, aspect of the money question during the 1865–73 period. But though the commercial group was more diversified than the bankers, it took a more rigorous and consistent hard-money position.

There were a few exceptions. Persons engaged wholly in buying and selling on domestic markets did not need to worry about currency so long as it was abundant and accepted at face value anywhere in the country, qualities possessed equally by greenbacks and national bank notes. Railroad builders were not enthusiastic about the shrivelling up of their bond markets, and in some areas, notably parts of Pennsylvania, Careyism was prevalent enough to swing men of commerce away from monetary rigor and free trade.

Aside from these few, however, the mercantile group classed tariff protection and "inflation" among "artificial" interferences with "legitimate commerce."[5] For those who dealt in exports and imports, and for the many people who as jobbers, wholesalers, and commission merchants brought imported goods from ports of entry to local markets, the instability and the depreciated quality of the greenbacks were the severest handicap to business. The Chamber of Commerce of New York petitioned the Senate for assistance to American foreign trade in the form of tariff reductions, ship subsidies, and greenback contraction; it pointed out that while costs of labor and materials had increased greatly since the Civil War because of "our excessive issue of irredeemable paper money," there had not been a "corresponding increase in the premium on gold coin." The automatic price-money mechanism evidently had some sand in its works. In effect, the price of goods purchased abroad to be sold in the United States had risen faster than the prices of goods produced domestically. Ships, for example, "are built with currency at an increased cost of fifty per cent, and they [the domestic shipbuilders] are paid for their services in coin, which will command only nine per cent premium in exchange for currency." Contraction of the greenbacks was the best of several remedies, they believed. Imported goods had to be priced to meet their actual cost, plus customs duties (tariffs) payable in coin only, less whatever the gold premium happened to be at the moment, while on the other hand American goods to be sold abroad had to be purchased by these merchants at greenback prices. Depreciation of the greenbacks below their par value thus caught the foreign trader, and the commission merchants and others who handled the goods and who had to meet some of these costs themselves, from either direction.

But depreciation was only part of it. The prices of greenbacks also fluctuated irritatingly. Commercial spokesmen often complained that the greenbacks made gold speculations inevitable. The gold premium fluctuated hourly, and the merchant could choose either to price as competitively as he could and hope for the best, or to set his price high enough to meet possible gold premium fluctuations, which meant risking his competitive position. According to Joseph S. Ropes, an articulate Boston merchant and sympathizer with Hugh McCulloch, "all legitimate business with foreign countries is turned into sheer speculation, gambling and stock jobbing." Greenbacks were a "great barrier" to the normal operations of the natural laws of trade; not only merchants, but farmers, laborers, and manufacturers would receive nothing but benefits from the contraction of the greenbacks right out of existence.

Throughout the period 1865–73, in fact, the mercantile group believed specie resumption was urgent, and contraction the proper way to get it. They were more consistently contractionist than any other economic group, even the bankers. The rhetoric of the mercantile group was the rhetoric of gold monometallism, reinforced by the arguments of the counting-house. The natural laws of trade, hatred of speculation, the view that "labor is the source of wealth, and that its productive power is proportioned to its virtue, intelligence, and skill," could only be realized by gold; the sooner gold returned, the better.[6]

Manufacturers differed astonishingly from merchants or bankers on the money question. This was not illogical: unlike merchants they produced goods rather than bought and sold them, and unlike bankers they borrowed money rather than lent it, in order to produce more goods more abundantly, efficiently, and profitably. The manufacturer—at least, the manufacturers in "growth" industries like iron and steel—was a producer, and he was usually a debtor. What is more important, he realized this and saw himself naturally allied with other producer-debtors rather than with other "businessmen," or capitalists.

"Capital itself is nothing more than labor—the surplus of yesterday's labor over yesterday's needs," said a manufacturer's journal aimed at the construction industry and the building trades. Labor and capital were a "harmonious alliance," the interests of "manufacturers and artisans" were identical.

As long as the manufacturer's self-image as a producer-debtor was stronger than his self-image as a "captain of industry," as long as the line separating artisans and manufacturers meant less than the line separating people with large investments and returns from those with small, the manufacturing group felt close to farmers and workers. After 1873 it was shocked when its allies complained—by strikes and other protest—that this harmony belied the facts of modern enterprise. Before that time, however, harmony reigned, and the manufacturers' understanding of civilization, law, and the producer philosophy led them to a stance on the money question which was "soft."

Producerism seems to have been part of the thinking even of manufacturers whose economic position made easy money less desirable. For example, the New England textile group, and others who were well established competitively, and for whom technological change was not at that moment rapid, counted themselves producers. For them, the placid and conservative aspects of producerism—social harmony, social order, anti-speculation, morality—counted most heavily. The rhetoric led toward monometallism rather than greenbackism. But manufacturers in rapidly growing and technologically shifting industries looked upon currency expansion as a positive good. To the *Iron Age*, Carey was "the veteran exponent of the truths of economic science." The Careyite principle of harmonious association led many manufacturers to reassure themselves that despite the sometimes threatening aspects of trade unions," "there is much less apparent danger here than in any other of the great producing counties [sic] of the world, of a conflict of classes." They even approved positively of Grangerite principles, which they thought conducive to class harmony; railroad leaders, more directly affected by Grangerism as targets of it, definitely did not agree. Although some Careyites, such as William D. Kelley, damned banks for "perverted practices" such as making loans on deposits, most manufacturing spokesmen approved of bank money as well as greenbacks. Currency expansion of almost any sort, together with tariff protection, stimulated production and, therefore, helped realize the good society.[7]

Labor during the 1865-73 period understood the money question first as the question of how to preserve paper currency (silver was not yet an issue), secondly as the need to pay the public debt equitably. As a group, laborites were currency expansionists. But paper money had to be greenbacks, not the notes of "monopolistic" national banks. Unlike many manufacturers, for whom "free banking" (i.e., the absence of a legal limit on total national bank note issue as long as the notes were secured) seemed legitimate, laborites almost to a man called for the abolition of the national banking system and a paper currency issued by the government alone.

Despite considerable internal cleavages within the labor group, whose membership ranged from people almost indistinguishable from Careyite manufacturers all the way to radical socialists, greenbackism was a common denominator. While the locomotive engineers' journal glowed warm-heartedly that "full reward for labor" and "just returns for capital, contentment, happiness, prosperity" indissolubly "go together," the *Workingman's Advocate* on the other extreme could let slip that there was an "irrepressible conflict" between capital and labor. But in the great majority of cases, even in that journal, the keynote was social harmony. Greenbacks were the chief means to this end, not only for the National Labor Union, and its offspring, the National Labor Reform party of 1872, but for other laborites as well.[8]

It had not been always thus. In Jacksonian days, labor had lost no love on banks or bank notes, and it still felt the same way in the seventies. But in the meantime its allegiance switched from specie to greenbacks. Most of the labor interest in the post-Civil War years was not interested in "cheap money" for reasons of indebtedness, heavy mortgages, or the ordinary borrowing requirements of small business. The latter may have affected the artisans who were part of the labor interest at that time, but to wage-earners it would not have mattered. Their real worry was high interest—on public debts as well as private—and to this worry, greenbacks seemed the solution.[9]

Why were they so concerned about high interest and ready to use greenbacks to combat it? The answer lies in their adaptation of producerite rhetoric. Producerism, with its suspicion of non-producers, made them steadfast bullionists before the Civil War and steadfast greenbackers after it. Producerism was moral and economic bedrock, and in the producerite scheme of things, money was the midwife of production. William Sylvis, the founder of the National Labor Union, put it well. Why, Sylvis asked, should interest rates concern working men, who are neither borrowers nor lenders? Simply because the nation's real wealth increased at a rate of 3 per cent to 4 per cent a year, and it followed that "any rate of interest above 4 per cent, is direct robbery upon labor, and is running the nation in debt." In truth, he continued, the actual rate was about 3 per cent. But the interest rate averaged about 15 per cent: which meant that "the 3 per cent consumes all that is produced, after feeding and clothing the producers; and the 12 per cent is a lien upon future labor. It is a mortgage upon the productive industry of the country." Interest *produced* nothing; labor alone produced. "The manufacturer, the farmer, the business man of any kind . . . the mechanic, the common laborer," Sylvis complained, had to pay interest at a rate set by "a few bankers, brokers and usurers." The result was disharmony. With the rate of interest higher than the annual increase in national wealth,

> the employer, to keep his works going must borrow money, and must pay more interest for the use of it, than his return in profit; to save himself he reduces wages, the workmen not being able to see where the true difficulty is, go on a strike— the works are closed, and employer and workmen go to ruin together.

Prewar bank issues and postwar national banknotes "purported to be the representatives of money, when, in fact, they represented nothing," in Sylvis' opinion.

Another writer in the *Workingmen's Advocate* argued that specie was no essential basis for money, and thus specie resumption would benefit nobody except a few bankers who controlled specie and therefore the value of production and property. Naturally, he continued, those people would deny government the power to determine the monetary standard by law, because that power strikes at the root of their "incurably vicious" specie system. Laborites agreed with the strictest bullionists that money and prices should not fluctuate, that supply and demand operated inexorably, that the quantity of money had a direct bearing on wages and prices, and of course that "labor is the creator of all wealth." But they went on to deny that money had any intrinsic value whatever. Money, to them, was nothing more than the measure or yardstick of what labor produced, and labor "is entitled to all which it creates."[10]

What then? Abolish interest or capital? Not at all. Capital was nothing other than deferred labor, essential to production. As such, however, as labor "inactive" or "dormant," the return on it should never be quite as high as the return on labor actively employed. This was another way of saying that the return on capital should never go above, and ideally should be slightly below, the rate of increase in national wealth.

Government bonds, as a form of deferred labor, should bear interest according to that principle. They should be replaced by an "interconvertible" bond that paid 3.65 per cent interest (since they figured the rate of increase in national wealth to be 1/100th of one per cent per day). A man had a right to a return on his accumulated labor, as long as the return did not outstrip productivity; he could put that accumulated labor into 3.65 per cent bonds. If he chose to put it to active use, he could convert the bonds into greenbacks. (That bonds might not be saleable at 3.65 per cent, especially to foreign investors who had no use for greenbacks, did not bother the laborites).

The 3.65 per cent interconvertible bond scheme, as Professor Unger pointed out, was the distinctive feature of laborite political economy. It was, in its way, the logical conclusion of the producer philosophy just as the extreme bullionism of Newcomb or Bowen represented the logical conclusion of the mechanistic natural-law attitude. Yet both extremes recognized the goodness of the productive function, and the existence of natural laws, often derived from classical economics; both were seekers after civilization and harmonious social order.[11]

Even more radical elements welcomed coalition with other groups. Greenbacks, "the people's currency—elastic, cheap and inexportable, based on the entire wealth of the country," would insure equitable distribution of earnings to labor and capital, and would be adequate to the "legitimate demands of . . . business." Greenbacks were more than the currency of labor: shipbuilders, farmers, manufacturers—all of whom were fellow producers—would benefit from their use. Gold, "the gambler's currency," and "this wild-cat national-bond-double-interest-bank-paper currency," should be repudiated and their evil effects obliterated.[12] In spite of sporadic appearances of bellicose proletarianism in the *Workingman's Advocate,* harmony and cooperation among the classes was the common theme both there and in other labor journals during most of the period from 1865 into 1873.[13]

Before 1873, agriculturists were virtually a silent group. Farm spokesmen expressed themselves rarely on the money question, and on those few occasions, they leaned toward hard money: the "fluctuating measure of value—an unconvertible currency," one farm paper said, was to blame for "oppressive taxation which falls heaviest on the laborer and lightest on the capitalist." More often than not, agrarian spokesmen before 1873 also favored lower tariffs, a "free market," and free competition.[14]

The one issue sure to win support from farmers prior to 1873 was the destruction of railroad monopoly, as well as lesser monopolies such as those suspected in warehousing, insurance, telegraphs, and mining. Anti-monopoly, an ancient and very general agrarian attitude, stemmed from producerism. Agrarian versions of producer rhetoric, at least in the late sixties, were less willing to accord producerite status to others (laborites, etc.), than those others were willing to accord to farmers. But then, most American lived on farms in those days. While national prosperity, they admitted, rests on the value of its production, "The soil is the source from whence we derive all that constitutes wealth; without it we would have no agriculture, no manufactures, no commerce." Labor, to the extent that it was urban, was prone in some agrarians' eyes to the sybaritic parasitism that infected city-dwellers in general.

Some agrarians, to be sure, emphasized the ideal of unity among the producing classes and the similar positions af farmers, workingmen, and businessmen. Still, agrarian producerism was noticeably more exclusive than manufacturing or labor producerism, just as the agrarians' involvement with issues was more closely restricted to those issues, such as railroad rates, that touched their own interests obviously and directly.[15]

Agrarians also used the rhetoric of natural law more often than manufacturer or labor spokesmen did. Business enterprise, even railroading, was not intrinsically evil, but it behooved monopoly-prone businessmen to conform, as farmers did, to the "hidden forces of Nature," "God's Great Engine," "the grand economy of God." Debt, speculation, corruption, special government subsidies, were to be shunned in favor of "retrenchment," the "economical use of public money," honesty and observance of law. As one Granger put it, "The productions of the earth are subject to the influence of natural laws, invariable and indisputable; the amount produced will consequently be in proportion to the intelligence of the producer, and success will depend upon his knowledge of the action of these laws, and the proper application of their principles." Grangerism's ultimate object, in fact, was to "expand the mind by tracing the beautiful laws the great Creator has established in the Universe, and to enlarge our views of Creative wisdom and power." Be moral, produce, and observe the divine laws of the universe, and ye shall have higher corn prices.[16]

These deeply ingrained ideas were to provide abundant support for a soft-money position when agrarians awoke after 1873 to the ways in which the money question directly affected them. Before 1873, however, they were less concerned with monetary policy than any other major economic group. Agrarians were soon to take their place on the left of the spectrum of group positions, but until that happened, the spectrum read, from left to right, laborites, manufacturers, bankers, and men of commerce.

7

THINGS NOT SHARED:

PARTY, SECTION,

AND NATION

Partisan and sectional divisions over the money question existed along with ideological and economic divisions. But analysis according to party and section sheds much less light on the dynamics of social organization. This may seem odd, especially since such differences have traditionally been thought crucial to the understanding of American political events, but the reasons for it are not obscure.

Parties did not demonstrate social differences very well simply because the first purpose of the parties—especially the major parties—was to unite people, not divide them; to blur differences, not to stress them. Doctrine deferred to the requirements of electoral success. Democrats, Republicans, and even members of the larger splinter parties (Liberal Republicans and National Labor Reformers in 1872, Greenbackers later) were everywhere on the ideological spectrum. Party requirements played a key role in the development of the money question, but this role—to make policy decisions, gather support for them, and put them into effect—was basically different from the division-sharpening role of ideological and economic groupings.

The major parties, for practical purposes, did not have "positions" on the money question, except in the sense that specific leaders used partisan ties to further specific policies at specific moments in specific circumstances. The Democratic party included greenbackers, midwestern moderates, and contractionists such as Hugh McCulloch; the Republican party ranged from Yankee monometallists to Careyites such as William D. Kelley. For that reason, it is virtually impossible to talk of party positions outside of a narrative of events. To be sure, the Democratic party perhaps leaned toward soft-money more often, as in its 1868 platform, than the Republic party did. But so many Republicans and Democrats were exceptions to the broad party tendencies, and the issues were so complicated, that nothing more definite than that ought to be said. Members of both parties shared the rhetorics of civilization, law, and producerism, and this too helped both major parties achieve their coalition-building function. But there was no clear line between a "Republican" rhetoric and a "Democratic" one.[1]

Sectional divisions are not especially revealing because they represented little more than economic regionalism—the tendency of people in, say, a staple-crop-producing region or a manufacturing region to react similarly to legislation. Where sectionalism has been used to analyze post-Civil War economic policy it has often been used badly, for example when it led to the enormously oversimplified belief that Northeastern business during Reconstruction ran roughshod under robber-baron command over the helpless agrarian victims of South and West.[2] Nevertheless, some notable sectional variations on general rhetorical themes did exist.

The Northeast, i.e., New York and New England but excepting Pennsylvania, was outstandingly the section of gold-monometallist ideologues and members of the hard-money wings of both major parties. There are two obvious reasons for this. Geography and tradition placed on the Northeastern seaboard the greater share of American foreign commerce and banking; hence these two monometallist-leaning economic groups were strongly represented there. New York and New England, moreover, were the home of the "quality press," and the great opinion-leading periodicals of the day nearly all tended strongly toward the monometallist viewpoint. The *Popular Science Monthly* assumed coinage and political economy to have the exactitude of astronomy, and proclaimed gold and silver "the most fit of all known substances" to serve monetary purposes. The *Nation* called any kind of inflation, even the conservative bond-refunding program which the Treasury undertook after 1870, "repudiation" and "mischievous delusion." Thaddeus Stevens and John Sherman (!) were "partisans of disgrace" because of their greenback proclivities, said *Harper's Weekly*, and in New York City, the *Times* and the *World* fought the monometallist-free-trade fight. There were many exceptions, but austerity usually marked Northeastern opinion in money matters.[3]

The South was more self-consciously sectional about money during this period than any other area. Southern spokesmen sought the rebirth of their section's economic power, which had been destroyed by the War. This meant surplus cotton production, and the sale of the surplus cotton and other staples from farther up the Mississippi, on world markets. Southerners chafed at their dependence on the Northeast for development capital: "Monopolies of Eastern capital and transportation" bothered New Orleans writers who hoped for a Southern-Western coalition. Northeastern financiers, not manufacturers, interested themselves in the South during Reconstruction. These financiers often came from areas of Copperhead strength; Radicals, such as Thaddeus Stevens, had little interest in restoring the South's economic power.[4] But dependence on the Northeast was momentarily unavoidable. The national banking system, which Southerners called a Radical tool, destroyed state bank notes without giving the South a proportionate share of national bank issues. Thus the area was chronically short of cash. Careyism, with its antislavery and protectionist elements, was "Northern," said *De*

Bow's Review, and that leading Southern journal and several others demanded rapid specie resumption. But many Southerners supported free banking, and though there was little talk of greenbacks before 1873, many Southerners would embrace green-backism later. Sectional needs pulled in opposite ways: restore King Cotton or industrialize? Most Southerners who were vocal on money matters were deeply aware of the region's need for money and other capital, but were even more impressed by the need to sell on world markets. "We sell our great staples for currency, and are, therefore, interested in having that currency as nearly gold as possible." Southern editorialists wavered very little throughout the pre-1873 period on the need for resumption to end "speculation" and put Southern recovery on a solid basis. Production was the root of wealth, and in the South this meant staple agricultural production in surplus.[5]

Midwestern monetary thinking, and that of Pennsylvania, generally favored free banking or greenbacks rather than rapid specie resumption, and stressed producerism more than mecha-nistic rhetoric. This befitted an expanding region which lacked capital of its own. The North Central states had replaced the Northeast as the most populous census region by 1870. The Mid-west was growing fast in every sector, and it was money-shy most of the time. The Midwest felt consistently that national bank notes should be expanded; free banking, sometimes involving the retirement of greenbacks and sometimes not, was welcomed more widely there than in any other section. There was a realistic basis for Midwestern soft-money sentiment of this type. A chronic shortage of national bank notes and other currency not surpris-ingly made for economic sectionalism, as Redlich has explained. Western boards of trade were often contractionist, and the con-tractionist Treasury Secretary, Hugh McCulloch, was a Hoosier who had support from his home section. But the business inter-ests and the press of this producing region generally sympathized with the "respectable" versions of inflation, such as free banking, and even at times with greenbackism itself.[6]

The Pacific Coast and Mountain States were unique in that one of their chief products was bullion. They were no less avid for the protection of their own interests than was any other section: but self-protection for them meant a rigorous bullionism. California, in fact, was so distant and isolated from the rest of the country before the transcontinental railroad opened in 1869 that she never left specie payments all through the Civil War. For these reasons, the Far West was more sympathetic to speedy resumption and free trade than any other section. Californians were devoted to gold monometallism, while from Nevada came traces (virtually the only ones anywhere in the country) of bimetallist sentiment, including a number of petitions urging Congress to take steps to insure the monetary employment of American silver as well as gold. It was easy for westerners to talk of "the pernicious character of our irredeemable and fluctuating paper currency," and the need to "return to a specie basis with all the speed possible," in order to deal fairly with merchant, mechanic, and laborer alike. In the West, a producer might very well be a bullion producer, and the commodity nature of money was seldom questioned.[7]

Another kind of division on the money question crossed national boundaries: the policy interests of nation-states. In this context, the United States, for all its internal divisions, was a unit whose most influential rhetors expressed liberal values and whose policy-makers were convinced of the desirability of gold monometallism. America therefore shared, in international context, rhetoric and policy trends with other Western nations. The United States, Britain, France, and Prussia (after 1871, the German Empire) were tied to each other in several ways. They were the leading economic powers in the world; they traded to a great extent with each other; the bonds of one nation would largely be sold in the others; all agreed that precious metals were the one acceptable medium of international exchange. They also shared rhetoric: much of the contemporary rhetoric of money flowed across national boundaries as easily as did bullion itself, and was a theme with national variations.

The variations stemmed from national interests. America needed to grow, but at the same time it needed to protect zealously its overseas borrowing power. France wanted to gain, and

Britain wanted to keep, world commercial and manufacturing leadership, partly as a means to world political leadership. Germany sought economic expansion but her overriding task was national political unification. Each country shared and drew on the common rhetoric of civilization, natural law, and economic theory; each shared the social-Newtonian liberal outlook; each sought its own ends within the framework.

Britain, the first industrial nation, had been the first to adopt the single gold standard, in Lord Liverpool's Coinage Act of 1816. By the 1860's, she led the world in production and foreign trade. Quite naturally her sellers demanded to be paid in gold, since gold was the currency they used and needed at home. For these reasons, no outside firm, person, or nation seriously interested in world trade could ignore gold. Many Britons and some foreigners even regarded the gold standard as a main cause of British economic leadership. In such circumstances, gold was not likely to be dethroned in Britain except by events of extreme gravity. None such occurred for another sixty years. The gold standard reigned until the world economic collapse of the early 1930's.

Britons were patriotically proud also of their discovery of classical economics and its eternal laws. "Liberalism" was not the exclusive property of a single political party or economic group. In the late sixties and into the seventies, until depression struck, the British involved themselves in only one major controversy about the monetary standard, and this led only to a firmer reassertion than ever of gold monometallism. Civilization and law clearly demanded the unqualified retention of the gold standard; bimetallism was inane and even pernicious, despite its humanitarian desire to benefit all social groups by giving silver full monetary status, helping mankind while observing bullionist tenets. Orthodoxy in monetary affairs meant the gold standard, for Britons and also for the great body of educated and influential Americans within the British commercial or ideological orbit. As Amasa Walker wrote John Bright, "cordial sympathy with all your great designs and great accomplishments for human welfare" assured him their agreement on "free trade, sound currency, un-

trammelled industry, and permanent peace." Gold was the means
to these splendid universal ends.[8]

France, meanwhile, was bimetallic. There, monometallism was
the challenger to tradition. Powerful groups, including the Bank
of France and the Paris branch of the House of Rothschild, were
satisfied with bimetallism. Civilization and law were even more
common expressions in France in the last years of the Second
Empire than they were in Victorian England. But it was never
conceded in France that these terms led ineluctably to gold
monometallism. Before and after the Franco-Prussian War and
the Paris Commune, amidst the worst national trials, Louis Wolowski, Léon Say, and other bimetallists battled Esquirou de
Parieu, Michel Chevalier, and other monometallists for the soul
of the French monetary system, and always on the narrow battleground of bullionism. Despite a postwar suspension of specie
payments lasting through most of the seventies, no paper ideology
developed in France as it was doing in America. In the National
Assembly and in the journals, both sides claimed ownership of
civilization, order, and science, and flung their various versions
of this rhetoric at each other. Bimetallism, said Wolowski, was
shown "by the force of events" to effectuate free trade, economic
freedom, the "free field and natural play of unfettered relationships," while the monometallist Le Touzé viewed international
coinage unification on the gold standard as "a work of civilization, a work of progress, in a word one of the most beautiful
reforms of the century; let us unite all our efforts to hasten its
accomplishment, and above all let us profit from the good will
of foreign states."[9] But it was to be bullion prices and depression,
not argument, rhetoric, or even politics, that would force a suspension of silver coinage in the seventies.

The German states, traditionally and in the late sixties, were
on the single standard of silver. But beyond that simple fact lay
vast disorder. Many of the states had traditional coins whose
weights, finenesses, and denominations differed from others considerably. Unless they were somehow unified, political unity
would be at best imperfect. But to unify all of them into a single
coinage system on the basis of silver monometallism involved

insuperable difficulties, especially political ones; such a process would intensify particularism, rather than allay it. Yet particularism had to go. To Bismarck, monetary unification was part of the larger problem of how to create a united German Empire, the problem which far outweighed any considerations of monetary theory or political party. The Iron Chancellor's plan was to junk silver monometallism altogether, and replace it with another monetary standard. The choice was between bimetallism and gold monometallism: of the two, gold had more advantages.

From the time of the formation of the North German Union in 1866, after the war with Austria which assured that Prussia would lead any further German unification, Bismarck's advisers and other monetary and economic leaders in North Germany leaned toward gold monometallism. Domestic unity, foreign relations, and economic theory all seemed best satisfied by it. Particularism was most easily avoided by avoiding silver altogether. Also, monometallism would separate Germany completely from the French monetary orbit. The German commercial community favored it. So did the "German Manchesterdom," an influential group of economists whose ideas closely resembled the English liberals. For the Manchesterdom, gold and free trade manifested the "laws of political economy." Bismarck's Finance Minister, Rudolph von Delbrück, and the Liberal leader and Bundestag member Ludwig Bamberger, shared these views and propagated them tirelessly within the Prussian Government. Dr. Adolph Soetbeer of Hamburg, the translator of John Stuart Mill, used his position as consultant to the Hamburg and other chambers of commerce to become Germany's most active and influential private monometallist among such groups as the *Deutsche Handelstag,* a national business association, and the *Kongress deutscher Volkswirthe,* the Congress of German Economists. As a result of this conjunction of theory and policy, Germany was preeminently the country where silver or bimetallism was made to appear barbaric and unpatriotic, while gold monometallism became semi-officially "the money of the future," as Bamberger put it, and the monetary standard of united Germany.

Monetary liberalism was therefore much more nationalistic in

Germany than it was in England or the United States. When later, in the seventies, it seemed necessary for Bismarck to choose between liberal theory and national welfare, he made the choice easily: gold and liberalism could give way. With political unification accomplished, silver was no longer such an enemy. The nationalism that had always been present in the German Manchesterdom eased the shift toward the ideas of Henry C. Carey and the "historical school" of political economy, and toward protectionist and soft-money policies. To the architects of German unification, gold monometallism was a means to an end. But since it was just that, they pursued it tenaciously and irresistibly from the late sixties ino 1873.[10]

PART THREE

Narratives, 1865–1873:

The Spread of the

Gold Standard and the

Rhetoric of Harmony

. . . Money is *not a mere agency*, in our civilization, but is a *rationalizing ground* of action.

KENNETH BURKE, *A Grammar of Motives*

8

INTERNATIONAL COINAGE

AND THE PARIS

MONETARY CONFERENCE OF 1867

The wider adoption of the gold standard, and the obsolescence of the silver standard, were the major developments in world monetary affairs during the 1865–73 period. The United States was a leading participant in them, and its policy-makers, like policy-makers in other countries, considered them liberal and enlightened. They also considered them politically and economically desirable. An amalgam of idealism and interest was the stuff of which the rise of gold and the obsolescence of silver was built. Seldom was the amalgam more evident than in the International Monetary Conference of 1867, where the world's economic leaders agreed for the first time on the principle of gold monometallism.

The Conference, held in conjunction with the Paris Universal Exposition of 1867, was bathed in a blazing glare of liberalism and progress. A heady atmosphere of approaching millennium pervaded 1867: the American Union had been preserved and slavery ended; the Second Reform Bill brought about a Liberal (and liberal) dream in England, though under Tory auspices, and marked the onset of the Late Victorian Age; in Germany, Bismarck had just created the North German Union, by the slightly illiberal means of burying first the Danes and then the Austrians, but even Vienna could console itself with the preservation of Habsburg sovereignty as the ink dried on the *Ausgleich*. Napoleon III's Exposition splendidly displayed the glories of the modern world and particularly of France. As an American journalist enthusiastically reported,

> The magnificence of the Second Empire is beyond dispute. Paris is the unchallenged queen of cities, and Napoleon III has abundant reason to congratulate himself on the success that has attended his efforts to eclipse the world in making his capital the temporary emporium of all that is useful and lovely in the civilized world. . . . we are constrained to confess that the Paris Exposition of '67 was immeasurably in advance of every effort of the sort in the history of the world.[1]

Crowned heads the world over paid their respects to Napoleon, his city, and his Exposition. The delegates to the Monetary Conference were less noble, but they were still impressive: imperial and royal privy councillors, central bank presidents, the Master of Queen Victoria's Royal Mint; on the whole, the first-line financial diplomats of nineteen major countries. The task before them was to unify the coinages of the world, making them scientific and progressive. If certain delegates had their way, the unification would be based on the metric system, one of the glories of French science and the *ésprit géometrique,* by which the size and shape of money would rest on the meter, itself a decimal fraction of that most natural and eternal of intervals, the "quadrant of the terrestrial meridian," the circumference of the earth itself. The silver French franc was already scientific and natural, having been established as an integral fraction of the meter and the gram by the great Napoleon I. But coinage unification in 1867 was to rest on gold.

In retrospect, it is clear that these men had stared so long at the light of progress that it had blinded them. Yet at the time, universal coinage unification seemed a natural and promising development. People already believed political economy to be a science. Nature, laws, equilibrium, certainty should be attainable in monetary affairs just as it was in anything else. Men of good will, in an enlightened age, should be able to extend their discoveries of certain natural law to the whole world. Liberal ministers of finance viewed their offices as instruments of civilization and peace, and the chief monometallist in the French government, Vice-President of the *Conseil d'Etat* and Vice President of the Monetary Conference Marie-Louis-Pierre-Félix Esquirou de Parieu, was convinced that universal coinage on the basis of gold would mean the "gradual destruction in the economic order of one of the numerous barriers which formerly separated mankind, and whose fall facilitates their *mutual moral conquest*, serving as the prelude to the peaceful federations of the future."[2]

Much had already happened before 1867 to bring the promise of unification about. The idea was discussed at the London "Crystal Palace" Exhibition of 1851, and at International Statistical Congresses at Brussels in 1853, Paris in 1855, and Vienna in 1859; the British and American governments explored weights and measures unification officially in the late fifties; and eminent private citizens in several countries joined private associations to press for it.[3]

Until 1863, the international movement for unifying standards of weights and measures involved scarcely more than a desire for scientific neatness and accuracy and the hope of ridding the world of irritating and arbitrary differences. Coinage was included rather late among the things to be standardized, along with weights, distances, and temperature, and mainly because in France, the birthplace of the metric system, silver coins were weighed and measured by the gram and the meter. But at the Berlin International Statistical Congress of 1863, coinage unification began to take priority over weights and measures unification. Everyone agreed that the world needed a standard coinage unit. Everyone agreed also, for the last time in many years, that a universally accepted ratio between gold and silver was possible.

But how to unify coinages? The British delegate at Berlin proposed that the United States, which had suspended specie payments for the moment anyway, reduce slightly the gold content of the gold dollar to make it exactly one-fifth of a gold pound sterling, the British unit. Perhaps the Britisher's motive was anti-French; whatever it was, his plan completely ignored the metric system. But the American delegate, Samuel Bulkley Ruggles of New York City, promptly brought metricism to the fore again. Ruggles countered with the suggestion that *both* Britain and the United States reduce the gold content of their standard units, making the pound sterling and five dollars exactly "equiponderant" to twenty-five gold francs. The British idea, Ruggles said, would have created "a permanent antagonism" between the proposed British-American coin and the coins of Europe. But Ruggles had no doubt that British gold monometallism was the only sensible international standard, whatever the unit. The Congress supported neither plan, nor Ruggles' plea for gold monometallism. But it did agree that the metric system ought to be adopted universally for weights, measures, and coins, and it urged a world conference (ultimately the Paris Conference of 1867) to decide what the new coinage unit, and a worldwide gold-silver ratio, ought to be.[4]

The next moves were France's. The French monetary system was metric and bimetallic; to spread it was one of the means chosen by Napoleon III to spread French influence. But opinion divided sharply in French society and even at the very center of the Imperial Government over whether bimetallism ought to be preserved, or replaced by gold monometallism. From 1865 until late 1867 or early 1868, the monometallists controlled policy by a slim margin. French monometallists were a disparate group, some of them scientists, academics, and journalists primarily interested in the theoretical neatness of an international metric gold coinage, while others among them were motivated chiefly by the gold franc as a diplomatic weapon. During their ascendancy, however, the two wings of the monometallist group flew in unison.

On December 23, 1865, the French, Belgian, Swiss, and Italian governments signed the Monetary Treaty of Paris, which united them and their coinages into a "Latin Monetary Union." The French five-franc silver coin was the basic unit, with gold in ratio to it at one to fifteen-and-a-half. The Latin Union was bimetallic. But almost every delegate to the Latin Union conference declared for monometallism, including the French chief delegate, Esquirou de Parieu. The French insisted on preserving bimetallism for the moment, probably because it was traditional and because powerful elements within France, not only certain policy-makers but the House of Rothschild and the Bank of France, wanted it preserved. But bimetallism was on the defensive, and in the long run, the main consequence of the Latin Union treaty was more to hasten the coming of international gold monometallism than to spread the franc and the metric system.[5]

Three official bodies within the French government considered aspects of international standards and coinage unification between December, 1865, and the time of the 1867 conference. They polled foreign experts, the major chambers of commerce in France, French and foreign (especially British) private groups such as the British Association for the Advancement of Science, and policy-makers. The composite effect of these investigations was to publicize international standards and coinage unification as a great liberal reform. Bimetallists had a strong voice in the proceedings, but the gold-standard advocates were still stronger. Any Frenchman whose first objective was to preserve France's bimetallism had good reason to be nervous in 1866 and early 1867. But a Frenchman who was a gold monometallist, or who cared little about the monetary standard, could take satisfaction in a course of events that seemed to be bringing the world closer to France's monetary unit, her system of measurement, and her scientific and "moral" leadership. Books and journal articles advocating coinage unification appeared in Britain, America, and France; the British and American Associations for the Advancement of Science took a lively interest; the sun of progress was shining brightly, with golden rays.[6]

Official activity in the United States began on January 31, 1866, when President Andrew Johnson approved a House Resolution allowing the United States to participate in the Paris Universal Exposition. On May 17, Congressman John A. Kasson of Iowa, chairman of a special Committee on Coinage, Weights, and Measures in the House, reported out two bills giving legal force to contracts containing metric specifications. John Sherman and Charles Sumner immediately backed these bills in the Senate, and by the end of 1866 the statutes included a law permitting (but not compelling) the use of metric measurements in the United States. Kasson, Sherman, and Sumner showed even more interest in a resolution to authorize the President to appoint a special commissioner to discuss coinage unification with other countries. After vigorous advocacy and debate, in both houses, and forceful lobbying by the New York State Chamber of Commerce, the resolution passed, and Sherman, at least, was happy with the special commissioner on coinage appointed early in the fall.[7]

By the end of June, Secretary of State William H. Seward had appointed an American Commissioner General for the Universal Exposition, N. M. Beckwith, and Beckwith was already reporting from Paris. In all of his reports, Beckwith heavily emphasized coinage matters. He sent Seward a full report on French monetary activity, including extensive documents explaining the Latin Monetary Union agreement of 1865, and French legislative discussions of it. He also informed Seward of the desire of many French officials for gold monometallism. Beckwith volunteered the idea, which Samuel B. Ruggles had offered three years earlier at the Berlin Statistical Congress, that international unification of coinage could be achieved very easily on the gold standard by making five dollars, one pound sterling, and twenty-five francs identical. French monometallic sentiment Beckwith ascribed to economic facts: heavy Californian and Australian gold production since 1848, silver's undervaluation at legal ratios. In language that gold monometallists were to repeat almost verbatim in the years that followed, Beckwith told Secretary Seward that "Common sense undoubtedly decides in favor of a single standard, and it is logical; for how can law fix the relation of two values [gold and silver] that the nature of things and the vacilations [sic] of markets subject to incessant changes?"[8]

Beckwith, however, soon began to function solely as a majordomo of American preparations for the Exposition, for Seward

wrote him on October 4 that Beckwith's wish for a special coinage commissioner, to handle the coinage, weights, and measures
discussion at the Exposition, had been granted. The appointee
was Samuel Bulkley Ruggles. Ruggles, said the Secretary, "will
be charged with the subject of a common unit of coin"; he had
represented the United States at the Berlin Statistical Congress
in 1863, and "has already been in correspondence with the international committee, organized on that occasion, upon this important subject, to which he has devoted much study."[9]

Samuel Bulkley Ruggles, at the time Seward appointed him,
was a sixty-six-year-old Connecticut Yankee who had practiced
law and developed real estate in New York City since before the
opening of the Erie Canal. A planner and visionary whose
schemes and projects took him far beyond New York City, Ruggles served as Canal Commissioner of the State of New York from
1839 to 1858; then, as an acknowledged expert on public transportation, which for him was a great humanistic achievement, he
moved easily into railroad promotion, when railroads replaced
canals as the highways of the future. In late middle age Ruggles
was one of the guiding forces within the New York State Chamber of Commerce, represented it at the first meeting of the National Board of Trade, and served as chairman of its committees
on finance and on weights and measures.

Born literally in the first spring of the nineteenth century,
Ruggles was one of that spectacular breed of grand promoters of
whom America had many in that day, who knew not incredulity
nor recognized defeat. They blazed paths as bright as comets,
and often left works that were no more permanent. But they
often changed the minds and lives of their fellow men, and they
differed from their compatriots in only one main thing: they
had the same ebullience and vision raised to considerably higher
powers.[10] Ruggles, by the early 1860's, deserved the title of the
American apostle of coinage unification, and he continued to
work toward that end until just before his death in 1881. The
peroration of his report to Secretary Seward after the Paris Conference of 1867 was typically long-winded, but it reflects his style
and ideas beautifully. It is a first-class specimen of the American
Gilded-Age promoter mentality:

The fire but recently kindled [the Paris Conference agreements] is rapidly diffusing its light throughout the world. The farsighted negotiators of the quadripartite treaty of 1865, though seriously embarrassed by the fallacy of a double standard, now generally discarded, succeeded in establishing a uniform system, not only of gold but of silver, over a large and populous portion of Europe, since increased by the adhesion of the Pontifical States and of Greece; thus including, by a singular felicity, in this newly enlightened region of the globe, the two great seats of ancient civilization. With this wide-spread area extending off from the British Channel across Europe to the Mediterranean, and along its classic coast far into the east, the great reform [gold coinage unification] may be greatly advanced by the trans-atlantic co-operation of the American Union— by God's great providence, undivided and indivisible. Wisely limited by its own organic law to one common coinage between the two great oceans, the world needs only the assent of our own continental republic to give to the gold dollar and its multiples a free, unchallenged circulation, meeting no money changer or other impediment through the whole breadth of Christendom. The United States may alone complete the golden chain binding in one common monetary civilization the out-spread lands and waters of America and Europe, stretching from the "Golden Gate" of the Pacific over the auriferous "Oberlands" of our wide interior, and across Christian Europe to the Western bounds of the Ottoman Empire. To widen and extend still further this majestic belt, to embrace in the same great measure of civilization the residue of Europe with the wide extent of Asiatic Russia has been among the leading aims of the international monetary conference.[11]

Ruggles was obviously not the sort of man one would care to meet in a dark lecture hall, but he left behind for the cultural historian a compost of rare fertility.

At the Conference, Ruggles would reveal himself a true believer not only in universal coinage, but also in the universal gold standard. Bimetallism was already anathema to him in 1863 when he spoke for the union of the pound, the dollar, and the franc on the metric basis at Berlin. He jettisoned metricism later when it got in the way of the gold standard. But on May 17, 1866, he demonstrated its "admirable scientific harmony" to the New York Chamber of Commerce and called the permissive metric bill being discussed by Kasson in Congress that very day "a distinguishing feature in the history of American civilization." When he drew up a resolution to thank Congressman Kasson and Senator Sherman for steering through Congress a bill providing for the coinage of five-cent copper-nickel pieces weighing five metric grams and measuring an even fraction of the meter, the Chamber supported it, and it went to Washington.[12]

Four years after Ruggles' appointment as coinage commissioner to the Paris Exposition, George Opdyke, a prominent member of the New York Chamber, proudly told the convention of the National Board of Trade that Ruggles "has been the representative, partly of our Government and partly of the Chamber of Commerce of New York, in reference to the coinage question, in various conventions that have been held in Europe."[13] Not even the Bank of England or the Banque de France had such representation. If they had, it is doubtful that they could have picked a more effective agent.

Immediately after Seward appointed him, Ruggles got to work. More accurately, he continued earlier activities in a more public manner. Before the end of 1866, Ruggles and an "advisory committee" of New Yorkers, who had been preparing quietly for the Paris Exposition ever since the United States had been invited to it in March, 1865, produced a report describing how ten major sections of the American exhibit were in formation, with the indefatigable Ruggles in personal charge of the division on mines, metallurgy, forests, fisheries, chemistry, pharmacy, "& c." Five days after this massive report went in to Washington, Ruggles was writing Secretary Seward about how the conference on unification of weights, measures, and coinage, to be held as part of the Exposition, would fulfill the recommendation of the 1863 Berlin Statistical Congress. Early in March, 1867, American official preparations became complete when the Senate, after a week's debate, and the House, granted a supplemental appropriation of fifty thousand dollars for American exhibits and costs at the Exposition. Ruggles left for Paris a few days later.[14]

When he arrived, on March 23, 1867, French policy was still in flux; a full-scale International Monetary Conference, separate from the less elaborate unification discussions planned as part of the Exposition, was not yet definite. Ruggles' appointment was limited, strictly speaking, to cooperating with the Exposition authorities in setting up coinage, weights, and measures displays and discussing unification in the latter conference. But Ruggles and the French monometallists wanted something grander. The French chargé in Washington had already written Seward on January 4, 1867, to ask if the United States would be interested in joining the Latin Union outright, or at least in taking part in a coinage unification conference that would use the 1865 Latin Union treaty as its basis. Seward, after consulting with the Secretary of the Treasury, had answered that coinage unification was a long-time American aim; the United States would be happy to participate in such a conference. But the formal invitation for it did not come until May 27. The delay resulted from a struggle within the French Government ultimately resolved by the welding of a solid Franco-American front for gold monometallism.[15]

Bimetallism was still strong enough within the French Government to win votes in a monetary commission as late as April 1867. But the monometallists never let up. Diplomacy, for them, was but war carried on by other means. The monometallist leaders, Michel Chevalier and Esquirou de Parieu, searching about for new weapons, came across a one-man army in the person of the magnetic Samuel Bulkley Ruggles.[16] Ruggles was as delighted as ever to serve the monometallist cause. But his commission from the State Department was limited; he could not commit the United States officially, or even convincingly, to monometallism.

The situation called for reinforcements, franc-tireurs if possible, and by the happiest of circumstances, two appeared at that very moment. When the "City of Antwerp" sailed out of New York on April 10, the passenger list included Senator John Sherman of Ohio and just-retired Congressman John A. Kasson of Iowa, the men most responsible for seeing the metric weights bill of 1866 through each house of Congress, and who had long been on record in favor of international coinage unification.

Kasson bore a commission from the Post Office Department to negotiate international postal agreements with several countries, which he did successfully later in 1867. He was a convinced gold monometallist and advocate of international coinage unification and had founded the House Committee on Coinage, Weights, and Measures. But his role in Paris monetary events in 1867 was apparently limited to moral support; compared to Sherman's role, it was certainly slight.[17]

Sherman, then just forty-four, was chairman of the Committee on Finance of the United States Senate. A lawyer by profession, with Yankee forebears and anti-slavery and some Radical Republican connections, he was entering in 1867 the most productive phase of his long career, one of the most notable careers in late nineteenth-century American statesmanship. Elected to the House of Representatives four times beginning in 1855, Sherman spent thirty years in the Senate interrupted by four years as Hayes' Secretary of the Treasury, and closed his service in 1898 after a year as McKinley's Secretary of State. Sherman was chairman of either the Finance Committee or the Foreign Relations Committee almost the whole time he was a Senator, and from the late sixties to the late nineties he was consistently active and usually instrumental in every major financial or monetary law that went through Congress. He was a first-rate politician, as he had to be to survive in Ohio public life, and the fact that the Presidency eluded him says less about Sherman than it does about the fortune and circumstances required to attain that office. Throughout his active life, Sherman worked constantly to maintain the public credit. But although his general outlook changed very little, his views on certain measures shifted from time to time. Devoted to a point of view on finance, he always remembered that the worst enemy of that point of view was extremism or dogmatism. With Sherman it was always *fortiter in re,* but never forgetting *suaviter in modo.* His actions best make sense over the long run if he is understood as a politician with "conservative" financial views, rather than as a financial "conservative" in politics; the politics had to come first, and govern his tactics.

"Conservative" is of course anachronistic. What Sherman fought for, such as universal coinage unification on the gold basis in 1867, he and others believed to be liberal and progressive.[18] He was a pragmatic rightist, a moderator among contending interests, a Republican politician from the state of Ohio whose special competence happened to be public finance, a Congressional leader whose financial policies were as clear or as cloudy as the political atmosphere through which he had to aim them.

In his memoirs written thirty years later, Senator Sherman said that his European trip of 1867 had had no other object than "rest, a change of air and scene, and . . . a visit to the Exposition in Paris." Nothing concrete remains to disprove this, but his further statement that "I have no memoranda in respect to the voyage and preserved no letters about it" is belied by upwards of two dozen letters in his papers in the Library of Congress. His memoirs, however, are among the most notoriously unreliable of any American statesman's. They were written when his memory was unquestionably slipping, and in dealing with the late sixties he was so often wrong when he could have had no conceivable ulterior purpose in being wrong, that there is no valid reason for suspecting deliberate distortion or any dark conspiracy. But simple coincidence cannot explain why the one man in the United States Senate whose approval was essential to any coinage bill happened to journey to Paris at that crucial moment, and in the company of a man of Kasson's qualifications, and that both Sherman and Kasson had sponsored metric and coinage unification proposals in Congress on the very days twelve months earlier when Ruggles was securing resolutions on those matters from the New York Chamber of Commerce.

On his trip, Sherman mixed a little business with pleasure from the start. Jay Cooke, the Philadelphia banker, arranged introductions into Paris banking circles. Congressman Samuel Hooper of Massachusetts, a veteran House financial specialist, gave Sherman a letter to Thomas Baring of Baring Brothers, asking Baring to put Sherman in touch with a number of people "not generally accessible to Americans." In London, Sherman and Kasson met John Bright, Disraeli, and other eminent Victorians. In early May they were invited to dinner "to meet gentlemen interested in advancing the community of Measures, Weights, and Coins." By the time they arrived in Paris and joined General John A. Dix, the American Minister, they had had every opportunity to meet the key British politicians, international coinage advocates, and City financiers.[19]

By early May, the French gold monometallists and their ally, Ruggles, were ready to launch their final offensive. The coinage unification discussions of the Exposition were already in progress. For the French monometallists, now was the winter of their discontent made glorious summer by this son of New York. Ruggles thereupon repeated his 1863 Berlin proposal to Esquirou de Parieu: that France should coin a 25-franc gold piece. Then the United States would lower the gold content of the dollar to make the five-dollar gold piece exactly equivalent to the new French coin. The British could make a lesser adjustment in the pound, and universal coinage would be a fact; with the great trading nations of France, Britain, and America unified, the rest of the world would follow suit. Esquirou de Parieu asked for this in writing on May 7, Ruggles replied that this was beyond his authority, and probably beyond that of General Dix. But by then the reinforcements were at hand. Sherman and Kasson arrived from London either at that moment or within four or five days, and when the Exposition discussions met about May 22, Ruggles presented two letters that irrevocably scattered the bimetallic forces.[20]

The first was from Ruggles to Sherman, dated May 17. Ruggles stated that the drift of the Exposition discussions was toward adopting the existing French five-franc gold piece as the international unit. "May I ask what, in your opinion, is the probability that the Congress of the United States, at an early period, would agree to reduce the weight and value of our gold dollar, to correspond with the present weight and value of the gold five franc piece of France, and how far such a change would commend itself to your own judgment?" And could he, Ruggles asked in closing, submit Sherman's reply to the discussants?[21]

The second letter was Sherman's answer, dated May 18 from the Hotel du Jardins des Tuileries. As a matter of fact, said the Senator, the proposition had been so little debated in the Congress that he would be unable to say how it would be received. But several commercial organizations had discussed it, and "I feel quite sure that Congress will adopt any practical measure that will secure to the commercial world a uniform standard of value and exchange." The Latin Union of 1865, "and the probable acquiescence in that treaty by Prussia," are encouraging, and if Britain would reduce the sovereign by two pence and the United States the dollar by $3\frac{1}{2}$ cents, the major nations would have the same coinage unit, all equivalent to the gold franc and its multiples. Nothing was wrong with the sovereign or the dollar as units, but since seventy million people already used the franc, it was the most realistic basis.

The proposal was so good, in fact, that even the less attractive aspects of the Latin Union would be wiped out. If unification could be achieved on the gold franc basis, Sherman continued,

> France will surely abandon the impossible effort of making two standards of value. Gold coins will answer all the purposes of European commerce. A common gold standard will regulate silver coinage, of which the United States will furnish the greater part, especially for the Chinese trade. . . . It is clear that the United States cannot become a party to the [Latin Union]. They could not agree upon the silver standard; nor could we limit the amount of our coinage, as proposed by the treaty . . . we require more currency *per capita*.

Since the United States was at the moment on a currency of inconvertible paper, the time was ideal for the change. The only problem was existing contracts, which could not be infringed, but a distinction between the old and new dollars would be easy to provide for in both private and public contracts. "Certainly no more important object can excite the attentions of practical men than the adoption of universal standards of value, weights and measures," Sherman concluded. But the universal gold standard was the chief aim for him as it was for Ruggles.[22]

Ruggles and the French monometallists now had the bimetallists in disarray. The French already knew that Britain would never accept silver. If America opposed it too, and obviously no coinage bill that Sherman did not approve of could clear the Senate, international coinage unification on the metric basis or a bimetallic franc basis could go no farther. It provided the monometallists with the clinching argument that France had to support Ruggles' idea of a basic 25-franc gold coin if she wanted any success at all.

Some nerve-wracking moments had passed. For some reason, Sherman's letter failed to reach Ruggles for three days. By then, Sherman had already left for Berlin, and anxious telegrams went out from the Paris office of the American banking firm of Bowles, Drevet et Cie., probably Ruggles' cable headquarters, saying, "Ruggles has not received your financial letter" and asking for a copy. Sherman finally replied that it had been sent and that he had no copy. The anxiety was doubtless not only Ruggles': others awaited it. As soon as Ruggles finally received it, he took it to Esquirou de Parieu. The pair then brought it to the minister of foreign affairs, and then to Napoleon III himself. It sufficed. Thus cleared, the letters went to the Exposition coinage discussions.[23]

After the discussants heard Ruggles' letters, they immediately prepared a series of "recommendations" for the international monetary conference which was now a certainty. Ready engines began grinding at once: on May 27, the French chargé in Washington tendered to Seward a formal invitation to participate in an international monetary conference to begin June 17 at Paris, under the presidency of the French ministers of foreign affairs and finance. Seward accepted two days later and informed the French that Ruggles would be the American delegate.[24] In the next two weeks the Exposition discussions agreed on nine propositions, among them uniform gold coinage for all nations, uniform fineness of 900 for that coinage, the franc basis, the five-franc piece as a unit, decimal subdivisions, and the abolition of silver as a monetary standard, in Ruggles' words, "wherever it still exists." These became virtually the agenda for the International Monetary Conference.

After such careful preparations, the Conference was almost anticlimactically successful. Thirty-six delegates from nineteen countries attended the eight meetings which opened on the morning of June 17 at the Ministry of Foreign Affairs. Esquirou chaired the first half of the Conference. The delegates were not lightweights; some of them had been active in politics or public finance for nearly forty years, and among them were six of the nine delegates to the Latin Union conference of 1865. That many of them were the chief financial diplomats of their respective countries indicates the seriousness with which the leading governments regarded the Conference.

Ruggles was the only delegate who did not hold a permanent governmental or central banking office. Once the Franco-American *entente auréale* had been forged, however, he needed no further help. Sherman and Kasson remained in Paris, seeing Ruggles, General Dix, and others, and may even have dropped in on a session. Ruggles and the two legislators were doubtless gratified when, shortly after the Conference opened, Acting Secretary of State F. W. Seward thanked Ruggles for his efforts and said that the public and the Government would doubtless support Sherman's very able statement of May 18. Sherman and Kasson left for England at the end of June, after the Conference agreed on gold monometallism. Junius Spencer Morgan, a prominent London merchant banker and father of the later-renowned J. Pierpont, met them at Paddington Station for a visit to his country place, and after a few more days in London, Sherman left for home.[25]

The first meeting of the International Monetary Conference was organizational. Marquis de Moustier, the Foreign Minister, delivered an inspiring allocution to the delegates on the progressive nature of their task, and then turned the Chairmanship over to Esquirou. Esquirou forthwith appointed a seven-man subcommittee, including himself and Ruggles, to work out an agenda, in which the monetary standard was assumed to be the central question. At the second meeting, two days later, the agenda appeared. The Conference adopted it without debate, and spent the rest of the session discussing its first item, whether unification should take place on the basis of an existing monetary system or an entirely new one. The Dutch and Belgian delegates pointed out that science demanded a wholly new system. Not only would it avoid "national susceptibilities," but it would observe the obvious: The silver franc represented an integral metric weight, but the gold franc did not. A new unit, based on gold grams, was called for.[26]

Despite the cogency of these arguments, the Prussian, Russian, Swedish, and Portuguese delegates, plus Ruggles, Esquirou, and the influential Charles Feer-Herzog of Switzerland, demurred. Practicality demands the use of an existing system, they said, and of these, the Latin Union system was the obvious choice.

At this point, the metric system went by the boards. As Feer-Herzog put it,

> Without doubt, the metric system, in its application to weights and measures, satisfies by its admirable co-ordinations the necessities of practical character, together with the exigencies of theory; but to desire to impose it, coextensively, in all its rigor, in matters of coin, would be to encounter obstacles which mere considerations of practical utility would not have removed.

There is a school of thought in France, he continued, "important because of the scientific authority of its adepts," which demands a coinage unit measurable in a round number of metric grams (Michel Chevalier was one of these "adepts," which possibly explains why he was not a delegate to the Monetary Conference). But it would be unwise to demand a completely new unit, Feer-Herzog warned, if people really hoped practically to unify the franc, the pound sterling, the dollar, the [Austrian] florin, the thaler, and other units.

Since every delegate, it seems, winced at the idea of being thought a "scientific adept" rather than a practical man of affairs, Feer-Herzog had gained ground for the gold franc. But one battle did not win the war. The Prussian delegate said that while Prussia realized she would have to switch from silver monometallism to gold if unification were to be achieved, the switch would be very difficult. A few minutes later, Thomas Graham of Great Britain, even less encouragingly, declared that a reduction in the gold content of the pound to the 25-franc level would be neither easy nor likely.

Ruggles then intervened. In order to achieve unification, he said, the United States was prepared to reduce its whole gold coinage by 3½ cents in the dollar to conform with twenty-five francs, and asked in return only that Britain reduce the sovereign by two pence, and that France actually begin coining a 25-franc piece. This, of course, was the same proposal Ruggles had been repeating ever since the Berlin meeting of 1863. But Esquirou leaped at it: as chairman of the meeting, the Frenchman "expressed to Mr. Ruggles the satisfaction with which the Conference had listened to sentiments so favorable to monetary unification as those he had uttered in the name of the United States." Quickly, the delegates voted unanimously against a totally new basis for international coinage, unanimously in favor of some existing system, and then unanimously in favor of "the system of the monetary convention of 1865." With this, the session adjourned.

The last vote was understood explicitly not to "prejudge" the standards question. The system of 1865 was bimetallic; would the Conference keep silver or drop it? This was the question facing the third session, which met on June 20. The deck had been well stacked. No one, not even the delegates from silver-standard countries, spoke for silver monometallism. The Dutch delegate, echoed very faintly by the Austrian, was the only supporter of an international bimetallic standard. Gold was on the verge of triumph. While the delegates of Great Britain, the only major gold-standard country, watched in silence and did nothing to push the Conference either way, one great power after another put itself on record in favor of gold monometallism. The Austrian called it the only viable basis for international union; he would vote for it although his own country was on the single silver standard. Ruggles seized the occasion to affirm resoundingly his monometallist faith: he denied that the United States was really a bimetallic country except in the most theoretical and legal sense, silver dollars having disappeared with the increase in the world gold supply since 1848, "in obedience to the fundamental and inexorable law of demand and supply, which sets at naught all attempts made to fix by legislation the relative values of the two metals." American experience showed "that the system of a double standard is not only a fallacy, but an impossibility.

. . . The United States now share, without reserve, the conviction, more and more extended through the civilized world, that it is impossible to establish a double standard."

The most striking adhesion came a moment later from silver-monometallist Prussia. As long as the Conference provided for a transitional period, the Prussian delegate would vote for the single gold standard. Esquirou and Feer-Herzog each hailed this enormously gratifying development, making sure that no one missed it, and the Frenchman soothingly observed that the operation of Gresham's law would not be instantaneous anyway, and the silver countries could surely expect a transitional period.

The chief British delegate, speaking for the first time that day, moved a one-word amendment whose remarkable effect was to make monometallism certain. Silver standards would be retained only "temporarily," rather than simultaneously, with an international gold standard. The Conference thus adopted "the exclusive gold standard, leaving each state the liberty to keep its silver standard temporarily." The vote was unanimous except for the Netherlands. The British were not enthusiastic about the franc, but sought the adoption of gold, their own standard, everywhere.

Gold monometallism, which Ruggles later called "the cardinal, if not the all-important feature of the plan proposed by the Conference," had received the delegates' approval. They also approved some kind of gold coin, related to the franc. The remaining five sittings of the Conference were more momentous diplomatically than financially.

The fourth sitting opened with an air of nervousness on the part of several delegates who feared they may have overcommitted themselves the day before, but then it settled down to a discussion of the "transitional period" for the switch from silver to gold. This involved the question of a suitable and uniform price ratio between gold and silver. Most of the delegates assumed that there could and should be one, but Feer-Herzog, Esquirou, and Ruggles disagreed. Relentlessly, they warned that a fixed ratio would not only perpetuate the silver standard, but would inevitably run counter to the law of supply and demand.

The Prussian and Austrian delegates still held back. The

Prussian said that his government was still debating transitional measures and he was not empowered to discuss them. The Austrian, more significantly, stated openly what Berlin and Vienna were concerned about: Quite possibly the fall in the price of gold as compared to silver, which had been going on since the Californian and Australian gold discoveries of twenty years before, had gone as far as it was going to. Experts, notably Dr. Adolph Soetbeer of Hamburg, were already predicting publicly that gold would soon rise in relative value.

This was the first clear mention, either in the Conference or its preliminaries, that the movement toward the single gold standard might very well have been a movement to demonetize what was soon to become the cheaper of the two metals rather than the more valuable one. At this point, the Austrian moved to table the whole question of the transitional period and the bimetallic ratio. His motion passed unanimously, with Ruggles and the Prussian abstaining. But more cards were on the table than ever before; gold was to become, sooner or later, expensive or not, the sole monetary metal of the future.

The Conference did not meet again for five days. When it did, it had a new President. He was none other than Prince Jerôme Napoleon, cousin of the Emperor and not previously known for his interest or expertise in international coinage. But now His Imperial Highness looked forward, in spite of the incompetence he felt before such a distinguished gathering, not to "a fine report alone, or a good argument in favor of the unity of moneys," but "a useful result." Apparently the Bonapartes, now convinced that the Conference favored the franc basis, if not the metric system or French bimetallism, decided to assert their personal prestige at the half-way point in the Conference to insure some positive action. Probably too, they were hoping to secure a definite commitment from the British, as they already had from the United States, and, in the previous sitting, from Austria-Hungary and Prussia.

But the British, ever wary of "Gallic intrigue," recoiled. As soon as the discussion opened, one of the Britishers rose to declare that he and his colleagues thought it necessary "to indicate their delicate and exceptional situation." Although Her

Majesty's Government "will be always ready to aid any attempt to enlighten and guide public opinion in the appreciation of the question, and facilitate the discussion of the means by which such an assimilation, so advantageous in theory, may be effected," nevertheless "they cannot vote for any question tending to bind their government, nor express any opinion to induce the belief that Great Britain would adopt the Convention of 1865."

The Bonapartes had overplayed their hand. Prince Napoleon backed off quickly, saying that "the labors of the conference are essentially theoretical," and that the British delegates need have no fear; they would be voting for propositions which could be effectuated only by future meetings. This was an ineffective tourniquet; the Prussian, seconded by the delegates of Bavaria and Baden, made clear that what he had said earlier was "only intended as principle." The session adjourned after a long discussion of technical coinage matters.

At the sixth session, Ruggles made a fervent plea for his longtime objective, the 25-franc gold piece. It was adopted, as was the proposition that five gold francs would be the basic international unit and legal tender. But these agreements were achieved only at the expense of a Bonapartean cutting of losses. Prussia, though obviously ready to adopt gold as soon as she had the means, would not at that time support anything more specific than the principle of gold monometallism. For the moment Prussia abstained from specific measures such as the 25-franc basis. Britain, on the other hand, accepted the principle but positively refused to promise any action. Despite Ruggles' forceful presentation of America's willingness to reduce the dollar by an amount four times as great as the reduction his plan required of the pound sterling, so that the dollar and pound would equal five and twenty-five francs respectively, one of the Britons said he "placed himself in a purely theoretical point of view when speaking of the acceptability of the twenty-five franc piece." Prince Jerôme Napoleon, trying verbal force as a final resort, repeated that the Conference's aims were not toward "speculative studies," but were "definite and practical, to which it is the duty of all its members to direct their efforts." The Briton only replied that "England could not but appreciate the intention" behind the 25-franc proposal. With the rapid settling or discarding of the last four (and less important) questions on the agenda, the session adjourned. Ruggles and the French were not having things all their way.

On July 2, four days later, the seventh session met to discuss practical measures. Everyone, Ruggles observed, agreed that the first task of the Conference was to decide on a basis for future negotiations, which the Conference had done by adopting the gold standard, coins of equal weight and fineness, decimal subdivisions, and the five-franc unit. Yet it lacked the power to make final decisions. Even Prince Jerôme Napoleon knew he could lose nothing at that stage by admitting that French law would have to be changed, and a change would take time. (A very accurate prediction, in the event.) The Conference, including the British and the Prussians, decided that each delegation should take home the propositions agreed upon, make an official reply to France as the host government by the spring of 1868, and France would call another Conference, "if necessary," to set up an international monetary treaty.

The final session, on July 6, was virtually a solo performance by Esquirou de Parieu, summarizing the work of the Conference amidst quotations from Ovid, benevolent allusions to the wisdom of German thinkers, and frequent references to progress, civilization, science, the human family, and the dreams of poets and economists. All these were closer to realization, he said, because the Conference had adopted the gold five-franc piece as the basis for future universal coinage. After thanking Prince Napoleon for the labors of his "illustrious presidency," and the Emperor for his patronage, the delegates adjourned *sine die*.

Who had won what? The monometallists of all countries could now say that a great international convention, the greatest on monetary unification ever seen, had explicitly rejected bimetallism and declared for gold. In later years, Francis A. Walker, an American bimetallist, said that in its impact and political force the Conference was "unique," had "profoundly affected the public mind of Europe," and had placed every bimetallist and silver monometallist ". . . upon the defensive. The Conference stigmatized silver as unfit longer to be the money of

civilized countries. It had stamped the double standard as illogical and impossible in practice," and augured the future diplomatic victory of gold monometallism.[27] Britain apparently gained
by having assisted in universalizing the gold standard, yet had
not compromised in the slightest her own monometallic usage
or unique coinage system.[28] The Prussians returned to Berlin
having announced that Prussia already intended to change from
silver to gold, but had given no hint as to how or when they
would do it. The Austrians had the satisfaction of cooperating
with France, and moving toward the gold standard, as they too
already planned, while safeguarding their silver.[29] Ruggles went
home exhilarated that his arguments had been received so well,
but he doubtless could not forget (some of the delegates had
reminded him sharply) that the United States would have to
demonetize the silver dollar sooner or later.[30]

For France, the Conference was a forward step, but only a short
one, not only for the monometallists who still faced a very difficult legislative battle to change French coinage law, but also for
Napoleon III. Though the franc was apparently going to be the
basis of any future universal money system, the scientific metric
basis for that coinage, and the wishes of powerful bimetallist
groups within the country, had had to be sacrificed. Like so
many Napoleonic victories, this one had a mixed character.

Nevertheless, the French were grateful for Ruggles' work and
so informed Secretary of State Seward. Ruggles' report to Seward
in November was enthusiastic, as well it might have been since
his own 25-franc scheme of universal gold coinage had not only
received the vigorous support of Senator Sherman, but praise
from Seward and the "cordial concurrence" of Secretary of the
Treasury McCulloch, who said he would recommend it to Congress. Ruggles was at his orotund best in this final report. It was
replete with such phrases as "these pagan Asiatics" (whose bimetallic ratio was inaccurate), "the broad metalliferous mountain range stretching from Cape Horn to the Arctic Ocean," the
"Latin races who approach, to say the least, in general culture
and intelligence, some of the Teutonic and Sclavonic [sic] races
represented in the Conference," "the monetary movement in
these fifteen years on the waters of the globe," "powers of the

oceans . . . subdued by steam," the repeal of the French bimetallic law "by the natural and irresistible increase in the
value of silver in obedience to the superior and overruling law
of demand and supply." Ruggles apparently had no inkling,
though many others did, that a drop in the price of silver was
in the offing; universal gold monometallism glittered brightly
before his promoter's eyes for different reasons. America's duty
was clear, he coaxed:

> It now needs only a brief law of Congress, fixing the weight
> of the gold dollar at 1.61290 milligrams—to establish a
> permanent line of monetary unity spanning the Christian
> world from San Francisco to the confines of Constanti-
> nople.[31]

Except for minor difficulties such as the refusals of Britain and
Prussia to do likewise, the monetary millennium was but a short
step away.

As soon as he returned home, and for the rest of 1867, Ruggles
strove to bring that "brief law" before Congress. In his efforts,
he enjoyed the active help of Senator Sherman and Secretary of
the Treasury Hugh McCulloch.

9

MONETARY RECONSTRUCTION: CONTRACTION, THE FIRST GOLD STANDARD BILL, AND THE PUBLIC CREDIT ACT, 1867–69

Hugh McCulloch, in late 1867, was in a position that would have unnerved a lesser man. He was the second-ranking member of the Cabinet of a President whose congressional relations were so incredibly bad that that President would be impeached before the next summer. Yet McCulloch knew the critical task of the reconstruction of public finance would be impossible without congressional help. The immediate postwar years were as violently partisan as any in American history. How could McCulloch (himself a Democrat) succeed, or even proceed, without estranging himself from either President Andrew Johnson or the Republican leaders of Congress?

McCulloch succeeded in creating and executing a policy that moved generally, if roughly, in the direction he desired, because of two things: he was himself utterly convinced of a moralistic monetary theory that led in a definite policy direction, and at

the same time, neither the Democratic nor Republican parties
were united on the money question at all. McCulloch, a latter-
day Jacksonian, could muster support from various Democrats
and Republicans, some of the latter important congressional
leaders, for a policy that crossed party lines. Though ever loyal
to Andrew Johnson as President, McCulloch differed from his
chief on most of the important financial issues that arose—or,
they would have differed had they argued them out; they did
not, because Johnson left the Treasury alone most of the time.
Even more ironically, Johnson's greatest persecutors among the
Radical Republicans were at least as "unorthodox" (i.e., greenbackish) as he; the President and his impeachers were closer on
financial questions than either of them were to Secretary Mc-
Culloch or to the less militant Republicans who frequently had
charge of congressional monetary affairs. Thus it was that Mc-
Culloch was able to work effectively with Senator Sherman and
Samuel B. Ruggles, and a number of other people in and out
of government, toward generally hard-money ends and without
regard for party labels.

McCulloch set about resuming specie payments after Appomattox in the quickest way he could think of. Take greenbacks
out of circulation, and the demand for them would rise; soon
they would be at par. The gold premium would disappear and
the great end of specie resumption would be accomplished. This
method was called contraction. Although it amounted to further
deflation in an already deflationary cycle, large majorities in both
houses of Congress passed a law on April 12, 1866, approving the
Secretary's policy of "retiring" greenbacks.

McCulloch had a rationale for this hardest of hard-money
schemes, and it was not by any means a simple favoritism toward
capital-holding specie interests. His general approach to financial
matters was rigorously bullionist; the one-time state banker was
no wildcatter. Basing his bullionism on natural law and producerism, McCulloch saw contraction to be the obvious and
proper way to proceed, as he wrote Horace Greeley in mid-1866.
To resume, said the Secretary, he would compel the national
banks to redeem their notes at the "sea-board cities" if he had
the power, and he would retire enough of the greenbacks "to

check speculation and set the people at work." Contraction was
the road to resumption and, more importantly, to the good
society. "What we want," he told Greeley,

> is a restoration of industry, a diminution of importations
> and an increase of export. These we are not likely to have as
> long as a vast volume of irredeemable currency is kept in
> circulation. . . . *I care very little about specie or specie pay-
> ment in themselves considered.* What I do desire is that the
> business of the country be brought into a healthy condition;
> that the horrible immorality, which is the legitimate result of
> inflation, shall cease, that as a nation, we shall be independ-
> ent, that as individuals we shall become industrious, eco-
> nomical, honest.[1]

McCulloch continued to contract the grenbacks for another year
and a half. His papers are crowded with testimonials to his
wisdom from metropolitan financiers, country bankers, Elbridge
Gerry Spaulding (a wartime Congressman who had reluctantly
helped create the greenbacks), then a national banker in Buffalo,
German-American leader Charles Reemelin, Amasa Walker,
Francis Lieber, and others. In his annual report at the end of
1867, McCulloch reiterated his belief that the only real money
was gold coin, the "circulating medium of the world," which
by its nature resisted inflation perfectly and could do nothing
to labor, industry, and enterprise except stimulate them. But
paper money, he warned, was demoralizing and repudiatory.[2]

Yet by that time, McCulloch had had to reappraise the contraction policy. Since early 1866 he had had to try to build a
reserve of gold in the Treasury to anticipate demands for it on
resumption day. But at the same time, he had had to sell gold
for greenbacks and certain bonds, not only in order to retire
them but also to keep the open-market prices of both somewhere
remotely near par.

Treasury gold sales were not uniformly welcomed on Wall
Street, though McCulloch would have liked to think so. Mc-
Culloch and H. H. Van Dyck, the head of the New York Sub-
treasury, had to publish open letters in May, 1866, explaining
their policy. In McCulloch's mind, the stabilizing effect of the

gold sales benefited the "laboring and producing classes" and he considered his policy vindicated by the surprising "steadiness of the market [and] the gradual advance of currency to the true standard of value" since the War. Van Dyck, who did the actual selling, and at unannounced times and amounts, explained that without the gold sales, the gold premium would undoubtedly have shot up to panic levels, and all existing contracts would have suffered. Keeping the gold premium down, he said, met the unquestionable necessity of strengthening our foreign credit.[3]

McCulloch, in fact, was constantly being pushed toward making the maintenance of the public credit, rather than contraction, his first priority. This was a relief to certain business and political people unfavorable to contraction from the start. Manufacturers and others attempting to expand amidst deflation, even many financiers, looked forward to ultimate resumption but considered contraction a very ill-advised way of getting there. *Their chief aim was monetary stability.* Disliking either speculation or deflation, they considered contraction (especially during "natural" postwar deflation) a hindrance to the return of prosperity. It was even a danger to the public credit since it might damage trade and thus lower revenues to the point where the government would have to default on interest payments on the debt. The Wall-Streeter Henry Clews complained that business prostration was far worse than a few speculators. The New York Chamber of Commerce refused to endorse contraction openly, partly on Henry C. Carey's advice. Jay Cooke wrote Senator Sherman that refunding of the debt, not contraction, should be the government's first object. Cooke recognized that the gold premium acted as a supplement to tariff protection for productive enterprise, and that without protection it was just not possible to produce coal, iron, and other essentials economically. Increased production, not contraction, was to Cooke the road to resumption "in a reasonable time say 12 or 18 months and without any great disturbance to our industrial, mechanical or manufacturing interests." Sherman not only agreed, but had introduced a resolution in early March, 1866, forbidding contraction; voted against the bill of April 12, 1866, which authorized it; and continued to fight it throughout 1867 and 1868.[4]

Sherman and McCulloch, never intimate, were at loggerheads on the contraction question. Each had his business backers: with Sherman, there were those who looked toward ultimate resumption, even "speedy resumption," but without severe deflation; with McCulloch were those who thought immediate resumption imperative to active and honest business. In late 1867, the majority seemed to be with Sherman. Despite McCulloch's belief that contraction "has had no little influence in stimulating labor and increasing production," and his certainty (as he wrote Van Dyck) that Sherman was mistaken, he nevertheless gave in. He informed Sherman that although contraction was the wisest policy, he would suspend it if Congress wanted to reconsider his authority in the matter.[5]

Congress did. On December 7, 1867, Congressman Robert Schenck reported from the House Ways and Means Committee a bill to suspend the Secretary's power to reduce the currency by retiring or cancelling United States notes (greenbacks). It passed the House that day, 127 to 32. Soft-money Radical Republicans such as William D. Kelley called McCulloch's policy "as dishonest as it is unwise" since it palpably increased "the value of the rich man's hoarded or invested dollars" and "robs millions of laborers of their whole estate." To Kelley, "the contest is between the creditor and the debtor class—the men of investments and the men of enterprise; and during all such contests the laboring classes are inevitable sufferers." Production, not contraction, was the sure road to the specie resumption everyone desired. McCulloch himself could not have disagreed with that thought, but the Secretary could not conceive of full production except on a specie basis; but Kelley and his Pennsylvania manufacturer friends knew better.

Sherman, as Senate floor leader for the contraction repeal bill, put his whole stress on the stability of business conditions that the end of contraction would bring. The repeal bill was needed, he said, to convince the business community and investors that monetary stability was the government's foremost aim. After an anti-inflation amendment was beaten down (mainly by Midwesterners and Pennsylvanians), the bill passed overwhelmingly and became law without President Johnson's signature on February

5. The greenback currency was stabilized at $356-million, the amount circulating at that moment.

McCulloch and Sherman both wanted resumption. Both wanted business prosperity. Both were gold monometallists. McCulloch even more than Sherman talked in the accents of producerism. Both spoke of the need to support all economic groups and the national interest; both detested "repudiation"; both were Midwesterners of New England antecedents. Yet their policies on how to achieve specie resumption were exactly opposed. If contraction meant hard-money, repeal of it soft-money in early 1868, the high tide of Radical Republicanism (Johnson was impeached a few weeks later), then Sherman took the softer side. Clearly, however, it was political and economic stability, not soft money in any inflationary sense, that Sherman sought and won.[6]

Sherman and McCulloch did agree, however, on another stabilizing measure: the gold standard, as recommended by the Paris International Monetary Conference. The two men worked closely before and after the Conference, and in late 1867 and into 1868, Secretary and Senator moved to implement the Paris proposals. These moves were the first steps that led finally, in 1873, to America's demonetization of silver, discarding of bimetallism, and legal adoption of the gold standard.

Ruggles sent his official report on the Paris Conference to Washington in October, and in November, McCulloch sent his annual report to Congress. In it was a plea for Congress to put Ruggles' and the Conference's plan into law. On December 23, not very surprisingly, Senator Sherman wrote Secretary McCulloch that he was "strongly impressed" with the Paris Conference plan, and intended to implement it in the Congressional session just convened. American law, proclaimed Sherman, should provide full legal tender for gold, but should limit silver to payments of no more than ten dollars.

The 1867 report of the Director of the Mint, Henry R. Linderman, which went to Congress, as usual, as part of the Treasury Secretary's report, called for the same thing: adoption of the gold standard, "using silver only for subsidiary purposes." It hailed the Ruggles-Paris plan for international coinage unification, provided the reduction that Ruggles wanted in the gold dollar did not infringe existing contracts. Linderman, a Pennsylvania Democrat of German ancestry, was a surgeon by schooling, a coinage expert by training, and a politician by instinct. Appointed Mint Director by McCulloch when the Republican incumbent, James Pollock, resigned because of partisan differences, Linderman remained at Philadelphia until he, in turn, was replaced by Pollock when the Grant Administration came to power early in 1869. Linderman was a political asset to the beleaguered Johnson administration, was consulted on Pennsylvania patronage, and was in McCulloch's eyes a man "in whom we all have great confidence." But Linderman did not neglect his Republican contacts; and regardless of the party in power, he served gold monometallism faithfully and well.[7]

As Mint Director, Linderman had a style and grasp that contrasted markedly with the methods of the administrator-functionary, Pollock. When he took over at Philadelphia, Linderman had new stationery printed, with his own name on the outside of the triple-folded letter forms, above the words "U.S. Mint," and in bigger type. His letters to his Washington superiors were full of references to the chemical composition of ores, technical problems of refining, new machinery for assaying and coining, and other such matters which effectively precluded any substantive argument from Washington about his management and which surrounded him with an unimpeachable air of competence. Probably the only people in America who could have given Linderman a run for his money in an argument over the technical side of coinage were his own subordinates. But no letter left the Mint except from Linderman himself, or covered by a Linderman letter. He was not a man for anyone, even a Treasury Secretary, to treat lightly.

Linderman's 1867 report, advocating the Ruggles-Paris plan, brought him quickly into the planning of coinage legislation, a position he seldom vacated for the next decade. In late December, 1867, a flurry of letters passed between Secretary McCulloch, Senator Sherman, and Linderman. A meeting ensued between the three men and their aides in Washington just before New Year's. On January 2, 1868, Linderman sent McCulloch the coinage bill "prepared at your suggestion"; perhaps Senator Sherman would want to look it over. Four days later, Sherman presented to the Senate "a bill in relation to the coinage of gold and silver." This bill would have enacted the Ruggles-Paris plan to unify the franc, the pound sterling, and the dollar; adopt gold monometallism; and discard the silver standard in America. The bill immediately went to Sherman's Senate Finance Committee for consideration, and the United States bode fair to produce the first great results of the International Monetary Conference.[8]

Little evidence survives from the six-month period when the gold standard bill was in the Finance Committee. But there is enough to show, first, that Sherman was in touch about it with McCulloch, Linderman, and Representative William D. Kelley (which may seem odd, in view of Kelley's pronounced Careyism, which usually meant greenbackism, but Kelley had good reasons which will become clear later), and secondly, that Sherman, if one assumes that he was not trying to sabotage his own bill, got his wires crossed.

Sherman finally reported the bill to the Senate on June 9, shortly after President Johnson's impeachment trial. He floated it on a broad raft of arguments roped together with all the relevant rhetoric he could scavenge. The overriding object of the measure, Sherman announced candidly, was to make the monetary standard "fixed and invariable." Dismissing the greenbacks, he crowned precious metals the best standard for this purpose, "for the value of property and all internal commerce adapts itself to [their] intrinsic value." He had plenty of other arguments: international coinage would benefit civilization. America as a bullion producer would benefit from the ability of an international unit to travel the world over without exchange costs. If the dollar were legal tender everywhere, debts would be easier to pay. The time was ripe. Gold monometallism was "an American idea, yielded reluctantly by France and other countries." Finally, bimetallism, the use of silver along with gold, foolishly contravened Gresham's Law and the inexorable law of supply and demand.

Silver, therefore, had to go. Of course the bill had no other real point than to demonetize silver, since the United States was already on a precious-metals standard even though not on specie payments; all the other arguments advocated what already existed. Sherman argued that the dropping of the silver dollar, the debasement of lower-valued silver coins in order to keep them circulating (which also already existed), and limiting the legal tender power of silver coins to ten dollars, "are urged by the director of the mint [Linderman] to secure harmony between the present market value [sic] of gold and silver . . . without disturbing the sole legal standard of value for large sums." Silver, like gold, was an American product whose use in coinage ought to be maintained and protected. But, although it admirably suited subsidiary coinage (except, oddly, five and three cent pieces, slated to disappear along with the dollar—which, as will be seen, was a peculiarly Philadelphian contribution to the bill), silver could not be allowed to interfere with the internationality, the stability, the conformity to natural laws, the protection to existing capital investments, that gold afforded.[9]

Thus were Sherman's arguments for his gold standard bill in June 1868. Was silver such a threat to established values? More to the point, were Sherman, Linderman, and McCulloch aware that it was becoming a threat?

There is every indication that they were. Sherman's bill was meant not only to fulfill the ideal of international coinage unification, such as that ideal was, and to make the Paris Conference plan a reality in America. It was also undertaken—the evidence is circumstantial but very considerable—to neutralize an impending decline in silver prices relative to gold, which, if it occurred, would severely injure countries in which silver was a legal standard but many of whose international payments had to be made in gold; a country, in short, such as the United States.

Every key aspect of American monetary policy—the gold sales, bond purchases, resumption plans, the stabilization of currency values—would fail dismally. Exporters and importers dealing in goods payable in gold on the London market would be hard put to buy that gold with depreciated silver. Public creditors would lose confidence, bond prices would plummet, Treasury gold reserves would drain away endlessly in a futile attempt to support the bonds or absorb the silver. Creditors would obviously be hurt, since they would be repaid in money of lower value than they had expected. But a case could be made that every economic interest, certainly any having to do, however indirectly, with foreign markets, producers, distributors, and consumers, would suffer.

The machinery by which silver, if it did fall drastically, could thus bombard existing arrangements, was not complicated. Suppose that silver bullion, for whatever reason, began to appear on world markets in great bulk. Any nation legally on a bimetallic standard, such as the United States or France, would have to accept silver with as good grace as it accepted gold. Under the American ratio by which one ounce of silver was legally worth sixteen ounces of silver, as soon as the price of sixteen ounces of silver dropped significantly below the price of an ounce of gold, bullion sellers naturally would keep the gold and present only silver to the Mint for coinage. Moreover, they would melt down gold coins, exchange the gold bullion at the Mint for silver coins, and end up with more dollars than they originally had, and dollars equally legal. Gresham's Law, that "bad money drives out good money," would operate as long as the fixed parity ratio and legal equality of the two metals existed. This, in reverse, was the very process that had made silver dollars so scarce in America: gold prices had dropped below the one-to-sixteen level in the 1830's, silver had disappeared, and the country was, for practical purposes (and by the sixties, habitually), on the gold standard. What now threatened was the replacement of gold by silver.

In these circumstances and by such reasoning, Sherman, McCulloch, Linderman, Kelley, and the other seekers after gold monometallism should only be praised for preparing for what they viewed as a horrible eventuality rather than condemned for rigging legislation to protect the bondholding interest. If silver prices faced a severe drop, and if, as their understanding of political economy predicted, the whole American credit, debt, and production structure would be turned upside down, the efforts to secure gold monometallism—a good idea in any event according to the rhetoric of civilization, law, and their version of producerism—became urgent. Motivated perhaps by the interests of commercial, bond-holding, and banking groups (though there is little evidence for this), motivated also by the ideology of gold monometallism and the prevailing civilization—natural-law—producerite rhetoric of the day (there is much direct evidence for this), these men were planning consciously and working actively, as early as the beginning of 1867, to demonetize silver as a monetary standard in America.

The circumstantial evidence for this judgment is impressive. Sherman's memoirs can be construed in several places as attempting to hide his real purpose in going to Paris at the time of the Monetary Conference in 1867, yet he was instrumental in creating the Franco-American *entente auréale* that underlay the Conference and brought about its declaration for gold. Ruggles and Sherman were in day-to-day touch with American and British bankers and creditor interests at the time of the Conference. Sherman, Kasson, and very probably Ruggles were in contact about metric coinage a year before the Conference. Sherman, Ruggles, McCulloch, and Secretary of State Seward were aware of what the Conference was for. Ruggles was described three years later (by George Opdyke) as an agent not only of the American government, but of the New York Chamber of Commerce. Ruggles admitted years later that the New York Chamber of Commerce was much interested at the time of the Conference in a "general unification of the gold coin."[10]

But all of this activity on behalf of gold and against silver means nothing unless Ruggles and Sherman and McCulloch, or at least the latter two, were expecting silver prices to drop, for only then would silver threaten the investments of bondholders. Silver did drop precipitously in the seventies, but before then, and in 1867, it was still actually worth more in the open market than it was at the U.S. Mint at the one-to-sixteen ratio. Could Sherman, or McCulloch, or anyone, have known then what would happen several years later?

Remarkably, it is more than likely that they could. In Britain, a month before the Paris Conference opened, the *Economist* published an article by Professor William Stanley Jevons in which Jevons noted that gold prices had started to rise; the long-term decline in gold had in fact stopped sometime before, and silver was slipping to very near the French one to fifteen-and-a-half ratio, at which point it would return to circulation in the Latin Union. In Germany, Dr. Adolph Soetbeer of Hamburg, a respected authority, held similar views, which some German delegates to the Paris Conference stated flatly. The most direct warning of the new trend came in April, 1867, when the silver price slid below the French parity ratio. The Prussians were actively considering a switch from silver monometallism to gold, and other German states would likely follow suit, thus changing world supply-demand patterns for the two metals. The foreign exchanges of India, considered "the sink of the world's silver," i.e., able to swallow up any available silver for her domestic exchanges, were shaky and might get shakier, which also meant a declining demand for silver.[11]

This evidence was imposing. To coinage experts and to American policy-makers such as Sherman, McCulloch, and Linderman, it could not have been unknown; it was common knowledge in such circles all over Europe, for some of it had been stated outright at the Paris Conference. For Americans, however, there was even more direct evidence for a silver decline, and it was definitely known to McCulloch, Linderman, and Sherman. This evidence was the strong probability of great new silver discoveries in America, and the technology to mine it, refine it, and bring it quickly to world markets. This, to believers in the mechanical inexorability of supply and demand, meant silver prices were about to drop.

Most accounts of late nineteenth-century American silver politics blame much of its intensity on a coincidence: that silver demonetization in early 1873 was immediately followed by the enormous, but wholly fortuitous, silver strike at Nevada's Comstock Lode, which wrecked silver prices around the world and infuriated silver producers when they found the Mint, which they had ignored for years, suddenly closed to them. After the original Comstock strike in 1859, the mines had supposedly played out until Mackay and Fair happened on their colossal quarter-billion-dollar bonanza in 1873.

That is not how it happened. The 1873 strike was a surprise only in its magnitude. Lesser but significant discoveries punctuated the years before 1859 and 1873; major strikes occurred in 1866 and 1870. The Treasury Department watched them all. Two months before Sherman introduced his gold standard bill, McCulloch revealed in his annual report that he had recently been reading not only Ruggles' communications about the Paris Conference, but other reports, begun months earlier, to survey the mineral resources of the American West.

In 1865, a Treasury agent visiting the Denver branch of the Mint had reported that the branch might soon need new silver refining equipment because of fresh ore discoveries nearby. McCulloch followed up. Extracting a special appropriation from Congress on July 28, 1866, he immediately appointed J. Ross Browne and James W. Taylor "special commissioners" to survey mineral resources, Browne in the Rockies and Far West, and Taylor east of the Rockies. McCulloch gave them detailed instructions, and they presented long "preliminary reports" early in 1867. Taylor's was only mildly optimistic about bullion sites, but the Browne report must have given Treasury officials an uncomfortable mixture of horror and patriotic pride.

Browne did not guarantee that silver strikes would take place at the Comstock or anywhere else. But he did say more than enough to frighten any thinking gold monometallist. The Comstock Lode, Browne's report read, is geologically similar to the great argentiferous lodes of South America, "and mining geologists say that the class [of veins] are inexhaustibly rich in silver. It is presumed that they are rich in ore far beyond any depth which miners can reach." The ore did assay less as the lode deepened, but mining companies using proper equipment and the newest technology would nevertheless find them hugely worthwhile. At the moment, Browne continued, silver mining procedures in the Comstock were unsatisfactory, but with the Sutro Tunnel project [which would allow mining to new depths] under way, a splendid increase in silver production was in sight. Meanwhile, sorry to say, California gold production was declining, improved technology was not so likely to bring results there, and "the chief gold mines of California, high as their product is, are small affairs when compared with the vast works of the chief silver companies of Nevada."

McCulloch understandably secured a further appropriation for Browne to continue his researches in 1867. Also, whether Browne knew about them or not (Linderman certainly did), other technological improvements made his forecasts even more ominous. As an expert on bullion refining, Linderman knew of cheaper methods about to become widely available. The transcontinental railroad would shortly end most of the difficulty in getting American bullion out of the mountains and around the continent; distance and terrain would no longer insulate the world from sudden price shifts. Linderman, in his annual reports for 1866 and 1867, called it a happy fact that American precious metals resources were vast, would shortly be produced "to an extent hitherto unknown," and would become easily and quickly transportable to world markets. But privately his joy was tempered by the urgency this gave to the demonetization of silver.[12]

In 1867, then, at the time Sherman drew up his gold standard bill and even seven months earlier, at the Paris International Monetary Conference, a decline in silver prices was apparent to policy-makers and monetary experts in France, Britain, Germany, and most obviously of all, the United States. Silver might very well return to circulation in America. At the same time, many of these people, certainly the Americans, looked upon silver as a threat to "established values," which to them meant gold values. Bimetallism was not only illogical and inconvenient, but dangerous. Bimetallism had to go. The Paris Monetary Conference, at which Sherman and Ruggles played crucial roles, proclaimed the necessity for universal gold monometallism in large part as a hedge against the future. Silver's threat to "established values" was not the only reason for the Paris recommendations or for Sherman's gold standard bill of early 1868—the prevailing rhetoric, the ideology of gold monometallism, the interests of domestic groups, all figured in—but it was one of the reasons. The threat to "established values" was not adduced at that early date as the main reason for snuffing out bimetallism, nor is there good evidence that anyone suspected then how far silver would fall or how demonetization would affect economic or sectional or political groups over the next thirty years. The point is that American policy-makers, among others, had good reason to fear silver, in

1867, as a force for fiscal (and hence social) instability; they therefore sought to put an end to the silver standard, *because to do so was in the public interest, as they understood the public interest.*

Yet Sherman's gold standard bill foundered in 1868! When the Ohioan reported it on the Senate floor on June 9, 1868, he produced many arguments in favor of it,[13] but despite them, recommended that it be postponed until the next session, to afford "fuller discussion by the people." He ordered five thousand copies of the Finance Committee report on the bill to be printed, and copies of the Browne and Ruggles reports printed also. Sherman had lost the battle within the Finance Committee itself. His report included a minority view from Senator Edwin D. Morgan, a New York Republican, of which the main argument, ironically, was that Sherman's bill did not sufficiently protect creditors. Morgan, citing Browne's report, stolidly observed that the impending increases in bullion production would bring a depreciation of existing values, but private and public creditors would simply have to "abide" this. Depreciating the dollar further, however, which the Ruggles-Paris plan called for, was indefensible; it would aggravate an unfortunate natural trend by legislative interference. Not that Morgan disliked silver for non-standard purposes. In fact, another defect in the bill, as he saw it, was its failure to provide adequately for keeping silver in circulation domestically and in Latin American and Far Eastern trade. But the change in the gold content of the gold dollar was his main objection: this would deprive public creditors alone of one hundred million dollars, would only benefit hoarders and speculators, and would be just another obstacle to specie resumption. Appending a statement from two Mint officials to the effect that the French coinage system was impractical, complaining that there was no public consensus on the measure, Morgan wanted it postponed. Sherman capitulated, and gold-standard legislation lay dormant for the rest of the year.[14]

The principle of gold monometallism was never at issue between Sherman and Morgan; the argument was over means. Private discussions of international coinage unification in 1867 and 1868 likewise agreed on the principle but diverged on method, so much that they prolonged, rather than hastened, the coming of the gold standard. Endorsements of universal coinage were not helpful. Although the proceedings of the Paris Conference should have made it obvious that unification on the metric basis, though desirable, had to take second place to gold monometallism, which Ruggles had called "the cardinal feature," metricism continued to be linked, like an albatross, to the coinage movement. The International Geodetic Association, meeting at Berlin, and the International Statistical Congress, at Florence, plumped for the metric system of weights, measures, and coinage, in late 1867. The American Association for the Advancement of Science, and the American Statistical Association, sent resolutions to Congress urging international metric-based coinage—the ASA urging a reduction in the legal-tender power of silver coins to ten dollars (which was a feature of the Sherman bill), the AAAS advising against tampering with the "existing monetary unit of the United States, viz., the gold dollar," which the Sherman bill would have done. In France, the monometallists began to split openly between more "practical" men such as Esquirou, who favored international coinage on the basis of the existing gold franc, which was not really metric, and "metric decagrammists," theorists such as Michel Chevalier, who wanted an entirely new coinage unit weighing a decimal round number of gold grams. The effect of all of this agitation was to divide the monometallist camp into metricists and nonmetricicsts. The division was never healed, and it meant eventually the defeat of universal coinage unification. But it helped assure the success of gold monometallism.[15]

While gold-standard legislation languished in late 1868, there was no lack of interest in two more visible aspects of the money question: greenbacks and the public debt. A presidential election was only weeks away, and for the first (but definitely not the last) time in the late nineteenth century, money was a major issue. Sherman's coinage bill had not satisfied Senator Morgan, but to the *New York Times*, it was "the first-born offspring of the Chicago [Republican] platform, denouncing national repudiation in every shape and form," since it underwrote the "existing legal and moral duty" of the Treasury to pay the bondholders "principal and interest in gold of the full weight to which he was

entitled at the time of the contract." ("Repudiation," to these
Eastern Republicans, meant payment of the bonds in anything
other than gold.) The Republican platform of 1868, approved at
the Chicago national convention in May, devoted three of its
fourteen sections to the national debt. But, like all good platforms, it was strongest just where it was the most vague. Though
it denounced "all forms of repudiation as a national crime," it
practically admitted that specie payment of the bonds was seriously open to question when it demanded that the interest-
bearing dept be paid "not only according to the letter, but the
spirit" of the contract. Thus it could appeal to voters less hard-
money than those who agreed with the *Times*. In a more sensible
vein, the platform called for refunding of the debt not only at
lower rates of interest but in such a way as to remove any suspicion of "repudiation" in the minds of bondholders, present or
future.

The Democratic platform approved in New York in July was
much clearer and much less clever. Embodying the "Pendleton
Plan" of George H. Pendleton of Ohio, it wanted bonds paid in
"lawful money," meaning greenbacks, unless they expressly stipulated coin payment. This firm stand cost the Democrats accusa-
tions of "financial heresy" and the support of nervous voters.[16]
The Republicans, therefore, could unify people and interests
who were by any interpretation "hard"; the Democrats could
only divide themselves by explicitly appealing to those who were
"soft." As the Republicans strove to avoid a split between their
hard-money wing and the more greenbackish Radicals such as
Thaddeus Stevens, Ben Wade, and William D. Kelley, the Democrats acted to create one. In state platforms, too, Republican
vagueness contrasted with Democratic greenbackism and anti-
national-bank slogans. While Democratic newspapers defensively
denied that their "Pendleton Plan" to redeem national bank
notes and bank-held bonds with greenbacks was "repudiation,"
Republican papers, depending on their readership, could either
pound out hard-money editorials or point to the fact that both
parties had hard and soft money wings, that platforms were
"mere breath," and that superior leadership was what counted.[17]

By mid-campaign, the *Commercial and Financial Chronicle,* a bellwether of Northeastern mercantile-banker thinking, discarded contraction as a resumption method—"to jump at one bound from where we are to the old coin standard would unsettle every contract in the country"—and argued that stability was the *summum desideratum*, even though the long-range effects of the gold premium adversely affected farmers, planters, labor, and manufacturers alike, and "an irredeemable and depreciated currency [meant] fluctuations in gold so affecting values that chance reigns instead of law, chaos instead of order."

The newly organized National Board of Trade, at its annual convention, heard occasional "repudiationist" or "inflationist" murmurings. Most delegates agreed with a Louisvillian who declared that irredeemable currency "induces wild and extravagant speculation, enhances values far beyond a safe limit, turns aside the great natural laws of trade that should control the prices of the products of the country . . . and supplies illegitimate influences in their stead." But this group, the country's largest and most diversified business association, also sought stability even more.

Both the *Commercial and Financial Chronicle* and the overwhelming majority of the National Board of Trade delegates, however, called for the "honest" payment of government bonds, which meant payment in coin, not in greenbacks. Why? To give a windfall to bondholders? Hardly. To create stability in commerce, production, and standards of value; to thereby stimulate honest labor and enterprise; to uphold the public credit; to pay the bonds as promised, according to the spirit of the contract. This in itself ruled out contraction. Yet whatever the advantages of greenbacks, and large numbers of businessmen and Republicans as well as laborites and Democrats understood those advantages well, greenbacks as a means of paying the interest-bearing debt were to these people inadmissible. Whatever the plausibilities of the Democrats' "Pendleton Plan," or the laborite interconvertible bond scheme, their putative benefits could not outweigh existing moral obligations. The Democratic intepretation, that morality lay in paying the bonds in "lawful money," and that the real danger of repudiation lay in paying the bonds in coin when the contracts did not explicitly call for it, seemed slightly shady to the majority of the voters.[18]

The Republicans won, and immediately set about making coin payment irrevocably certain. They did this very simply, without disturbing the existing quantity of greenbacks or national bank notes, without contraction or inflation, without directly changing a single bond contract. Congress simply passed a law promising that the bonds would be paid, principal and interest, in coin, unless a bond expressly stipulated otherwise.

The electoral victory and a timely intervention by the despised Andrew Johnson gave Republican leaders a splendid opportunity for a hard-money victory at a bargain. In his last annual message, Johnson declared that "Our national credit should be sacredly observed; but in making provision for our creditors we should not forget what is due to the masses of the people." Johnson saw no reason why the people should continue to pay on the bonds; bondholders had already cleared much more than their original investment. He recommended that "the six per cent interest now paid by the Government should be applied to the reduction of the principal in semi-annual installments, which in sixteen years and eight months would liquidate the entire national debt." This would give "the public creditors a fair and liberal compensation for the use of their capital, and with this they should be satisfied." However the bondholders felt, the Republicans professed horror. Johnson's statements cost him censure resolutions from both houses, and the support of Secretary McCulloch as well, while it won for the Republicans more unity on money than they had enjoyed in years.[19]

Sherman summed up the Republican response in a Senate resolution of December 16. "Public policy" and the "good faith of the nation" demanded, he said, that the five-twenties (the largest Civil War bond issue, then largely in foreign hands) be made equivalent to coin, and that Congress should take "measures" (unspecified) to bring about specie resumption "at as early a period as practicable." Another Ohioan, Robert Schenck, introduced a more resounding version in the House on January 20, 1869. After some debate, during which its supporters praised the intrinsic stability of gold and silver coinage, and Democrats complained that they could not make themselves heard, the measure passed, 121–60, on February 24. A vanguard of Republican Radicals, including William D. Kelley and John Covode, together with Democrats chiefly from the West and South, voted against; the mass of Republicans and some Eastern Democrats voted for. The division in the Senate was much the same three days later, when an intersectional coalition of Republicans, plus one Democrat, defeated a contingent of Western and Radical Republicans, 30–16. Republican Oliver Morton of Indiana and Democrat James P. Doolittle of Wisconsin argued that to pay in coin what had been borrowed in greenbacks was to line the pockets of bondholders at the expense of the public; this was truly "repudiation," and it damaged rather than helped the public credit. But hard-money men won, and this time Sherman was impeccably orthodox. After a conference, the bill passed in final form on March 3. Johnson, of course, vetoed it, but Schenck and Sherman reintroduced it several days later (by which time Ulysses S. Grant was President).

By March 18, the new President signed it into law as the Public Credit Act of 1869. It pledged the United States to pay the greenbacks and the interest-bearing debt in "coin" except for bonds expressly stipulating payment in "lawful money or other currency than gold or silver." Many Democrats and Republicans had been claiming for months that quite a few of the laws authorizing the wartime bond issues permitted payment in greenbacks, and in those laws Congress had not only separated interest (payable in coin) from principal (payable in paper), but coin interest from paper interest. Did the "spirit" of the laws require coin payment of principal and interest? The point was arguable. The Public Credit Act seemed to settle the argument by stipulating coin payment, and subsequent bond authorizations always included coin payment clauses. Although the Act did nothing to set up machinery for refunding or specie resumption, it did declare for coin payment in an irreversible manner.[20]

But did coin mean gold or silver?

10

PROGRESS AND POLICY

IN FRANCE, PRUSSIA,

AND BRITAIN, 1867–71

In Europe the aftermath of the 1867 Paris International Monetary Conference paralleled, in general, its aftermath in America: international coinage unification languished, while gold monometallism progressed. French, British, and Prussian policy never again intertwined as closely with American policy after the 1867 Conference as they did before and during it, but the comparisons are instructive. Monetary rhetoric continued to be trans-Atlantic, as was the business cycle. The most important impingement of European events on American ones, from mid-1867 into 1873, was a function of the supply and demand for gold and silver: in a simple but vicious circle, a drop in the demand for silver in any major country caused the price of silver, relative to gold, to fall; the price fall lessened the demand further, causing a further price fall. An increase in the supply of silver that was available to the world's mints had the same price-depressing effect. Furthermore, declines in the demand for silver usually involved an increase in the demand and price of gold. But the supply of gold was not increasing significantly. A bimetallic world was a possible world when there was some kind of supply-demand balance between gold and silver. Such balance had existed traditionally with Britain gold-monometallic, America and France bimetallic, the Germanies and Austria on silver. Any major change in this pattern threatened the existence of *de facto* bimetallism in the world. Between 1867 and 1873, all of these things—a drop in silver demand, a rise in silver supply, a rise in gold demand, and changes in monetary standards by important nations—occurred.

The British delegates to the International Monetary Conference returned to London beaming over the prospect of a spread to other countries of the delights of gold monometallism. They were not enthusiastic about the reduction of the gold content of the pound by two pence, which the Ruggles-Paris plan involved, and they puzzled over the diplomatic ramifications of the Conference, especially the willingness of the United States to ally itself with France, even if that meant reducing the gold content of the dollar by three and a half percent. The Government decided to turn over the whole coinage question to a Royal Commission. Appointed in 1868, the Commission included the delegates to the Paris Conference and, among others, the bankers Thomas Baring and Lionel Nathan Rothschild. Rather predictably, the Commission reported that gold monometallism was "essential to *any* scheme of international coinage," and it doubted the practical utility of reducing the pound to conform with twenty-five gold francs. But it suggested a loophole through which coinage unification might still slide: If the Government instituted a slight coinage charge, or "seignorage," the pound could remain the same domestically while its international value would decrease by that amount. With a coinage charge of two pence in the pound (1/120th), Britain could maintain the "integrity" of existing contracts and yet avoid standing in the path of progress.

Robert Lowe, Chancellor of the Exchequer in the new Gladstone Government, seized upon this idea and brought it before the Commons in 1869. In doing so, Lowe touched off the greatest

public controversy over money that Britain had seen in years.[1]
For people completely convinced that money must have an "intrinsic" value, that gold possessed intrinsic value preeminently,
that civilization's forward progress lay directly along the path of
free-trade liberalism and the laws of classic political economy,
Lowe's plan had all the earmarks of some kind of devaluation of
the pound, which, of course, was the essence of public immorality.

Everything about the "Gold Coinage Controversy" in Britain
in 1869 and 1870 underscores the difficulties in a purely rhetorical
interpretation of history. The predictability of action from known
rhetoric is never completely possible, but for France, Germany,
and even the United States, it was simple compared to the British
situation, where anomaly conquered all. Lowe the Liberal, who
believed ardently in the scientific laws of political economy, supply and demand, free trade, and the rest of it, proclaimed his
disbelief in the intrinsic value of the precious metals. In calling
for a seignorage, he seemed to be advocating a retrogressive
measure; perhaps, like Gladstone, not realizing that free coinage
was by then as much part of the liberal monetary canon as the
"great commercial community" he and Gladstone sought. Lowe
let himself appear the enemy of bourgeois property rights and
fixity of contracts. The monometallist Chancellor was asserting
that monetary value could be set by law and not, as thinking
men knew, by the free market. Even bimetallists (and the most
prominent disliked Lowe's proposal) knew better than that. On
the other hand, Lowe was one of the few Britons who accepted
the broad liberal view that international coinage unification was
worth making sacrifices for.

The anomalies would have evaporated if Lowe and some of the
controversialists had known more about the practical workings
of coinage and bullion exchanges. Incompetence, not malice,
marred the liberalism of that exceptional man on that occasion.
Lowe had not the slightest intention of defrauding creditors. It
was simply that he and his supporters rejected the idea that gold
was intrinsically valuable. For this they could thank their too-
close reading of Adam Smith: value came from labor. More
classic than the liberals, Lowe had many supporters, from Wil-

liam Stanley Jevons to Frederick Hendriks to the Association of Chambers of Commerce of the United Kingdom, which came out in January, 1870, in favor of the Paris Conference plan.

Nevertheless, while doctrinaire metricism was crippling the Conference plan in France, doctrinaire intrinsicism defeated it in England. Britain did pass a new Coinage Act in 1870, but the Conference plan was not part of it. The coinage that Lowe wanted was rejected; silver remained a legal tender to forty shillings only; the gold pound remained the same size, slightly different from twenty-five gold francs. With the Coinage Act of 1870, Britain legalized the status quo, and maimed the chances of the Paris Conference plan irrecoverably.[2] Britain saw no reason to discuss the money standard again until world economic conditions forced a reappraisal in 1875–76.

The Paris Conference plan fared no better in France, but for quite different reasons. The plan did not ask the French to change the bullion content of their coinage unit. Instead, it asked something more: a change in the French monetary standard from bimetallism to gold monometallism. For several reasons, among them the Franco-Prussian War, this did not happen.

One reason was the power, in government and in banking, of bimetallic traditionalists. Another was the lack of a clear majority for change among the French Chambers of Commerce and provincial treasury officials. Another was the split within monometallist ranks between monetary politicians such as Esquirou de Parieu, who were anxious to get the gold standard adopted by whatever plan would work, and men such as Michel Chevalier who were not interested in a change unless the new gold coinage were strictly metric.

These difficulties began almost as soon as the Paris Conference ended in mid-1867. Esquirou and others kept up a barrage of articles in the popular journals about monetary trends in other countries. They were thrilled that "through the voice of Mr. Ruggles the opinion of the American government on this great question of monetary uniformity" could not have been phrased "more precisely nor more conciliatorily" when it "asked us to sacrifice the double standard." But journals were not enough to win the battle.[3]

Esquirou, from his powerful position as Vice President of the *Conseil d'Etat,* arranged the appointment in 1868 of a Monetary Commission which, he apparently hoped, would affirm the need for monometallism and force it through the national assembly. The Commission heard witnesses and circulated questionnaires around the country. The strongest opposition to a change from bimetallism came from the very largest financial institutions: Baron Alphonse de Rothschild and the Governor of the Bank of France used rhetorical arguments—a change would be "contrary to the spirit of the *Code Napoléon*—and practical arguments—a change would raise gold prices by raising demand for gold, and lower silver prices correspondingly, and many bank reserves were in silver. The majority of the Commission disagreed. Gold was the actual standard anyway. Silver did not circulate. Gold production far outstripped silver production. Silver was chronically undervalued and would remain so. These arguments, of course, were at odds with the facts, though perhaps the Commission did not realize that they were. It seems likely that the French Chambers of Commerce, and the leading financial civil servants in the provinces (the *Trésoriers-payeurs généraux*), whom the Commission circularized, did not realize that the undervaluation of silver was ending. Of the sixty-six Chambers polled by the Commission, forty-four favored the shift to monometallism, twenty opposed it, two were doubtful; the *Trésoriers-payeurs généraux* supported it 64–14, with nine in doubt. Thus fortified by public opinion, the Commission recommended the shift to gold monometallism along the lines of the Paris Conference plan, telling the Emperor with a flourish of rhetoric that a fixed ratio between gold and silver would be "in flagrant contradiction with the principles of political economy as well as with the nature of things."[4]

Still there was no legislative action. Esquirou, despite his powerful position and despite several years of agitation, had to confront bimetallist Ministers of Finance. Another fifteen months of journal warfare, in which the monometallists argued from rhetoric, practicality, and the progress of gold in other nations (especially the United States), only intensified the division between the "practical" monometallists and the metric doctrinaires. When the question of a shift to monometallism finally surfaced in the French Senate, in January 1870, the infighting was so bitter between Michel Chevalier, who sought an entirely new gold coin of ten grams, and Esquirou, who sought a gold 25-franc piece as the 1867 Conference had called for, that the monometallist drive was utterly stalemated. This was undoubtedly what the bimetallists, led by Senator Magne, a former Finance Minister, wanted. Ironically, the metric system—which had been the vehicle for universal gold monometallism through the mid-sixties—was the wedge in 1870 which split the monometallist forces in the French Senate itself.

About two months before that episode, the Emperor appointed another monetary commission to examine the monetary standards question. It was probably another device to stall the monometallist drive, and if so, it worked. It also revealed interesting divisions of opinion throughout the country. The usual split among the monometallists between the "practical" men and the "decagrammists" quickly became obvious. More important, the investigation laid bare a strong disagreement between the great financiers of the country, who were bimetallists, and certain major Chambers of Commerce. The most significant development, however, was that gold monometallism was beginning to be based in France, as it already was in the United States, on the realization and the fear of an impending drop in the price of silver.

The Governor of the Banque de France, and Baron Rothschild, derided the usual arguments for gold-monometallic international unification. In rapid exchanges with Esquirou and Chevalier, the great financiers declared that "monetary science" did not correspond immediately or exactly to practical affairs. Economic science was a good thing, but "you are still in the night of uncertainty; you are still at the beginning of economic study, at the beginning of those great searches which are indispensable for learning the truth. . . . you are still in the ABC's of it. Study, study a long time; wait for universal agreement. What have you got to lose?" So spoke the Governor of the Banque de France. To demonetize silver, he continued, would disrupt world monetary arrangements. It would destroy billions of silver francs and require their replacement with gold that was, in fact, not being produced.

Gold never prevented financial crises in Britain; it would not do so in France. There was not gold enough for monetary purposes even as it was, as the American suspension of specie payments showed. Rothschild and the Governor of the Bank thus quoted the facts of life against whatever "science" seemed to demand.

But the Chambers of Commerce of Paris, Lyons, and Le Havre all supported gold monometallism, on grounds of civilization, convenience, science, and national advantage—a blend of nationalism and the usual rhetoric. Only Rouen's, of the several major Chambers polled, wanted bimetallism retained. At the same time, not less than four witnesses before the commission forecast a drop in silver prices. The drop was well understood, then, by mid-1869 in France. But the four witnesses drew different conclusions from the fact. Ernest Seyd of London pleaded with passion *not* to switch to gold monometallism, because the switch would deprive the world of much of its money stock. Others cried that the switch was all the more imperative, because without it debtors would be able to defraud their creditors by paying debts in a depreciated money. Chevalier and Esquirou as good as admitted—which they had not done before this time—that their chief aim in demonetizing silver was to protect creditors against an anticipated decline in the price of silver. Rothschild and the Bank Governor, of all people, were not worried. Why the divergence? One major reason, unquestionably, was that the bankers understood from experience that scarce money made panics and uncertainty more likely. The economists and politicians, on the other hand, were gripped by rhetoric and ideology. They believed fervently in equilibrium, balance, science, natural laws. Any attempt to legislate a gold-silver bimetallic ratio would fail, they said, and this Baron Rothschild explicitly denied: the legal parity ratio actually helped stabilize market prices, and if a silver decline seemed to impend, nothing disastrous had come of the enormous gold discoveries of the late forties; why all the fear of silver discoveries now?

But monetary liberalism in France, whatever the case elsewhere, meant the protection of creditors against silver declines and, at the same time, outright opposition to the views of the country's central bank and its greatest private banker. The commission voted for the plan of the Paris Conference of 1867, meaning gold monometallism. Before any legislation could be seriously considered, however, monetary reform in France was halted completely, a casualty of the Franco-Prussian War.[5]

Stubbornly, France suffered and survived not only the shock of military defeat and the overturning of the Second Empire, but the social upheaval of the Paris Commune and a financial crisis as well. The Third Republic not surprisingly began with economic policies less liberal, in the economic sense, than those of the Second Empire. New leaders, many of whom were in eclipse during the last years of Napoléon III, dictated this change, as did the expense of the war and the exaction by the Germans of a five-billion-franc war indemnity, payable in gold.

Under Thiers' leadership, the Republican Government met the situation "illiberally," and France became the first of the major nations to junk liberalism and put economic nationalism into effect. Other countries would do so later in the decade. The Banque de France suspended specie payments in August, 1870, and did not resume until 1878. As happened in the United States a few years earlier, an absence of specie payments did not prevent the government from issuing and selling large amounts of bonds in 1871 and 1872, and paying its war indemnity despite a high gold premium. Thiers also terminated the free-trade treaty between France and Britain that had been worked out by Richard Cobden and Michel Chevalier in 1860; Thiers, who leaned toward tariff protectionism anyway, needed revenue. All of these steps had been taken by the United States at the beginning of the Civil War. Opinion, or some opinion, still favored gold monometallism; the report of the 1869–70 commission finally appeared in 1872, and its very appearance testified to the durability of ideological and economic group positions despite devastating political and social upheavals. Nevertheless, the indemnity to Germany, the suspension of specie payments, heavy taxation, tight money markets, and the overriding need to put industry and the rest of the French economy on its feet, all combined to put the quietus on monometallist pressure. Until the mid-seventies, when the silver decline seemed hopeless, France attended to more pressing problems.[6]

Prussia presented a very different set of monetary developments. In the sixties and the early seventies, the monetary standard of the German states completely changed. In 1857, Prussia led the Germanies in creating a *silver* coinage, based on the metric system, binding together the thaler area (Prussia and north Germany), the florin area (Bavaria and south Germany), and the Habsburg Empire. But Prussia gradually shifted toward the gold standard during the sixties. By 1865, when the *Deutsche Handelstag* met at Frankfurt, the great majority favored a gold coinage. The Frankfurt meeting also showed that the commercial community played an effective and organized role in shaping future Prussian and German policy. Private opinion, led by monetary experts such as Dr. Adolph Soetbeer, and expressed by organized groups such as the *Handelstag* and the *Kongress deutscher Volkswirthe,* became a vocal and useful prop for, and perhaps a determinant of, the monetary policy of Prussia and the North German Union.[7]

Why were the Germans interested in gold monometallism just then? For several reasons. For one, in German areas where the one- to fifteen-and-a-half ratio of gold to silver prevailed, the threat posed by declining silver prices was already visible in 1867, at the time of the Paris Monetary Conference, as the price of silver in the market began to flutter around that parity level. For another, German commentators on the Conference were dazzled by how the French coinage system—metric, decimal, and (soon to be) gold monometallic—promised the unity of "law, trade, commerce, customs, weights, measures, and coinage" that augured the community of mankind so yearned for by scholars and poets. These Germans were particularly impressed by the noble and laudable sentiments of Mr. Ruggles, the American delegate to the Paris Conference. But the biggest attraction of the gold standard was its usefulness as a spur to national unification.[8]

In late August, 1867, the sixth meeting of the *Kongress deutscher Volkswirthe* convened at Hamburg. Soetbeer opened the monetary discussion, declaring that "It is very timely and highly desirable that the obstacles and temporary hindrances confronting complete monetary unification in Germany be removed soon, and that before long the plans contemplated by the

Paris Monetary Conference of 1865 (the Latin Union) and of 1867 be embraced appropriately." He outlined the steps needed to achieve "a complete practical coinage union in Germany," by gradually subsuming the mark, thaler, and South German coinages into a single gold standard, using the franc system.

The dream of German political unification underlay the whole discussion. Other considerations, Soetbeer and the Prussian government realized, were secondary and would have to be sacrificed. Soetbeer admitted that "to provoke an impression of favor to the [Prussian] thaler would be, I hold, extremely dangerous with regard to the South Germans, who are inclined without exception to the franc system." Amid exclamations that gold was the wave of the future, that silver was the standard of "half-civilized peoples" and gold the key to "higher cultural development," the Congress adopted Soetbeer's recommendations of the franc-oriented, decimal, gold-monometallic basis for general German coinage.[9]

The *Deutsche Handelstag* met at Berlin about a year later, in October 1868, and gave gold monometallism an even greater boost. Soetbeer led the assembled delegates of 120 North German commercial organizations through nearly two days of discussion on monetary standards.[10] Soetbeer again combined Manchester liberalism, pan-German nationalism, and the rhetoric of science and progress in his argument, as he had done the previous year, but his audience in 1868 was larger and not so academic. Several factors made German adoption of the gold standard urgent, Soetbeer proclaimed; among them, the shakiness of silver. "In general," Soetbeer noted, "the demand for silver by India, has dropped greatly since 1866, and therefore the price of silver has sunk, at the exact time as a new and considerable supply of silver (of which production otherwise was somewhat in decline) has emerged on account of conditions in Mexico, through the discovery and putting into production of rich silver deposits . . . in Nevada, and so forth." New railroads would soon bring the North American silver to market. There were other reasons for getting rid of silver; the double standard, of course, was illogical to begin with, Soetbeer reminded the delegates.

But Soetbeer's most compelling argument was political, not

economic. The Prussian government, he told the convention, wanted gold monometallism and international coinage unification on the five-franc basis, the plan of the 1867 Paris Conference. Whether Soetbeer was making an educated guess about Berlin's policy, or was actually a mouthpiece for it, is unclear, but he certainly helped it along, whatever his connection. The Paris recommendations were convenient talking points. Soetbeer recalled that the statements of "Herr Ruggles" at Paris showed how anxious the United States was for international coinage unification, even to the point of reducing the gold content of the dollar to conform to five gold francs. Germany should be equally amenable. With America about to enter the ranks of the leaders of world trade, the unification of the thaler and the dollar, and the unhindered intercourse of the two great nations, was something worth working for.

Soetbeer's final argument was the overriding one: coinage unification among the German states would be a preliminary to political unification, another step toward "Deutschland" as a political entity. Soetbeer and the policy-makers of Prussia knew that German coinage unification would not come on the basis of silver, or with any existing unit, including the Prussian thaler, as the base. There would have to be a wholly new gold coin. If not, particularism would wreck coinage unification and endanger political unification. In 1868, the five-franc gold basis recommended by the 1867 Paris Conference seemed as good a device as any for a new all-German gold coin. This device would soon be discarded, but the policy did not change.

The *Handelstag* delegates voted for three resolutions Soetbeer presented, which together meant gold monometallism embodied in a new coinage system. Another Soetbeer resolution, however, nearly failed: it would have adopted the five-franc basis. Many delegates also disliked a reference in one resolution to the Paris Conference. It was clear to Soetbeer, and no doubt to the Prussian government, that gold monometallism and a new coinage unit was favored all over North Germany, but things French were not. The *Handelstag* was serving not only as a sounding-board for Prussian policy, but was helping to modify and channel it. The *Handelstag* response, in fact, cleared the air for the

Prussians: they could push ahead for a new gold unit, but it needed no connection with the franc or any other existing unit.[11]

The demonetization of silver meant a much greater change for Germany than it did for the United States. Silver actually circulated in Germany; it was the sole standard; the value of existing silver stocks was huge compared to America's; a shift to gold should have benefited tremendously a few people with invested capital. Yet the consensus among commercial, manufacturing, and probably other groups was greater in Germany than in America. Why?

In the first place, the interests of economic groups differed between the two countries. Many important German manufacturing interests were competitively secure. Like American textile manufacturers, but quite unlike American iron makers, a deflation following a monetary change would not hurt. It might even help, by making their international competitive position better. German agriculturists, especially those with large holdings, needed cheap imports more than they did protection; the gold standard would help them, while deflation did not help American agriculturists. Inter-German and international commerce, of course, could only benefit from unifying the coinages of the German states and Germany's major overseas customers.[12]

Another reason was that a unity of rhetoric and ideas prevailed among groups in Germany more than in the United States. The 1868 conventions of the *Deutsche Handelstag* and the American National Board of Trade took what were, in their respective contexts, hard-money positions. But the German commercial people were closer to other economic groups than their American counterparts were. Also, the distance between monetary theory and government policy was shorter, on the whole, in Germany; not only was German legislation more "doctrinaire," but the views of theorists such as Soetbeer met with less resistance. The decision-making process was less cluttered; the pressures on policy-makers were much less diverse. Perhaps this is only to say that certain groups could not gain a hearing. The fact, nevertheless, was an alignment between private and public interests that made policy-making relatively simple.

The Franco-Prussian War created the final conditions for

change. As France in her travail retained her bimetallic standard, Germany in her triumph shifted to gold monometallism. German productive enterprise reached new heights in 1871 and 1872; the "German Manchesterdom," with its low-tariff and gold-standard policies, was in the ascendant; major economic groups either favored or did not oppose the change; the French war indemnity assured an influx of gold. Bismarck and the Germans, their liberal mood reinforced by military victory and economic well-being, grasped that it was also the hour for monetary nationalism. As Karl Knies said, "The maintenance of the Silver Standard is bound up with our former condition as a League of States, and the introduction of the Gold Standard is far more closely allied than one would suppose, with Emperor and Empire."[13]

At the state opening of the Reichstag on October 16, 1871, Emperor Wilhelm I called for a new imperial gold coinage, with the mark to be the unit. Within a few days, Bismarck brought a coinage bill before the Reichstag, together with a statement that the French indemnity could not possibly be assimilated unless Germany adopted the gold standard. Since one may reasonably assume that Bismarck had had something to do with Germany's getting the gold indemnity in the first place, he must have considered the opposition to gold within the Reichstag still strong enough to require this "argument from necessity." His bill, moreover, was gentle: it did not abolish existing or future silver coinages in the *Länder.*

These tactics seemed to work. Delbrück, the Finance Minister, and Bamberger, the leading monetary liberal, introduced the bill with extended oratory on November 11, and only one delegate among all the speakers, and only one Chamber of Commerce among the several dozen petitioners, openly requested a silver or bimetallic standard. The members discussed certain sections of the bill exhaustively, but the debate on the monetary standard, though clear and intense, was one-sided. An imperial gold standard was acceptable especially if local coinage were still to exist. The Government was taking special pains to stress national unity and to avoid arousing particularistic sentiments; having done so, the outcome was never in any doubt. The bill became the Imperial Gold Coinage Law of December 4, 1871.[14]

This basic statute provided new gold coins of ten and twenty marks. The coins were not metric. No other gold coins, and no silver coins of consequence, could be minted in the Empire, and the Imperial Chancellor received the power to withdraw existing silver coins at his discretion. Article VIII specified the legal ratio between the new gold marks and the existing assortment of thalers, schillings (of Lübeck), schillings (of Hamburg), florins, and Bremen gold thalers, and placed the gold-silver ratio at about one to 15.55. Germany had in this law done not one single thing to align her coinage with Britain's, France's, or anyone else's. Except for its gold monometallism, said the *Economist*, it was "nothing more or less than a new international vexation."[15]

Bismarck and Delbrück immediately moved forward toward a new law to make silver coins "correspond" with the imperial gold coinage. In 1873 the Reichstag took up this measure, which explicitly declared gold to be the sole legal monetary standard in the Empire, created imperial silver coins of five marks and smaller, and limited the tender powers and quantity of silver coins.

The 1873 bill came none too soon. Delbrück and Bamberger found that long speeches had less effect than they had had two years before. Important members fought to retain full-valued silver coinage, especially for South German states. Petitions bombarded the Reichstag from the Chambers of Commerce of Coblenz, Ulm, Nuremberg, Bayreuth, Munich, Leipzig, Regensburg, and other cities, and from private individuals, calling for the retention of silver or the introduction of bimetallism. The bill did become law in July, but storm warnings were obviously up. Even Bismarck had gone as far as he could, and in spite of the powers conferred on him by these laws, he would have to use his powers discreetly. The gold standard law of 1873 was indeed German monetary liberalism's last victory—just as repeal in 1873 of the tariff on iron was "the last act of the free-trade era" in Germany.[16]

Britain and America were, by 1872, the only major powers working toward international coinage unification, and neither was working very hard. The American and British governments carried on official correspondence on "the subject of a common unit and standard of an International Gold Coinage," and Sweden had attempted to awaken interest in the idea in 1870, but none of these discussions had much result. In Britain and in America, the keynote of monetary activity was stability; in France it was recovery; in Germany it was consolidation of nationhood. The gold standard, between 1867 and 1873, had been reaffirmed in Britain, and had overthrown traditional standards in America and Germany. International coinage unification, meanwhile, had become less likely than it had been in the mid-sixties.[17]

11

A LEGISLATIVE

TRIPLE PLAY,

1869–70

The Public Credit Act of 1869 had promised holders of American bonds that they would ultimately be paid in coin. It left other problems untouched, and raised as many questions as it answered. When Ulysses S. Grant and the Republican party took over the Executive Branch in March, 1869, they found waiting for them a set of financial decisions that had to be made quickly.

One problem was the refinancing of the public bonds. The interest-bearing debt was a floating debt with a face value of more than two billion dollars, much of which was becoming payable very quickly. Issued during the war emegrency, the bonds bore high interest and short terms of maturity. To refinance, or "refund" the debt, by replacing these existing bonds with longer-term, lower-interest ones, would greatly ease pressure on the Treasury, reduce immediate expenditure, and help insure specie resumption, since foreign bondholders would be less tempted to present bonds in payment for gold. But new bonds, if they were to be sold, would have to guarantee coin payment of principal and interest.

Another problem was scarcity of currency in certain sections, especially the Midwest. Sentiment was strongly against expanding the greenback issue. More national banks, however, seemed permissible and in several ways advantageous. Permissible, because to issue notes a national bank had to secure these notes by depositing government bonds, purchased in gold, with the Treasury: The national bank note had a kind of backing, while the greenback did not. Advantageous, because the creation of more national bank notes presupposed more national banks. The Civil War laws authorizing the creation of national banks limited the total amount of notes these banks could issue, and in effect limited the banks themselves to New England and the Middle Atlantic states because few people outside these areas had the capital during the War years to apply for a charter. By 1869, things were different: Midwesterners had the capital, and needed the currency and the banking facilities that more national banks would supply. More national banks would also benefit the Treasury, because new banks could be required to buy some of the new, refunded bonds the Treasury hoped to issue. New bank note currency might replace some of the interest-bearing debt, and perhaps some of the greenbacks. The clever way to solve the currency problem, therefore, was to remove the limit on national bank note issue, either partially or wholly, thus relieving sectional pressure and reducing several financial pressures.

Refunding the bonds and expanding the national bank notes would move the country toward specie resumption and stabilize values. No longer would the Treasury have to sell gold in the open market, as McCulloch had done, to keep bond prices steady; the Treasury could accumulate a gold reserve more easily. The greenbacks would not be contracted—McCulloch's contraction policy had proved too rigorous for almost everyone. But the greenbacks would be kept stable in amount and number, and their value would rise (and the gold premium decrease) as growing business needs brought them more into demand. The country would "grow up" to them. These were the general lines of administration thinking in 1869. Refund the bonds; loosen the controls over national bank note issue; neither contract nor expand the greenbacks. The intended result was economic, sectional, and national stability.

Yet the nagging fact of legal bimetallism remained. If silver ever returned to circulation—and there was good evidence by 1869 that it might—this whole financial policy would collapse. Specie resumption could take place in silver instead of gold. The Public Credit Act and any new refunding law might specify "coin" payment, instead of greenbacks, but coin could mean silver. Creditors were not interested in silver. To insure that the Public Credit Act, and a new act refunding the bonds, meant anything, the silver standard had to be got rid of. This was the third problem facing the Grant Administration. Less visible and seemingly less urgent than refunding and currency reform, less annoying to sectional and economic interests at that moment, it was nevertheless a *sine qua non* of a strong public credit, resumption, and economic stability as those things were then understood.

On each of these three questions—refunding, currency reform, and silver demonetization—bills came before Congress in 1869–70, and on each question there were strong differences of opinion. The 1869 annual meeting of the National Board of Trade revealed these differences and resolved them in such ways as to guide government policy in 1870. The Board brought together delegates from chambers of commerce and other business groups from all over the country. Many delegates were in some kind of commerce, wholesale or retail, but there were enough bankers and manufacturers present to make it representative of the more prominent businessmen of all sorts. The delegates were asked by the Executive Committee to vote on several resolutions on money and on the tariff. They supported specie resumption overwhelmingly, voted down contraction even when it was sugar-coated with bank-note expansion, and opposed tariff reductions by slight margins. The discussions, however, revealed more than the voting.

The Northeastern delegates divided evenly on tariff reduction and voted about two to one against contraction. Only Boston supported contraction; her delegates also supported lower tariffs, as did the delegates of Newark, Buffalo, and Portland (Maine). New York and Philadelphia opposed contraction as well as lower tariffs; Baltimore split on both issues. Since contraction and tariff reduction meant hard-money and "free trade" in that context, the voting at that meeting of the National Board of Trade did not tally at all with the hard money, free-trade emphasis in most of the Northeastern press. Furthermore, the New York vote (and discussion) showed that Careyism was not the sole property of Philadelphians.

Midwestern delegates generally favored contraction more than the Northeasterners, and took a hard-money line regularly, except for the notion, which they liked, that the Midwest and South should have a larger share of the national bank notes. They voted, as a section, about three to one for lower tariffs. But again there were marked differences among cities: the Chicago Board of Trade (the largest Midwestern group present) split on the money and tariff resolutions, while Milwaukee and Cincinnati wanted lower tariffs but easier money. Southerners agreed. There were few Southerners present, and they said little, but usually they too opposed contraction and wanted lower tariffs.

The Midwestern and Southern voting and discussion still reflected sectional concern with the marketing of raw or semi-processed agricultural products; the Northeasterners represented a more mixed economy. Everyone, however, was clearly and intensely interested in the money question. Even the more austere journals of the day opposed either "inflation" or "hasty resumption," and looked tolerantly at national bank expansion, as did the delegates to the National Board of Trade meeting. As a consequence, Senator Sherman, Secretary of the Treasury George Boutwell, and other policy-makers in Congress and in the Grant Administration had their path to consensus well marked out.[1]

Boutwell and Sherman worked well together throughout Grant's first Administration. Not only were they both Republican politicians interested in party unity and party victory, but they also shared similar views about what the economy needed from them: stability in business conditions, the jealous protection of the public credit, and ultimate (not hasty) resumption on the gold standard. Boutwell, a former Massachusetts Congressman with a reasonably Radical record, had not been Grant's first choice for the Treasury Secretaryship, and he promised at the outset to lack distinction at least as much as Grant's other Cabinet appointees. He was not the first choice of the Republican hard-money extremists either, because he was not doctrinaire and not particularly experienced in public finance. In Boutwell, the doggedness, experience, and sometimes frightening consistency to principle that characterized Hugh McCulloch were not present (though McCulloch later called Boutwell's stewardship of the Treasury "conservative and judicious"). Yet Boutwell could succeed where McCulloch could not, not only because of his less inflammatory party label, but because his conservatism was always, like Sherman's, tempered by a feel for the political practicalities. Boutwell had to continue McCulloch's gold sales policy, and his inexperienced techniques in doing so probably contributed to the "gold corner" and "Black Friday" panic of September 1869, which earned him a Congressional investigation. But he survived, took hold of things, and by early 1870 had earned considerable confidence from commercial, agricultural, and banking groups—from nearly everyone, in fact, except radical labor, which talked of the "Boutwell gold-gambling and stock-jobbing system"; but radical labor was greenbackish and outside the main stream. The mainstream was where Boutwell wanted to be, and once in it, he stayed there.[2]

Sherman and Boutwell were guided by their own "conservative and judicious" tendencies, by the requirements of party unity, and by the opinions and sentiments of economic groups all over the country, when they sat down to formulate legislation in the public interest in late 1869. The gold standard, and the public credit, had to be protected; the new legislation also had to satisfy ideological, economic, and sectional groups. Sherman brought three bills before the tumultuous second session of the Forty-first Congress. The first, a currency bill, would expand national bank note issues but without "inflation," by replacing rather than adding to part of the circulating medium—new national bank notes would replace other issues. The second bill would authorize a refunding of the national debt. The third, the last to appear, was a complicated coinage bill which would have demonetized silver, have placed the United States on the gold standard, and have assisted international coinage unification.

The currency bill came before the Senate on January 24, 1870, and touched off a six-day debate. As Sherman reported it, the measure authorized $45-million in new national bank notes, chiefly for the Midwest and South. The new notes would replace three per cent "temporary loan certificates," an interest-bearing note that circulated as currency; the greenback issue would remain stable. Hence the bill was neither "inflationary" nor "deflationary," in the sense that it did not expand or contract the currency; but it was supposed to satisfy sectional pressure. The hard-money elements were to be mollified by a provision allowing banks to issue notes redeemable in gold if they chose to; there would be no legal barrier to specie resumption by a private bank.

For early 1870, this was a middle-of-the-road bill. On the left lay laborites and Careyite-greenbackish Republicans; on the right, the extant contractionists and those who wanted national bank notes to replace greenbacks one-for-one. The *Workingman's Advocate* called for an end to the "national bank swindle," for the interconvertible bond, and for more greenbacks; but it was not a serious political threat. Contraction, on the other hand, was moribund; even the *Commercial and Financial Chronicle* pigeon-holed it. But not all of the brethren dwelt in unity. Some Republican Congressmen, including William D. Kelley, sought greenback expansion, and within the Treasury Department, the Comptroller of the Currency urged the replacement of the greenbacks by national bank notes. Sherman's bill, therefore, had the beauty of appearing to avoid extremes, allaying sectional tension, uniting the mass of Republicans, and approximating "sound finance."[3]

The Senate debate on the currency bill revealed that phenomenon so common to financial policy-making through the whole period: agreement on rhetoric, divergent interpretation according to interest. Western and Eastern Senators both condemned "speculation," "inflation," and unstable business conditions. To the Westerners, however, these catch-terms meant over-rapid resumption, and replacing greenbacks with national bank notes. To Easterners the catch-terms demanded a complete refusal to issue any further currency of any kind. The Westerners had a point about their section's dearth of circulating currency, and the complaint was bipartisan. Allen Thurman of Ohio, a Democrat, and Oliver Morton of Indiana, a Republican, argued similarly. As Morton put it, "The ten-dollar bill which is used in a county in Iowa will not change hands half a dozen times while the same ten-dollar bill would change hands a hundred times in Massachusetts or in London. . . . because the [Western] population [is] comparatively sparse, money does not pass from hand to hand so readily, and actual currency must supply the place of bank credits, bank checks, and savings institutions." He was quite right; the national money supply, but not the Western, was increasing; currency, so often the only form of money in the Midwest, was even diminishing *per capita*.

Sherman agreed with the Western complaint. When Senator Charles Sumner of Massachusetts, representing a state with plenty of national banks and newer forms of money, presented a substitute bill that would have replaced greenbacks with national bank notes generally, Sherman talked like a die-hard Westerner. But when Morton amended the bill to enlarge the new bank note authorization by a few million dollars, Sherman joined the Easterners. The bill passed the Senate on February 2, much as Sherman had presented it. Though the vote reflected sectional lines, it reflected party lines as well; party unity was apparently intact.[4]

Sherman brought the funding bill before the Senate the next day. The opposition and support for it, in and out of Congress, was much the same as the alignment on the currency bill, except that many Northeasterners who had opposed the currency bill eventually voted for the funding measure. The remarkable feature of the long debate on the funding bill was that it hardly touched on the technical aspects of the bond flotation but instead devoted weeks to highly rhetorical and ideological arguments over the question of the standard of money and value. Sherman's original bill provided for three bonds (5 per cent, 4½ per cent, 4 per cent), payable principal and interest in coin, and tax-exempt; purchase could be in foreign currencies and interest payable in foreign cities; the national banks would have to replace their existing security bonds with the new bonds. Sherman hoped that the foreign payability feature would promote international coinage unification. But most Senators worried about other things.

The debate was a tussle over "repudiation," "speculation," "city stock-gamblers," "productive enterprise." Why such broad terms? Because, as Sherman proclaimed on March 11, this was not just a funding bill, but a bill "to bring about specie payments without any material contraction." The mechanics were that "We give to every holder of a greenback, which is the dishonored promise of the nation, the right to present to the Treasury of the United States [that greenback] and convert it into a bond bearing four per cent interest in gold." Thus the new bonds tied the greenbacks to gold, Sherman said. Producer rhetoric was employed by Senators at both extremes: rigorists, such as Reuben Fenton of New York and Justin Morrill of Vermont, scored greenbacks, resumption postponement, and low-interest bonds because they led to speculation, repudiation, and immorality harmful to the producing classes and capitalists alike. Currency expansion ignored "the natural laws of distribution," Fenton grumbled, and Morrill warned that "there is an insurmountable infecundity in paper money. Speculation indeed fattens upon it, driving a coach and four-in-hand, but in its presence honest labor pines for opportunity; substantial business becomes a lottery with more blanks than prizes; and foreign commerce is reduced to the contemptible dimensions of barter." But Senator Morton of Indiana employed producerism in his argument that the bill was really contractionist and harmful to producers! The long discussion hardly changed the bill, except to delete the foreign payability clause (its nod to the international coinage idea), and it passed in mid-March without recognizable sectional division. Sherman had taken the middle of the road even more surefootedly than on the currency bill.[5]

Sherman introduced his third measure, the coinage bill, on April 28, and immediately had it sent to his Finance Committee. This bill was a revamped and more complex version of the gold standard bill he had presented in 1868. The 1870 bill, unlike the bill of 1868, did not embody the international coinage scheme of Samuel B. Ruggles and the Paris International Monetary Conference of 1867. But it was just as definitely a measure to transfer the United States from bimetallism to gold monometallism.

There were several reasons why the Ruggles-Paris plan went by the boards. Congressman William D. Kelley had become the leading coinage spokesman in the House of Representatives by 1868, and within two weeks after Sherman's gold-standard bill was shelved in June of that year, Kelley presented a more strictly metric gold coinage bill reflecting the views of E. B. Elliott of the U.S. Mint, the American Association for the Advancement of Science, and the American Statistical Association. Kelley was playing a role very similar to that of Michel Chevalier in France: more rigorously scientific than monetary politicians like Sherman, unhappy with the flabbiness of the Paris Conference plan, supported by private groups, Kelley, like Chevalier, stalled the progress of gold monometallism by his doctrinaire single-mindedness.[6]

Besides the split among the American monometallists, coinage legislation had to wait through much of 1869 because the change in administration of the Treasury and the Mint had to be digested. Linderman, a Democrat, was replaced by James Pollock as Mint Director when the Republican took office in the spring of 1869. Although Linderman rather quickly returned to favor despite his party label (Boutwell employed him to make a fact-finding tour of Western branch mints in the fall of 1869), different people and different political circumstances prevailing in the Treasury suggested a postponement of the coinage bill.[7]

Nevertheless, the coinage bill that Sherman introduced in April, 1870, had been in preparation at the Treasury at least as early as December, 1869. At that time, Boutwell asked John Jay Knox, the young Deputy Comptroller of the Currency, to draft a coinage bill with Linderman's assistance. Knox was a good choice. A central-New-Yorker, he had come to the Treasury during the Civil War, and McCulloch soon gave him his first major responsibility, which was to supervise mint and coinage correspondence and undertake special tasks relating to the Mint. Knox uncovered a million-dollar defalcation at the New Orleans branch, inspected the Carson City and San Francisco branches in the pre-railroad (but not pre-silver-bonanza) days, and kept his eyes wide open. McCulloch called him "a gentleman of excellent judgment and business habits"—he might also have added, of great native quickness. A Republican, Knox kept his post when Boutwell took over.

Knox and Linderman had known each other since mid-1867, if not before that, and in all probability they had hammered out the main lines of the 1870 coinage bill well before the end of 1869. Both were freshly familiar with western mining conditions, with the increase in silver deposits at the Mint, and recent demands for silver coins, with new mining technology, with European coinage developments, and with the likelihood that silver production was about to expand greatly. They took all of these things into account when they prepared their bill.[8]

Knox's procedure, as he explained it publicly, was to codify existing laws and his and Linderman's own ideas into a draft, and then to send the draft to Mint and Treasury officials and "such other gentlemen as are known to be intelligent upon metallurgical and numismatical subjects." Returns from about thirty such experts were in Knox's hands by early March, 1870. Knox and Linderman then redrafted the bill, incorporated some of the suggestions. The redraft went to Boutwell, then to Sherman, then to the Senate.

The bill as Sherman presented it to the Senate contained no silver dollar, and thereby abolished the silver standard, since the gold dollar was defined as the standard and unit. Knox's original draft had included a 384-grain silver dollar, which would have been a subsidiary coin quite different from the traditional 412½-grain silver dollar. But virtually none of the experts they consulted wanted any silver dollar kept, and none at all wanted it kept as a standard.

The draft included many other provisions, but only a few affected its legislative history. It would have created a Mint Director at the Treasury who would be superior to the Philadelphia Mint and all the other branches. (This ultimately created a new job for Linderman.) It abolished the coinage charge on gold, conforming to British practice. It recommended but did not require metric weights for American coins. It discontinued two minor silver coins—of three and five cents—and added nickel coins of one, three, and five cents. These changes were ultimately insignificant compared to the dropping of the silver dollar, but, ironically, they exercised Congress much more at the time.

Knox in no way tried to hide what was happening to the silver dollar. In fact, he took pains to point it out. His letter to Boutwell transmitting the draft bill included a long explanatory footnote, prominently marked, entitled "Silver Dollar—Its Discontinuance as a Standard," in which Knox made it perfectly clear that he understood, as others unquestionably did too, that without the discontinuance of the silver dollar the United States was and would remain a bimetallic country. Admitting that the earliest American coinage laws made the silver dollar the primary unit, and that the gold dollar was a later addition, Knox stated that "The present laws consequently authorize both a gold dollar unit and a silver dollar unit, differing from each other in intrinsic value. The present gold dollar is made the dollar unit in the proposed bill, and the silver dollar piece is discontinued." The bill reduced the legal-tender powers of all silver coins— halves, quarters, dimes, and any old dollars that might possibly still exist—to one dollar. If we have to have a silver dollar, Knox added, it ought to be a "commercial dollar" with more, not less, silver than the 412½-grain dollar, to use American silver but to circulate only in foreign trade, and not domestically. But the bill, as it first went to Congress, included no silver dollar at all.[9]

While Knox, Linderman, Boutwell, and Sherman were busy with their coinage bill, William D. Kelley was active in the House of Representatives on a gold-monometallist scheme, but one so different from the Treasury-Senate bill that it quite stymied progress in 1870. Kelley succeeded in resuscitating two international coinage plans that Sherman and the Treasury considered dead.

On February 7, 1870, Kelley reported to the House a bill to unify the world's major coinages on a strictly metric basis. Ten days later, Samuel Bulkley Ruggles appeared before the Coinage, Weights, and Measures Committee on behalf of his own plan, the

old 25-franc idea he had talked about since 1863 and which had
been approved by the Paris Conference in 1867 (but not by the
U.S. Senate in 1868). Ruggles apparently staggered the metricist
opposition in the Committee. He showed up again at the Committee meeting of March 12, which must have been a donny-
brook, with Ruggles and other nonmetricists battling face to face
with Kelley and the metric advocate E. B. Elliott of the Mint.
The victory in that showdown went to Ruggles and the French
system. Four days later, Congressman Samuel Hooper of Massachusetts, a Boston merchant prince and the most redoubtable
Republican financial expert in the House, introduced a bill
embodying the Ruggles-Paris plan for international coinage.
Hooper sought support from James Pollock, the Mint Director,
and House members. Kelley, meanwhile, remained intransigent;
he was still in a position to torpedo any coinage bill he did not
like. The consequence was that although everyone concerned
sought gold monometallism, they so checked each other that
nothing but inaction could come out of the House of Representatives.[10]

Were Knox, Linderman, Boutwell, Sherman, and others aware
of what they were doing when they planned to drop the silver
dollar? It is inconceivable that they were not; Knox's statement
was explicit. But did they urge it because they feared a drop in
silver prices? No one made an explicit statement to that effect,
but it was undoubtedly the case. It was general knowledge two
and a half years earlier, in Europe and America, that silver was
about to fall. How far, no one knew; but that it might threaten
"established values," which to those people meant, for various
reasons, gold values, was likely. True, no one said flatly that
"this coinage bill will change the American monetary standard
from bimetallism to gold monometallism, and will protect vested
interests when the bottom falls out of the silver market in three
or four years." But no one would have wanted to. The switch
to gold was undertaken as part of a general monetary policy to
stabilize values and uphold the public credit, the *prima desider-
ata* not just of creditors but of many economic groups. It suited
contemporary rhetoric far better than bimetallism did. It prudently confronted a predictable decline in silver prices. Other

hypotheses may be entertained; but there is ample evidence to indicate that the move to gold was well understood, and was taken to represent nothing other than the long-term public interest as policy-makers saw it.

Sherman did not press the coinage bill in the 1870 session. Circumstances dictated caution: the currency and funding bills were more urgent, and even if the Senate approved it, Kelley and Hooper would undoubtedly battle over it in the House in a way that might split the Republican party three months before a general election. Sherman could wait.

The postponement was wise, because the House of Representatives had its hands full with the currency and funding bills. James A. Garfield presented the House with a currency bill that amounted to free banking, and would have retired millions of greenbacks. This passed the House in June, and it took two hard-fighting conference committees to bring the Representatives into conformity with the Senate version. The currency bill finally passed on July 7, 1870, providing $54-million in new national bank notes to replace temporary loan certificates, but not greenbacks. Sectional discontent with the national banking system had been allayed, without significant expansion or contraction of the currency. The final House vote divided along party, not sectional, lines. The Republicans united, which was one of Sherman's chief aims, and "confidence in the ultimate value of our greenback is established."[11]

The funding bill got away less cleanly. The House version provided only for one bond, at 4 per cent, and removed the clause requiring the national banks to exchange their existing bonds for the new ones. It took two conference committees to work out a solution, which restored 4½ per cent and 5 per cent bonds, but in smaller amounts than in the Senate version, but did not restore the bank-buying requirement. Boutwell had had to advise Sherman that "It is better I think to abandon the Bank Clauses than to abandon the Bill." Sherman presented the conference report to the Senate on July 13, with the comment that the banks, through their influence in the House, could wreck the whole refunding process, but he saw the conference version through the Senate.

The House's actions revealed the great extent to which unrestricted banking was a Midwestern interest. The Representatives had refused the first conference committee's report, which included the bank clause, and the negative voters included forty-four Republicans (twenty-five Midwestern, thirteen Southern, six Northeastern). But the second report, without the bank clauses, passed along straight party lines. The Funding Act of 1870 preserved the interests of party and section.[12]

By mid-summer of 1870, American financial affairs had been given considerable stability. Though the sectional demons had amputated the bank clause of the Funding Act, which did make the sale of the new bonds more difficult, the Funding Act and the Currency Act, taken together, solved two of the thorniest problems left by the Civil War.[13] The French, Prussians, and British were also working out their various accommodations to rhetoric and practicality, and only the demonetization of the silver standard stood in the way of America's achievement of monetary stability as policy-makers understood it. That job, however, was not proving to be simple.

12

AMERICA

DEMONETIZES SILVER

Congress, battle-weary after passing the Currency and
Funding Acts, adjourned in July, 1870, without acting further
on "a bill revising the laws relative to the mints, assay offices,
and coinage of the United States." Two and a half years were to
go by before the coinage bill, polished to the satisfaction of many
diverse people, became law. Later in the nineteenth century, the
Coinage Act of February 12, 1873, became notorious as the
"Crime of 73," the symbol of political, sectional, and class conflict. While it was being considered in Congress, however, the
public paid virtually no attention to it at all. Except for fleeting
glances from the New York Chamber of Commerce, the National
Board of Trade, and certain mining and refining interests, the
coinage bill wound its tortuous way through Congress attracting
no public notice. Monetary experts and policy-makers, in and out
of Congress, in Europe as well as in America, watched it very

carefully; most others did not. Far and away the chief characteristic of American public finance in 1871, 1872, and early 1873 was
the desire to produce and expand amid the modicum of monetary and financial stability that existed, to avoid rocking the boat.
The money question was not of great public concern from mid-
1870 to late 1873. So great was the inter-group harmony that
those three years were almost soporific. A few voices on the left
urged greenbackism, a few on the right urged contraction. But
the majority opted for dynamic equilibrium in the middle of the
road. The gold premium over greenbacks dropped in 1870 to a
steady twelve to fifteen per cent from the previous thirty-two to
forty per cent, the bonds were being refunded, money seemed
plentiful, the economy expanded. Who could argue with prosperity?

Boutwell and the Treasury accepted this situation readily and
saw no need to initiate any major policy changes, except to continue working toward silver demonetization. Refunding started
slowly in 1871, partly because of capital-market dislocations
arising from the Franco-Prussian War and a number of foreign
government flotations, but the new loan gradually found its buyers. Laborites wanted the bonds paid in greenbacks, others urged
speedier resumption of specie payments, bills to amend the funding policy were plentiful in Congress; but the keynote in Congress and at the Treasury was stability, neither increasing nor
rapidly decreasing the public debt.[1] As for the paper currency,
Boutwell took the popular view that contraction was unwise,
harsh, and a threat to stability, as McCulloch's contraction policy
from 1866 to 1868 had seemed to prove. Better to let the greenbacks "grow up to the needs of the country"—to issue no more
of them, but let rising population and economic activity increase
demand to the point, sometime in the future, when the greenbacks would reach par with gold. Boutwell even released, on
dubious authority, five million dollars in greenbacks in the fall
of 1872 to relieve a seasonal shortage. Sherman concurred in
Boutwell's gentle approach, and the only adjustments to the
financial statutes during the early seventies, except for the silver
bill, were aimed at stabilizing national bank, clearing house, and
certain other technical currency matters.[2]

Opposition did exist to the government's centrist tendency. On the left, the greenback-laborite *Workingman's Advocate* demurred from Boutwell's policy and the whole "specie basis fallacy." Calling for a paper money interconvertible with a new three per cent bond, to replace national bank notes and existing greenbacks, and existing government bonds, the *Advocate* insisted that its plan

> would make money cheap and plenty, destroy the present iniquitous and usurous [sic] rates of interest, develop the resources of the country, give profitable employment to our work people, stability to our financial system, enable us to successfully compete with European powers as common carriers on nature's highway.

To the *Advocate,* the money question was the greatest public question of the time; it could not understand the farmers' failure to pay any attention to the question. On the right, the *Banker's Magazine* still called the lack of specie payments "a condition which every merchant regards as a disgrace"; it called, though with diffidence, for contraction. As a rule, however, commercial and banking people were not convinced in the early seventies that contraction was the proper route to the specie resumption they all wanted. Jay Cooke, the Philadelphia banker, even went so far in late 1872 as to urge Boutwell to issue another forty million dollars in greenbacks.[3]

The National Board of Trade, the nation's major clearing house of business opinion, reflected many divisions within the "business community" at its four annual conventions from 1870 through 1873. At each of these meetings, the Executive Committee of the Board placed contractionist resolutions before the membership, and each time the opposition to contraction was vigorous. In 1870, the delegates agreed only on the hope that resumption would come "at the earliest practicable time," and defeated a resolution calling on the government for contraction of the greenbacks. The New England delegates unanimously favored contraction; New York, Philadelphia, and Newark unanimously opposed it; the Midwestern delegations split. Interurban rivalry played a large role among the Midwesterners, but the Easterners diverged for another reason: the commercial orientation of New England against the increasing manufacturing orientation of the Middle Atlantic states.

The National Board did pass a contractionist resolution in 1871, but at the heavy cost of a considerable drop in the number of voting delegates. The debate was long and acrimonious, and for the first time a sizable group within the Board clearly preferred to postpone specie resumption indefinitely, perhaps forever. Proponents and opponents of contraction drew on the same rhetoric, applying it to different policies. To George Buzby of Philadelphia and George Opdyke of New York, greenbacks satisfied, as well as coin ever did, the requirements of useful money —stability, aid to enterprise, and the measurement of value. But the Bostonians Joseph Ropes and Edward Atkinson could not conceive of money not having "intrinsic" value. Speakers on both sides had a poor opinion of national bank notes, incidentally. In 1872 the Board reversed itself, voted against contraction, but fought so bitterly that the number of voting delegates dwindled still further, to the point that the Board was falling apart as a barometer of business opinion. Its Executive Committee was in hard-money hands, which was why the Board, between meetings, could pressure Washington in a hard-money direction. But the mass of business opinion, outside of New England and a few Midwestern cities, disagreed.[4]

The election campaign of 1872 also reflected the nation's "don't rock the boat" mood in monetary matters. Republicans ran on their record of stability; the Democratic platform contained no sign of the Pendleton Plan of 1868 and duplicated the Republican money planks almost word for word; state platforms were similarly noncommittal. Outright greenbackism found expression only in the minuscule National Labor Reform party, an emanation of the National Labor Union. On the right, hard-money, free-traders formed a large part of the Liberal Republican movement, but their rigorous liberalism was decisively muted by the Liberal Republic nomination of Horace Greeley and the Democrats' embrace of that quixotic man. It was not a year for monetary dogmatism. Most of the voters, to judge by the campaign, were not concerned with the money question; those who were, to judge by the outcome, apparently agreed with the *New York Times,* that "Greeley's election would lead to all sorts of wild and chaotic experiments in our financial policy. Grant's re-election would insure perseverance in a course which has met, in the main, with the approbation of the country." Grant and Bout-well were finding no real quarrel with their mandate for stability.[5]

Through those years, the coinage bill demonetizing silver, a further guarantee of stability, proceeded slowly toward enactment. Despite the nearly total absence of public notice of it, Treasury and Congressional leaders tended it carefully, because they knew that the quickening decline in silver prices threatened to bring the standard silver dollar into circulation again. If that happened, the unthinkable would follow: specie resumption and bond repayment in silver instead of gold. The coinage law was the keystone in the whole arch of stability-promoting policy that Boutwell and Sherman had been building.

The bill had almost seventy sections, but only five affected its legislative history. Ironically, there was less argument about de-standardizing the silver dollar (its most important provision by far) and its recommendation of metric weights in coins (its sole reflection of the vast debate during the sixties on international coinage unification) than there was about three other matters— the changes in minor coins of silver, nickel, and bronze, the centralizing of the Mint administration, and the charge to be made for coining gold.

During the summer and fall of 1870, while the Knox-Linder-man draft lay in Sherman's Senate Finance Committee, Knox solicited additional comments on the draft and passed them through official channels to Sherman. The comments revealed that the framers had given up trying to write an international coinage scheme into the bill. Caught between the Scylla of the Ruggles-Paris plan and the Charybdis of the Kelley-Elliott metric plan, they left the gold coinage as it was, conforming neither to French nor English patterns. The coinage charge was another problem: some commentators argued for its abolition, claiming that a coinage charge tampered with the "intrinsic value" of the gold dollar, and that Britain's lack of a coinage charge invited gold bullion to flee to the Royal Mint, out of American hands. Others, admitting that the existing charge of .5 per cent was too high, nevertheless saw virtue in some small charge, simply as a fee for service. None of the commentators objected to the overriding point of the bill, the shift from bimetallism to the gold standard, but several of them wanted some kind of silver dollar, if only for foreign trade.[6]

Sherman brought the bill out of the Finance Committee and before the Senate on January 9, 1871, and the debate that day and the next revolved almost entirely around the coinage charge. The Finance Committee wanted .3 per cent; Mint officials had wanted the existing .5 per cent; West Coast Senators wanted no charge at all. (Britain had a "free coinage" system—ostensibly—and France charged .2 per cent.) These differences seem inconsequential, but they were of great moment to the Senate, because an important economic interest, bullion producers and refiners, was affected. West Coast Senators argued that America, if she kept a coinage charge on gold, would lose that gold to Britain. America would be impoverishing herself, and discriminating against her own producing class (the gold-mining interest).

To put the matter less generously, the gold producers were asking, through the two California Senators and others, that the Mint coin their gold for nothing, so that it could be shipped as coin rather than as bullion. At the same time, the California Senators were responding to pressure to transfer bullion assaying and refining from the Mint to a private refinery in San Francisco (which would cost the public more). Sherman saw these moves as legislation in a special interest, and opposed them. Arguing that the British were going to introduce a coinage charge (Chancellor Lowe indeed had proposed this, but a full year before), Sherman said there was no point abolishing the American coinage charge to keep bullion in the country.[7] The Senate debate lasted a day and a half, and at the end, the bill passed the Senate, 36–14. Sherman and the coinage charge were defeated by Senatorial deference toward the West Coast Senators who wanted to protect producers and refiners, and, apparently, East Coast Senators who were protecting their own shipping and arbitrage interests. The rhetoric of free-trade liberalism, which militated against a "legislative interference" so "artificial" as a coinage charge, assisted them. Sherman and several other members of the Finance Committee voted in the minority, against the coinage bill.

The Senate's consideration of the coinage bill was curious. In the first place, nothing about it was discussed except the coinage charge on gold; this, despite the statement in the *Congressional Globe* that the whole bill, and the Finance Committee amendments to the original draft, were read in entirety. Also, special interests helped shape the bill, but the only concern of the West Coast Senators was the gold coinage charge; they ignored the changes in silver.

Sherman's actions were even more curious. He insisted, on the Senate floor, that the bill made no major changes in existing law. The bill did not provide for international coinage unification, "because that is not a codification of the existing law, but a great and important and radical change of the law." But so was the change in standards; yet Sherman not only kept silent on that point, but did everything he could to minimize the bill's importance. It is incredible that he did not understand what effect the bill had on the monetary standard, in view of his activity at the Paris Conference in 1867, his gold-standard bill of 1868, his connection with the drafting of the coinage bill (when John Jay Knox explicitly discussed the discontinuance of silver as a standard), and the place of the coinage bill in the context of the funding and currency bills of 1870.[8] Why was Sherman so disingenuous?

Later critics would say that he wanted to drop the silver dollar in order to enhance gold values and thereby provide bondholders and other creditors with a great windfall. But this simplistic economic interpretation is insufficient. The bill did indeed benefit creditors, but that was a by-product of Sherman's (and other policy-makers') deep desire to protect the public credit. Sherman, like most everyone else, took a mechanistic view of things: the inexorable laws of political economy said that a flood of silver would be inflationary and would destroy some of the value of fixed contracts. Such a flood threatened. The only way to stop it was to get the "anachronism," the "barbarism," of the silver standard off the statute books. By his own lights, Sherman (and Boutwell and others involved) were acting in the public interest. If any turpitude was involved, there is no evidence of it. Another reason why he was so tight-lipped about the contents of the coinage bill was that, like any politician putting a possibly divisive measure through Congress, he was not obligated to reveal his every motive. The Senators had heard the bill and any interested person was free to read it. It was not Sherman's job to reduce its chances by pointing out possible objections. Given the political conditions, the financial problems, and the rhetoric of that day, as almost universally held by "responsible men," Sherman and the others believed they were acting prudently; indeed, they could hardly think otherwise.

It was another year before the coinage bill came before the House of Representatives. Having passed the Senate, it was out of Sherman's hands, and in the much less firm grip of William D. Kelley, the Philadelphia Congressman who was a disciple of Henry C. Carey. The coinage bill bobbed up briefly in 1871, but the House did not discuss it until January, 1872.[9] By that time the evidence of a silver boom was mounting rapidly. Mint Director Pollock was surprised by increased silver production not only in the Far West but in the Lake Superior region, and reported to Boutwell that so much silver was coming into the Mint that it "will soon compel the inquiry whether we cannot make more use of it at home than we are now doing." Linderman and Boutwell were not surprised. J. Ross Browne's investigations of western mining conditions in the late sixties, and a further report by Rossiter W. Raymond in 1870, confirmed the huge silver potential of the Comstock Lode. Pollock's printed annual reports showed that deposits at the Mint of American-produced silver had jumped upward in 1867, and rose from $902,000 in 1869, to $1.3-million in 1870, to $3.65-million in 1871, to over $7-million in 1872. More and more of this silver was being coined into standard 412½-grain dollars: 55,000 in fiscal 1868, 231,000 in 1869, 576,000 in 1870, 658,000 in 1871, and more than a million in 1872. Subsidiary silver coinage also rose. Gold coinage fell in those same years. In fiscal 1871, while the Philadelphia Mint coined those 658,000 silver dollars, it coined not quite 4,000 gold dollars. In the teeth of these trends, Pollock insisted on the virtues of gold monometallism in his 1871 report:

> In general, the country's currency must always be, as it has been, chiefly in paper redeemable in gold. A perfect domestic money system, would seem to be, bank or government notes for large payments; gold coin for occasional use in large or small; silver coins for fractions of the dollar down to the tenth part; and an inferior alloy for smaller denominations.

Trends in American bullion production were not the only reason why silver was falling and gold was rising in price. European demand was changing too—but to exacerbate, not moderate, the changes in supply. Linderman was undoubtedly aware of both processes, because Boutwell sent him to investigate the mint branches around the United States in 1870, and then the European mint and coinage situations in 1871. Linderman must have learned, if he did not know earlier, of silver sales by Norway, begun in 1869 to prepare for a shift to gold; that Sweden and the Netherlands planned to adopt the gold standard imminently; that Germany had just passed its Imperial Gold Coinage Law and intended to get rid of its silver in the near future.

From Linderman, if from no other source, Secretary Boutwell became quite aware of what was happening. He maintained, then and later, that the facts demanded the demonetization of silver. Twenty years later, when Congress was debating another silver bill, and the demonetization of 1873 was being attacked from certain quarters, Boutwell published a piece in the *Boston Herald* justifying his policy:

> In 1860 the American silver dollar was more valuable than the gold dollar, according to the statute ratio between the metals, in the sum of about 4 cents. From that time onward the difference in favor of silver diminished gradually, and in 1872 the difference had disappeared. At that time the power drill had been invented and its value established. The use of dynamite was well understood, and the number and richness of the silver mines in the Rocky Mountains justified the conclusion that silver would deteriorate in value with each

succeeding year. On this theory of the then future my policy was based. We were then on a gold basis as far as the use of the metals had a part in our financial affairs; we were a principal producer of gold, and the most important steps had been taken in the work of bringing the Treasury note [the greenback] to the standard of gold coin.

This was no retrospective rationalization, but a simple gloss on his annual report for 1872. Boutwell, with Knox, Linderman, and Sherman, knew what was happening, had known for years, and were acting to stave off what they considered would be a monetary calamity.[10]

William D. Kelley's participation is more puzzling. With E. B. Elliott of the Mint, he advocated a metric coinage bill in 1869 and 1870; as Chairman of the House Committee on Coinage, Weights, and Measures, he superintended coinage legislation through this period and had charge of the silver demonetization bill throughout 1871 and into 1872. He was anxious for the coinage bill to pass. But there is no evidence that he knew what was happening to silver, as Boutwell, Sherman, *et al.*, did; or if he knew, that he cared. As a disciple of Henry C. Carey, Kelley should have been interested in greenbackism and any other kind of plentiful currency, including silver. He was, in fact, a greenbacker, and later in the seventies became the leading Republican free-silverite in the House.

Despite all this, Kelley had a good reason for wanting the coinage bill to pass. "Judge" Kelley was elected to Congress for the first of sixteen terms in 1860 after a career in Philadelphia as a lawyer, anti-slavery advocate, and judge of the common pleas court. As Carey's noisiest follower, he was renowned for his efforts from the late sixties onward to protect Pennsylvania iron interests with high tariffs. But Kelley and Pennsylvania had more to protect than iron. Another Pennsylvanian, indeed Philadelphian, interest was nickel, and Kelley worked so hard to protect nickel that he lost sight completely of the easy-money side of Careyism in his zeal for Careyite protectionism. He swallowed the camel of silver demonetization while trying to protect the gnat of an all-nickel minor coinage; abolishing the silver dollar meant nothing to Kelley, but the coinage bill's replacement of three- and five-cent silver coins and smaller bronze coins with nickel ones did. Kelley was trying to help a local interest. There seems to be no evidence that he received any personal material reward from the beneficiary, and indeed the fervor of his Carey-ism and the strength of his loyalty to friends accounts plausibly for his action. But Kelley's efforts to protect nickel are a sharp example of how easily late nineteenth-century protectionist activity could take on the appearance of corruption.[11]

The nickel-purchasing policy of the United States Mint could stand as a prime exhibit of lax, shabby, and politically-involved administration in government during the Gilded Age. No law compelled the Mint officials to buy nickel through competitive bidding, nothing except a general desire they may or may not have had to keep down expenses. No law except that of minimum functional necessity stood in the way of subjecting the whole Mint staff to the uncertainties of political patronage. The Mint official had to buy his nickel from sellers who had the confidence of politicians.

Through the late sixties, Joseph Wharton, a Philadelphia businessman who owned a nickel refinery across the Delaware in Camden, sold nickel to the Mint at prices five to sixteen cents a pound (about four to ten per cent) higher than prices quoted by foreign sellers for metal equally good, and in such amounts that a Mint official complained in 1870 of a several-years' stockpile. McCulloch, Boutwell, Knox, and Linderman were not happy with the arrangement but could do nothing about it. Pollock poignantly wrote Boutwell in late 1869 advising against buying any more of Wharton's nickel. According to the troubled Mint Director, Wharton was asking $1.25 in gold while foreign prices were $1.18 to $1.20, the demand was down for three- and five-cent pieces, and there was a fifteen-month inventory on hand. "Yet to encourage our own manufactures," Pollock wrote, "the price named . . . would not be objectionable. . . . Whilst earnestly desiring to promote the personal interests of Mr. Wharton, I feel that my first duty is to the Government, and therefore cannot recommend the purchase at this time of any additional quantity of nickel." Kelley, the Philadelphia Congressman, naturally had a lively interest in the Philadelphia Mint and a Philadelphia businessman like Wharton; as Chairman of the House coinage committee, Kelley was in a position to help his constituents. It was not that he hated silver, but that he loved nickel the more.[12]

Kelley finally brought the coinage bill before the House on January 9, 1872, nearly a year after it had passed the Senate. By that time it was intensely anti-silver: no silver dollar, no silver three- and five-cent pieces, no coining of silver by the Mint for private persons. Kelley had some inkling of the degree of this hostility to silver, for he ostentatiously entered a resolution the previous day to "protect" silver by debasing it sufficiently to keep it circulating as minor coinage. But the ruse was unnecessary. Congressmen attacked the bill, not for its silver provisions, but for its favoritism to nickel and its creation of a new Mint official. The nickel debate revealed Kelley's bungling overeagerness; the administrative change nearly killed the bill.[13]

Soon after the debate began, Congressman Clarkson Potter, a New York Republican, quizzed Kelley on the bill's coinage provisions. Kelley stated that the bill made no change in the standard, weight, or fineness of gold or silver coins, and that it simply replaced copper and bronze minor coins with nickel ones. He added that "as I was charged with a bill that looked only to a codification of the mint laws, or mainly that, I did not feel it well to interject into that bill any of my own peculiar views," such as his desire to "make a wide difference between our silver and gold coinage," as Britain did, or "to have made the gold dollar uniform with the French system of weights, taking the gram as the unit."

Kelley compounded this obfuscation the next day. He rose to explain that when he had answered Potter's "categorical question," he had not had the bill in front of him and had erred in one of his statements. His error, however, concerned the salaries to be paid the new officials the bill would create; his misleading or wildly absent-minded statements on the coinage, he let stand. But his explanation reopened the salaries question, and it went on for two days and twenty-one columns in the *Congressional Globe*.

Finally a Democrat from New York, Dwight Townshend,

moved to strike the enacting clause of the bill. Again, the dropping of the silver dollar had nothing to do with his action: Townshend was simply disgusted, he said, with a Congress that had done almost nothing for a year and wasted its time debating the salary of one official when soon there would be no revenue with which to pay him or anyone else. Townshend's motion actually passed, but without a quorum, passed again by voice vote, but finally lost, 77–100, on a roll call.

Another Democrat, James R. McCormick of Missouri, did manage to scotch it. McCormick moved to recommit the bill with instructions to amend it to provide for competitive bids on any nickel bought by the Mint. "My impression is that the primary object of this bill is to affect the manner in which nickel shall be purchased. . . . There are in the United States more places producing nickel than the State of Pennsylvania." Missouri was one of them. McCormick's motion also would have abolished any "new bureau, new office, or increase of the aggregate amount of salaries."

Kelley recommitted the bill himself. In his solicitude for Pennsylvania nickel, he had almost managed to have the coinage bill killed entirely. Yet in the whole debate, neither he nor anyone else in the House made one reference to the dropping of the silver standard.[14]

When the bill reappeared a month later, Samuel Hooper of Massachusetts presented it instead of Kelley. Hooper, Chairman of the House Committee on Banking and Currency and a member of Kelley's Coinage committee, was a native of Marblehead who had made a fortune as a shipper, Boston bank director, railroad director, and holder of iron properties; some considered him the richest man in Boston. As a Congressman, he had been instrumental, early in the Civil War, in creating the national banking and greenback laws. Hooper had supported McCulloch's contraction policy, while Kelley had opposed it; Hooper had advocated the Ruggles-Paris international coinage plan in 1870, while Kelley had backed E. B. Elliott's metric scheme. The differences between the Careyite Pennsylvanian and the Yankee from Marblehead testify to the diversity of post-Civil War Republican leadership.[15]

Hooper was as interested in the coinage bill as Kelley was, but he understood it better and handled it far more smoothly. Hooper took charge quickly (so quickly that a Democrat on the Committee complained in the House that nobody had told him), contacted Pollock, Boutwell, and probably Linderman, and set about polishing the bill to make it more palatable to various interests. Boutwell advised him to clarify the silver provisions, still omitting the silver dollar, and to have the bill state clearly that the gold dollar would be the "unit of value." Others pressed him on the coinage charge, which he lowered from .3 per cent to .2 per cent. The most important change was the restoration of a silver dollar—not the old standard dollar of 412½-grains, but a 384 grain debased coin with limited tender power.[16] This change, for Hooper, was a compromise with the first bimetallist advice that he or any other American policy-maker had received. As soon as Hooper took charge of the bill, he got in touch with Alfred Latham of the Bank of England. Latham turned Hooper's letter over to a London monetary theorist and bullion merchant named Ernest Seyd, who had published a book in 1871 called *Suggestions in Reference to the Metallic Currency of the United States of America*. Hooper knew the book and asked Latham for Seyd's views, and Seyd wrote Hooper from London on February 17.

The essence of Seyd's position, which was later to be thoroughly misunderstood by critics of the Coinage Act of 1873, was a straightforward bullionist bimetallism which was fairly common in Continental Europe but almost unique in Britain or the United States at that time. For Seyd, metallic money was "the only real and most perfect medium of exchange," a fact adduceable from "metaphysical science downwards to practical reality." Bullion had "intrinsic value"; it was progressive, civilized, and followed natural laws like clockwork. Gold alone, however, was not enough: monometallism was economically false, socially pernicious, and morally wrong. A sufficient quantity of money, provided by gold and silver together, was the only means of providing all mankind with the production and exchange of goods so essential to their moral and physical well-being. "Money," wrote Seyd, "is a noble God-given thing; 'purity and truth' in

regard to it, in more than one sense, are much closer connected
with material and moral purity and truth, than most people are
able of perceiving." The common argument that gold was the
standard of "civilization" was "grandiloquent claptrap." Gold
monometallism would mean discarding half the world's money
supply. It would set off a great deflation of labor and commodities, while "the value of invested capital would undeservedly
and greatly increase, to the detriment of all social relations."
Certainly, the monetary standard should oscillate as little as possible; certainly, currencies should not be debased to benefit
debtors at the expense of creditors. But bimetallism insured
against these things far better than monometallism. In fact, to
change to monometallism to benefit creditors was a greater sin,
leading to "pauperism, misery, starvation and crime." Seyd hated
irredeemable paper, he was a thorough bullionist, a nineteenth-
century natural-law liberal. But he also considered the social
consequences of monetary laws, and hence condemned deflation
as far worse than inflation, and preferred bimetallic stability to
either.

Seyd was aware in 1871 that American silver production was
increasing and that the coinage bill before Congress proposed
to drop the silver dollar. He opposed the change. He said as
much in his letter to Hooper. He recommended a coinage charge
of no more than .2 per cent, which was just about the flat cost,
and advocated a 400-grain silver dollar which he hoped would
be the basis for an international agreement. If it was absolutely
necessary, he said, this dollar could be limited in legal-tender
power to fifty or a hundred dollars. But that point was untypical
(and was possibly an interpolation into the available versions,
all copies, of his letter to Hooper); in season and out, for twenty-
five years, Seyd called gold monometallism immoral, and advocated universal gold-silver bimetallism.[17]

Hooper read Seyd's letter carefully, and took some of it to
heart. He changed the coinage bill to make the coinage charge
.2 per cent, and restored a silver dollar of 384-grains. But Seyd's
bimetallism was not incorporated; to Hooper, on his own admission, the "double valuation" was incomprehensible. These two
changes also accommodated existing pressures. Linderman pub-

lished a pamphlet just then, advocating no coinage charge at all, which was the California position; Kelley's bill set it at .3 per cent; Hooper compromised at .2 per cent, which was just about cost. As for the silver dollar, people were beginning to awaken to the existence of growing silver stocks, and the 384-grain dollar in Hooper's bill would make use of some of the silver, for Oriental trade, without endangering monometallism. Sherman, in his memoirs, recalled that the "trade dollar" indeed "met all the demands of the silver producing states"; Sherman also noted that "since gold was then only coined for the benefit of private depositors," those depositors should not have objected to paying .2 per cent for the Mint's services.

All of these things suggest strongly that the lowered coinage charges and the inclusion of the nonstandard silver dollar for Oriental commerce were a package compromise to make the bill palatable to West Coast legislators. It may even have happened, though there is no direct evidence for it, that the Congressional silver guardians understood quite well that the standard silver dollar was being dropped, but did not realize how disastrously low silver prices were about to sink. Bought off to their own satisfaction in 1872, their only remaining weapon after silver fell in the mid-seventies (and they used it) was to profess shocked incredulity at how demonetization could ever have reached the statute books in 1873.[18]

Hooper brought the coinage bill back to the House floor on April 9, 1872. On that day and the next, the House discussed the bill's effect on the monetary standard for the first and last time. Hooper was clear and direct. The bill had "the sanction of the Treasury" and the advice of "Mr. Ernest Seyd, of London, a distinguished writer." Presenting the bill section by section, Hooper pointed out that the gold dollar became the "unit of value." The silver dollar was then the legal unit, but it did not bear a correct relative proportion to the gold dollar, and the latter had been for years, in practice, the "standard or measure of value, as it is legally in Great Britain and most of the European countries." The five-cent silver coin would be replaced by one of nickel, and silver coinage was otherwise unchanged "except in relation to the silver dollar, which is reduced in weight from 412½ to 384 grains; thus making it a subsidiary coin in harmony with the silver coins of less denomination, to secure its concurrent circulation with them." Silver's tender powers were reduced to five dollars (which thoroughly ended it as a standard). Congressman Stoughton of Michigan followed Hooper with another explicit statement about the standards change, and the ensuing discussion showed that Clarkson Potter and William D. Kelley understood it too. But no one opposed it.

Instead, the Representatives argued over other provisions. The bill favored private bullion refining. Two New York Congressmen (Republican Potter and Democrat Fernando Wood) protested this, but Hooper and Aaron Sargent of California claimed it was economical. Like the debased silver dollar, of course, it was a sop to the West Coast. Potter also scored the administrative change creating a Mint Director at Washington, claiming it was meant solely to "make a place" for a certain person. Potter suggested bluntly that since the present Director at Philadelphia, Pollock, refused to support Kelley's all-nickel minor coinage, he either had to be fired or overruled. (In fact an investigation begun the previous August under Boutwell's direction into allegations that Pollock had mishandled the Mint had just ended on April 3, less than a week before this debate, giving Pollock a clean bill of health. Linderman got the new job a year later, while Pollock stayed in Philadelphia, subordinate to his one-time employee. Another investigation in 1872, which Hooper's Banking and Currency Committee undertook, dismissed the Comptroller of the Currency on Hooper's House motion of March 26, and John Jay Knox became the new Comptroller. By mid-1873, by an odd series of circumstances (to say the very least), the two drafters of the coinage bill, Knox and Linderman, had become major bureau chiefs in the Treasury Department.) Potter was evidently not shooting blindly.

Yet the bill foundered one more time. Kelley, who was getting what he wanted, could not leave well enough alone. In the April 9 debate, he accused Potter of trying to protect New York bullion merchants who, under existing arrangements, could take silver bullion to the Mint and receive fractional coins worth five per cent more than the bullion value. Kelley's attack accomplished nothing, except to arouse the intense ire of several New York Congressmen, and Hooper had to withdraw the bill quickly into committee.[19]

Hooper eased the bill before the House one final time on May 27, 1872. In the intervening six weeks, Samuel B. Ruggles and the New York Chamber of Commerce strongly urged him to make the new American silver coins metric, as a step toward international coinage unification. Hooper did redefine the half-dollar and two smaller silver coins in metric terms, but left the silver dollar at 384-grains instead of 385.8 grains, as Ruggles asked, which would have made it "equiponderant" to five silver francs. The sole point at which the new American coinage took notice of international coinage schemes, after all that had happened, was the minor silver coins. Neither the silver nor gold dollars were internationalized in any way.

Another change met the objections of Kelley's foes. The Mint would buy its nickel through competitive bidding. The standards question did not arise again, the bill was not read, and the House voted to pass it, 110–13, without a roll call. It had to be repassed by the Senate, since the Senate that had passed it had expired long since, and Sherman took the bill in hand once again.[20]

Sherman and the Finance Committee made only one significant change in the bill while it was in their hands in the summer and fall of 1872, awaiting the reconvening of Congress in December. The nonstandard silver dollar of 384-grains that Hooper had inserted was enlarged to 420 grains, to constitute a "trade dollar," later called the "China dollar." It was to have no legal-tender power, or virtually none, in the United States, but was to circulate in Far Eastern and perhaps Latin American foreign commerce.

The Treasury Department suggested the 420-grain trade dollar, and Sherman accepted the Treasury's idea (meaning Boutwell's, Linderman's, and Knox's idea) instead of the strong representations of his old ally, Samuel B. Ruggles, to make the silver dollar and other silver coins metric and "equiponderant" with the Latin Union silver coinage. Ruggles pushed a metric resolution through the National Board of Trade in October, as he had done in the

New York Chamber of Commerce in May. In December, Ruggles bombarded every Congressman with documents and statements on international coinage unification. But in vain. Sherman and the Treasury leaders watched silver production mount, and silver prices decline. By late 1872, it was urgently necessary to demonetize silver as a standard, but at the same time to assure silver producers a place for their product at the Mint. The 420-grain "trade dollar" was their way of providing the largest possible protection for American silver, consistent with the principle of gold monometallism.[21]

Silver poured into the Mint in 1872 faster than ever before. Records remain of hundreds of currency and bullion transfers made by the Mint at that time, and in not one of those transfers did anyone send in gold dollars and ask for silver, despite frequent claims by monometallists that silver was at a premium over gold. That fiction evaporated in 1872, when the silver deposited at the Mint was five times what it was in 1870, and was equivalent in value to nearly one-third of all the silver brought to the Mint in the preceding thirty years. In mid-October the head of the New York Assay Office asked Pollock to hurry the shipment of silver dollars to pay bullion depositors who were asking for more silver dollars almost daily. Two weeks later the London *Economist* reported that the German silver demonetization was taking effect: silver prices were at their lowest since the early 1850's.[22]

Treasury officials knew silver was in trouble and understood the implications. Even the usually self-effacing Pollock suggested in his annual report that autumn that perhaps changes in minor silver coins would be a good idea "if gold should ascend to a premium." Secretary Boutwell grasped perfectly what was happening—that silver was beginning to threaten the whole edifice of specie resumption and protection of the public credit—and he laid the situation before Congress in his annual report in November, 1872:

> In the last ten years the commercial value of silver has depreciated about three per cent as compared with gold, and its use as currency has been discontinued by Germany and

some other countries. The financial condition of the United States has prevented the use of silver as currency for more than ten years, and I am of the opinion that upon grounds of public policy no attempt should be made to introduce it, but that the coinage should be limited to commercial purposes, and designed exclusively for commercial uses with other nations. . . . Therefore, in renewing the recommendations heretofore made for the passage of the Mint Bill, I suggest such alterations as will prohibit the coinage of silver for circulation in this country, but that authority be given for the coinage of the silver dollar that shall be as valuable as the Mexican dollar [which circulated in the Orient]. . . . As the production of silver is rapidly increasing such a coinage will at once furnish a market for the raw material and facilitate commerce between the United States and China.

The answer, then, was the "trade dollar." Boutwell also made it very clear that silver could hurt specie resumption.

As the depreciation of silver is likely to continue it is impossible to issue coin redeemable in gold without ultimate loss to the government; for when the difference becomes considerable owners will present the silver for redemption, and leave it in the hands of the government to be disposed of subsequently at a loss. If the policy should be adopted of issuing silver coin irredeemable, but whose intrinsic and nominal value should correspond to gold, the time must come when the country would suffer from the presence of the depreciated silver currency, not redeemable by the government nor current in the channels of trade.[23]

Linderman, of course, knew of the silver drop and was a strong advocate of the trade dollar as a remedy. At Boutwell's request, Linderman visited the Pacific Coast in late 1872, partly to find ways to short-circuit private refiners from taking away the San Francisco Mint's refining business, but also to see what effects the German demonetization and other silver developments were having on Californian commerce. Linderman reported to Bout-

well in November that the effects were considerable. The standard silver dollar ought to be replaced with a coin

> which will meet certain commercial requirements becoming
> daily more pressing, without giving rise to any of those per-
> plexing questions or complications resulting from the vary-
> ing values of the precious metals, under a double standard,
> and at the same time afford some relief to our mining indus-
> tries, from the serious decline and further apparent deprecia-
> tions in the value of silver.

Linderman and Knox later stated that the trade dollar idea had
originated with certain San Francisco businessmen and bankers,
and as early as 1868 Senator Morgan of New York suggested it
in his critique of Sherman's gold-standard bill. Whoever the
author was, he had strong support by the end of 1872.[24]

On January 17, 1873, as soon as the trade dollar amendment
was formulated, Sherman brought the coinage bill before the
Senate. The debate was short, but it showed that the silver decline was clearly understood. Using the international coinage
idea as a talking point, Sherman deftly led the bill past the con-
tentious protectors of gold and silver. Senator Casserly of California disliked the slight increase in the bullion content of the
silver coins, even for the international coinage reasons Sherman
gave, but Casserly was mollified by the reduction in the coinage
charge to .2 per cent. This, Casserly admitted, would draw Australian gold to our shores, making specie resumption easier, while
"this silver which we do not want and which before a great while
may be at an absolute discount on our hands" would flow out
to England, who wanted silver for her Indian trade.

Senator William Stewart of Nevada, who screamed years later
that the demonetization of silver had been surreptitious, was
present and awake; but he made no response on behalf of Ne-
vadan silver to Casserly's candid admission of the California gold
producers' interest in the bill.

Sherman hurried the bill along, no one objected to the scuttling
of bimetallism, and the bill passed without a roll call. Sherman
and Hooper met in a House-Senate conference committee,
secured House agreement to the Senate version containing the

trade dollar, and President Grant signed it. Bimetallism and the standard silver dollar went out of the statutes; the 420-grain trade dollar and metric minor silver coins equivalent to Latin Union coins remained. The coinage charge for gold was .2 per cent. All Mint establishments, including Philadelphia, came under a Director at the Treasury (Linderman soon got the job). The three- and five-cent silver coins and the two-cent bronze coins were dropped, to be replaced by nickel ones. The gold dollar became the standard and unit of value.[25]

What was the reaction to the bill? Policy-makers at the Treasury and in Congress, together with gold, silver, and nickel interests, were happy. International coinage had come off badly, but Ruggles and others lived to fight again another day. Newspaper comments were extremely rare and brief; even the *Commercial and Financial Chronicle,* on February 8, believed "that no financial legislation of moment will be done during this session." The *Chronicle* was never more wrong.

13

THE LEGENDS

OF THE

CRIME OF '73

Within three years, the Coinage Act was being damned as a great conspiracy, indeed, the "Crime," of 1873. The Act, so the legend went, had been the offspring of a bondholders' cabal. Fed by sectional, class, and ideological rancor, the legend of the Crime flourished through the rest of the nineteenth century.

As it spread, Sherman and other participants rushed to defend themselves, and a counter-legend developed that claimed that Sherman, Boutwell, and the other policy-makers involved had staunchly defended gold and the national honor against the idiocies of greenbackism and the threat of silver. This counter-legend dominated the orthodox economic histories of the period almost down to the present day.

As early as 1876, by which time the country was in the middle of depression and silver prices had plummeted to an immemorial low, the Coinage Act of 1873 came under attack from Congressional inflationists for its "sneaky" character. The French mono-metallist leader, Esquirou de Parieu, even though he approved of it, called it much the same thing (*"sournoise"*). Congressmen present when the Act was passed insisted during the silver-coinage debates of 1876–78 that a small group of insiders had slipped the Act under their very noses by wilfully concealing its main element, the change from bimetallism to the gold standard. The debates on nickel, coinage charges, and the rest, had been diversionary. By 1878, they were saying, the United States was becoming a bondholders' paradise thanks to the Coinage Act: Specie payments, and payments on public bonds (many originally bought with greenbacks), would be made, not in greenbacks, not even in by-then depreciated silver, but in gold.[1]

In the Congressional debates of the late seventies over money, Richard P. Bland of Missouri, William D. Kelley (of all people), and others strove to establish the surreptitious, conspiratorial, and special-interest character of the 1873 Act. In 1876 an official monetary inquiry implied that a small group of men purposefully concealed the silver demonetization from the public and from President Grant, pushed the Act through Congress without its having been read except by title, and planned it as a device to overpay the public debt. Others even at that early date took a blunter line, saying that the Act was the creation pure and simple of a conspiracy of "bloated bondholders": foreign bondholders had sent an emissary to the United States in early 1872, armed with a slush fund of £100,000 and drawing power for more, to bribe the Congress into passing the demonetization. The bagman was supposed to have been Ernest Seyd. Kelley in late 1877 denied Seyd's complicity, but the story stuck.[2]

The story of the "Crime" receded from public notice during the relatively quiescent early eighties, but a radical fringe kept the story buzzing. It continued well into the nineties as part of the noise-making equipment of certain vocal extremists who attached themselves to the Populist movement. The mass of Populists and Bryanites confined themselves to lamenting the all-too-apparent consequences of the Act, but the radical fringe endowed the legend with a gaudy filigree. The villains were the Rothschilds and other banking bondholders, John Sherman was their chief congressional henchman, and Ernest Seyd the wicked go-between.

In 1887 a Michigan radical, Mrs. Sarah E. V. Emery, condemned the demonetization as one of the "seven conspiracies that shook the world." Her book was spread broadcast through the Midwest in the campaign of 1888. The trouble began, she said, in 1862. A London banker named Hazzard circularized bankers in America and abroad to support the national banking bill, the bond issues, and the Civil War greenback issues. Capital's control of labor by means of chattel slavery would soon end, but these new financial laws could easily provide even more complete control. Greenbacks would later be dropped, and capitalists would direct labor, wages, and the whole money supply. According to Mrs. Emery, subsequent legislation such as contraction, the Public Credit Act, and refunding, simply put the Hazzard Circular into effect. Then in 1873 came the demonetization:

In the Banker's Magazine of August, 1873, we find the following . . . : 'In 1872, silver being demonetized in France, England and Holland, a capital of $500,000 was raised, and Ernest Seyd of London was sent to this country with this fund, as agent of the foreign bond-holders and capitalists, to effect the same object (demonetization of silver), which was accomplished.' There you have it, a paid agent of English capitalists sent to this country with $500,000 to buy the American Congress and rob the American people.

This was mostly Rothschild money, Mrs. Emery said. She claimed corroboration from the *Congressional Record* of April 9, 1872, where Samuel Hooper was supposed to have said that "Earnest [sic] Seyd of London, a distinguished writer and bullionist, *who is now here,* has given great attention to the subject. . . .," and from a Greenback Congressmen, whom William D. Kelley told that the original draft of the coinage bill was in Seyd's handwriting. What was the result of Seyd's perfidy?

Bankruptcies and financial disaster brought in train their legitimate offspring; and the statistics of those and the ensuing years are voluminous with the most startling and loathsome crimes. Murder, insanity, suicide, divorce, drunkenness and all forms of immorality and crime have increased from that day to this in the most appalling ratio.

A few agrarian writers added further "proof," a document called the Luckenback Affidavit, in which an ex-New York merchant, resident in Denver, testified in 1892 that Ernest Seyd told him personally, at a dinner party in London, how he had bribed the Congress into demonetizing silver with £100,000 raised by London and German bankers.[3] Others, particularly Senator Stewart of Nevada, connected John Sherman with the "Crime". In 1893 Stewart said in the Senate that he had followed "the slimy tracks of the Act of 1873" through the congressional documents, and he found that "the Senator from Ohio [Sherman], through English influence, managed to destroy silver for the benefit of English creditors." Stewart claimed that Sherman steered the bill through the Senate without calling attention to the demonetization, thus giving the false impression that the new silver dollar in the bill matched the five-franc piece. Stewart also traced back Sherman's actions from the floor leadership in 1873 to the gold standard bill of 1868 to monometallist activity at the 1867 Paris Conference (in this, Stewart was right). To criticisms that he himself had voted for the Act, Stewart only replied that the concealment had been so slick that it had even fooled so lynx-eyed a Congressional watchman as himself. By no means all of the silverites or Populists swallowed these extreme versions of the legend, but many of them apparently did understand the Act to have been consciously planned and surreptitiously executed to benefit holders of government bonds.[4]

Thus the agrarian legend of the "Crime of '73": conspiratorial passage of an unjust law to benefit a few, and in its most extreme versions, implicating Ernest Seyd and John Sherman. This legend is, to put it calmly, open to question.

The attempt to implicate Ernest Seyd is baffling. He was not

essential to the indictment, and it would have been just as helpful to have stated, for example, that H. R. Linderman did the
dirty work. Boutwell had sent Linderman on a trip to Germany
and London in September and October of 1871, and had anyone
accused Linderman of being the bagman instead of Seyd, exculpa-
tion might have been harder. But Seyd became the scapegoat,
apparently for no other reason than that Hooper had mentioned
his name as a consultant on the coinage bill when he brought
it before the House in April, 1872. Seyd's involvement is extremely improbable. In the first place, Mrs. Emery's quotation
of Hooper interpolated the phrase "who is now here," which
does not appear in the *Congressional Globe*. (The *Record*, by the
way, did not exist until 1873.) Secondly, prominent Populists,
such as Congressman John Davis of Kansas, and the Colorado
Silver Republican Henry M. Teller, denied Seyd's complicity and
the credibility of the Luckenback Affidavit, and recalled that
Seyd was a bimetallist. Ernest Seyd, Jr., said in an 1893 American
newspaper article that Seyd (who died in 1881) had not been in
America after 1856. Above all, Seyd never once, in all his published writings, regarded silver demonetization in the least favor-
ably. In 1871 he wrote that if the United States demonetized
silver it would violate every existing contract, and be "tanta-
mount to a gratuitous addition to the power of invested capital
and fixed incomes, whilst . . . the burden of taxation would become the heavier in proportion, and labour would become more
enslaved than ever." Seyd was not likely to have been either a
bribe-giver or a monometallist.[5]

As for Sherman, no evidence suggests that he received any
financial reward from anyone for his floor leadership of the
coinage bill or for any of his efforts in 1867. What he and many
others were seeking in financial policy was economic stability and
steady progress, and the protection of the public credit, by means
of what they considered to be the only sound foundation for
money and credit, gold monometallism; to this, silver was known
to be an imminent threat.

Nor was the demonetization surreptitious. A slim basis exists
for later claims that the bill was not read in the Senate or House

and that it was hurried through both chambers to avoid its proper consideration, since it was read in the Senate only in January, 1871, and in the House (incompletely) a year later. Also, Hooper and Sherman obviously hurried it through their respective houses when it last appeared in each. But many bills, especially very long ones, were not fully read. That bill was reprinted many times without the standard silver dollar; Hooper brought that point explicitly to the House's attention in 1872; and the original accompanying documents included paragraphs by Knox carefully explaining the change. Senator Stewart, who later shouted that he had been duped, not only was present at the final Senate debate, not only had every opportunity to read the bill and the accompanying documents, but may even have participated in drafting some of its silver provisions.

Was the Act a conspiracy? Yes, if that means that only a few policy-makers were fully familiar with it. But since the process of drafting and passing any complicated bill reasonably and normally involved only a small group in Congress and in the appropriate Executive agency, then, naturally, only a few people, such as Boutwell, Knox, Linderman, Hooper, Sherman, and for a time, Kelley, knew what was in the bill. Not even all of them controlled its contents at all times. Was there a conspiracy between these men and special interests outside the Congress? Certainly the policy-makers consulted (or were pressured by) businessmen whose interests were affected, such as nickel, gold, and silver people. But policy-makers consulted affected interests on any major bill; coinage was no different in this respect from tariff or transportation bills. But the "bloated bondholders," the supposed beneficiaries according to the later indictment, were not consulted and did not pressure policy-makers as a group; in fact they did not exist as a pressure group. As for the bill's having been part of a long-term postwar conspiracy to defraud the public, the main "documentary" basis for this—Mrs. Emery's quotation from the *Banker's Magazine* of August, 1873—is fictitious.

The Act did, of course, benefit certain people. In the face of silver's threat to "established" values, it completed the work of protecting bondholders that began with the Public Credit Act of 1869. Prior to that Act, as the campaign of 1868 demonstrated, there was plenty of public pressure to pay the Civil War bonds in the greenbacks that many of them had been purchased with. The Public Credit Act promised that the bonds would be paid in coin. When silver began to increase in supply and drop in demand, the American bimetallic law had to be changed so that coin meant "gold coin." This certainly did protect bondholders. But it also protected the public credit, a matter considered basic to economic law and good morals, and this was the real aim. The rhetoric of monometallism, not the succubus of private avarice, was the operative force.

So much for the legend of the "Crime of 73." Fortunately for the reputation of silverites and Populists, few of them swallowed it in anything but the most generalized and diluted form. But there is another legend of the Coinage Act, the counter-legend drawn up by its creators in their own self-defense. It became the "orthodox" legend because it was accepted very uncritically by financial historians who should have known better. But they were prone to believe and propagate it because they worked under virtually the same rhetorical and ideological presuppositions as the respectable, monometallist lawmakers of the seventies.

When Sherman, Knox, Linderman, and Boutwell defended themselves and the Coinage Act in later years, they adduced several reasons for the demonetization that they had not bothered to present in 1870–73. Sherman and Linderman insisted that the dropping of the silver dollar simply rectified the omission of it in the Coinage Act of 1853, the Act that had debased and limited the tender power of all the other silver coins. The country effectively went on the gold standard then, they said, and the dropping of the silver dollar in 1873 simply cleared up an oversight in the 1853 Act. Furthermore, Linderman and Sherman said the silver dollar was an obsolete coin by 1873; it had not been coined for years; it did not circulate. The Coinage Act of 1873 simply codified a mass of confusing monetary statutes and recognized existing facts.

Sherman said again and again that the Act had been passed in full public view. He put it most bluntly in 1893:

It was debated, scrutinized, and passed unanimously [in the House], dropping the silver dollar as directly stated by Mr. Hooper. It was reported, debated, amended, and passed by the Senate unanimously. In every stage of the bill and every print[ing] the dollar of 412½ grains was prohibited, and the single gold standard recognized, proclaimed, and understood. It was not until silver was a cheaper dollar that anyone demanded it, and then it was to take advantage of a creditor.

Of course the votes were not unanimous, and the demonetization not "proclaimed" at every stage. But Sherman did realize that the Act shifted the United States from bimetallism to gold monometallism.

Boutwell, in his memoirs, was utterly candid on that point:

In 1873 I had come to believe that it was wise for every nation to recognize, establish, and maintain the gold standard. I was of the opinion then, as I am of the opinion now, that nations cannot escape from the gold standard in all interstate transactions. . . . hence it was that I determined to abandon the idea of a double standard. . . .

The ex-Secretary emphasized that this bill, his bill, "established the gold standard for the United States for all time."[6]

Was the decline in the price of silver known beforehand to the bill's creators? Linderman contradicted himself, Sherman avoided the point, and Boutwell proudly claimed that he acted on precisely that prior assumption. Was the bill drawn up and passed conspiratorially? All three, plus Knox, denied that charge heatedly. None of them, with the notable exception of Boutwell, were anxious to advertise their responsibility for the demonetization. In later accounts they remembered details faultily, but all revealed that they understood and planned the demonetization beforehand as the key feature of the bill. Sherman, Linderman, Knox, Boutwell, and Hooper wanted to get rid of the double standard. All of them knew that silver was declining in price and would decline more severely, that gold would probably soon arrive at a premium over silver, as it always had been over the greenbacks. Some of their later statements were disingenuous (that the 1873 Act simply codified earlier statutes) or plain false (that silver dollars were not being coined; over a million were coined in the year preceding the Act). But their basic aim was understandable: to protect existing values, maintain the public credit, insure that specie payments would be resumed on the gold standard. That they walked on eggshells as they pushed the Act along indicates that they knew, even in the early seventies, that the Act might not be universally popular, no matter how responsibly it was intended.

The self-defense offered in the seventies and the nineties by the participants in the 1873 Act was taken over, embellished at some points, and propagated soberly by respected financial historians from that day nearly to this. The counter-legend became the orthodox story; people who unhesitatingly threw out of court the legend of the "Crime" just as unhesitatingly took the participants' version and made it an apologia. The reason for this is simple: most of the later commentators shared with the participants the same nineteenth-century monometallist and mechanistic rhetoric and world-views.[7]

The legend of the "Crime of 73" is full of holes. But so too are the accounts of the participants, and the financial historians who became their tribunes. The legend of the Crime indicts, the orthodox legend exculpates. What is left?

The demonetization of silver in the Coinage Act of 1873 was known, planned, and brought off by Sherman, Boutwell, Linderman, Knox, Hooper and others in order to secure what they believed, and believed mistakenly, to be the public interest. Gold monometallism was the only monetary standard they understood, because they believed in its ideology and in the rhetoric which seemed to make it the embodiment of civilization, natural law, proper political economy, and good morals. That some of them, such as Kelley, tailored the bill with provisions meant to protect certain business groups is true but not to the point. The demonetization of silver, far and away the crucial provision, was not undertaken for the specific benefit of specific groups, including the "bloated bondholders."

The creators of the Act consciously changed the United States from a bimetallic to a gold-monometallic nation. They did so as a result of their group affiliations: but these affiliations were the affiliations of ideology, party, and rhetoric, not of economic self-interest.

PART FOUR

Groups and Rhetoric

in the Period

of Stress

1873–1879

14

THE CONSEQUENCES

OF DEPRESSION

The Coinage Act of 1873, and its counterpart in Germany, ended a several-year-long trend to institutionalize the liberal and monometallist versions of prevailing rhetoric; a trend, moreover, that occurred amid a context of general economic prosperity. In the United States, and in other countries, policy-makers had painstakingly built an edifice of legislation and other governmental activity that was supposed to have insured civilization's further progress within the necessary bounds of natural law. The future, they expected, was secure.

The policy-makers reckoned without the business cycle. It changed quite abruptly in 1873. In doing so, it catalyzed rhetoric and group relations into a very new set of equations from those prevailing in the preceding period. Sectional antagonisms reawoke in America; economic groups discarded former coalitions and formed new ones reflecting a more modern stage of industrialization; the policies of the major nations (especially Germany and France) swerved away from liberalism toward economic nationalism. The rhetoric that served to bind social groups together in the pre-1873 period fragmented, lost that binding function, and became little more than an adjunct to the slogans of contending ideological groups.

To be sure, the pre-1873 years were not tranquil in any ideal sense—not with Reconstruction in the South, the Johnson impeachment, Black Friday in 1869, Granger agitation, some of the worst scandals in the Grant Administration, the rise of the Ku Klux Klan, the Liberal Republican and National Labor Reform political protests in 1872. In context, however, compared to the six-year period of depression and social stress that followed them, the several years ending in 1873 were among the most tranquil of the late nineteenth century. In the United States, manufacturing output increased from 1867 into 1873, the gold price of commodities remained fairly stable, the gold premium on greenbacks dropped sharply in 1870 and rose only slightly for the next three years. Wages generally rose as greenback prices fell, and agricultural output and exports, the largest sector of the economy, increased. The legislative settlements of 1870, particularly the currency and funding acts, had committed the country in a vague way to ultimate specie resumption but had not disturbed any of the major economic sectors. Prosperity and legislation allayed the political and sectional disagreements of the late sixties, and while liberal rhetoric and gold-monometallist ideology went almost unchallenged, a widespread sense of harmony prevailed in society.

The end of this happy condition came swiftly. Financial panics struck Berlin and Vienna in mid-year, Philadelphia and New York in September; by early 1874, Britain too was slipping into depression. The panics of 1873, like the New York stock market crash of 1929, did not cause the subsequent depression. But they destroyed investor confidence in an economy that was already structurally shaky. In the United States, for example, the third quarter of 1873 saw a slackening of commodity prices, foreign trade, and manufacturing, together with a severe tightening in the money market. The financial community was very nervous by September, and when the great investment banking house of Jay Cooke closed its doors on September 18, technically still solvent but so overextended in railroad securities that it lacked enough liquidity to meet current obligations, panic followed. By late October, unemployment increased as demand for goods fell off. In November, a conservative labor journal had to ask its readers to be "reasonable, and try and act manly" in the face of layoffs and wage cuts, and the *Workingman's Advocate* hoped that employers would realize that their interests and those of their workers were "identical" and would hence deal fairly regarding any wage or hour cuts that became "inevitable." Seldom would a labor journal use the language of class harmony again.[1]

In the United States, however, 1873–78 brought a depression with a difference.[2] Most, but not all, of the pre-1873 trends changed. Bank clearances and interest rates dropped sharply, farm prices and the wages of all workers except foremen began to slip in late 1873 or early 1874, retail prices declined (though more slowly than wages), wholesale prices declined about as fast as wages, especially from early 1875.

On the other hand, while depression affected the personal income of farmers and workers, and the profits of financial, commercial, and manufacturing people, the total national output in manufacturing, agriculture, mining, and export volume actually increased during this "depression" period. The gold premium shrank, partly as a result of stringent Treasury policy but ultimately and more importantly because of a favorable trade balance. Specie payments, which had eluded the country during prosperity, were resumed at the close of the depression.[3] Consequently, the depression following the Panic of 1873 was mainly noticeable where it was most upsetting politically and socially; while it affected individual wages, prices received for agricultural products or finished goods, and interest rates, it was in aggregate statistics not very harmful if indeed it was harmful at all to the productive strength of the American economy and its position in the world. Its harshest effects were its most visible ones. It functioned less as an economic disaster than as an event which provoked divisions among the country's ideological, social, and political groups, and helped shatter the rhetoric that had helped bind them.

Nevertheless, the depression was real, and it was worldwide. It changed the economics and also the coinage and tariff policies of all the major nations. Depression overtook Germany following financial panics in May and November, 1873. It struck Britain shortly afterward. Though it was milder in France, that country too underwent a gradual recession by 1876 which became depression by 1878. In these countries, the depression not only affected wages, prices, and interest rates, but, unlike in America, productive output as well. In Britain, where the depression was most severe, manufacturing, foreign trade, and wholesale prices declined exceedingly from the end of 1873 until revival finally began in the middle of 1879. Germany was almost as hard-hit; though German wholesale prices did not drop as sharply as American or British, wages and trade were thoroughly depressed almost from the beginning of trouble in mid-1873 until revival came in early 1879. France, which had begun to recover nicely from the shock of the Franco-Prussian War and its aftermath, avoided the depression depths plumbed by Germany and Britain, but could not escape a marked decline in wages, commodity prices, manufacturing output, and foreign trade in 1876–78.

The general malaise was bad enough without the presence of peculiar complications. But a major complication was palpably present: The value of silver, relative to gold, plummeted so drastically after 1873 that the years 1873–76 were referred to as the time of the "great silver panic." For patients accustomed to a diet of metallic money, a diet that had been growing steadily richer as the major nations moved toward gold monometallism in the late sixties and early seventies, this was bad news indeed. They responded to this change with significant reversals in policy.

The economic crisis confirmed policy-makers in the belief, which was understandable but mistaken, that money had to be made of precious metals or had to be freely convertible into them. This commitment left them without much room to maneuver. It also meant inevitably that they would have to reconsider even the most steadfast gold-monometallist policy when silver dropped in price.

The reasons for this are fairly simple, stemming from changes in relative supply and demand for gold and silver that occurred in the early seventies. Germany was the major, and America the minor, villain. Ernest Seyd, the English bimetallist, explained the problem succinctly in 1876: when trade and industry expanded rapidly around the world in the nineteenth century, differences in monetary standard (Britain on gold, the Germanies on silver, France on both) turned out to be happy accidents, because these differences contributed to equilibrium in the world's money supplies. Even the huge increase in the world stock of gold following the Australian and Californian strikes of the late 1840's did not upset things, because an informal international bimetallic balance existed. Certain French writers talked of a "parachute effect" between gold and silver, whereby a heavy demand on, say, silver, in one country would be matched by a heavy demand for gold in another country; as silver flowed into the first country, gold would flow out, until silver became abundant, whereupon the process would reverse itself and gold would begin to flow back. What Seyd and the French writers were saying was that the aggregate demand for gold and for silver was about equal the world over; local imbalances would therefore have to be temporary.

The parachute effect actually seemed to work in the fifties and well into the sixties. But to monometallists, it lacked "logical and scientific rigor." It also involved minor fluctuations in values, and though these fluctuations were not remotely as great as changes in gold and silver stocks, pressure for gold monometallism grew. This was the main flaw in the "parachute" mechanism: not that it did not work, given roughly equal aggregate demand for each metal, but that many people became so convinced that only gold could serve the purposes of money that they ceased to believe in the mechanism; got rid of silver; went over to gold monometallism; and thereby destroyed the mechanism: a self-fulfilling prophecy. When Germany shifted from silver to gold, the parachute was riddled. With Britain on gold, Germany on gold, and France shakily bimetallic, gold demand rose greatly, and the equilibrium could hardly operate. Germany became a seller rather than a buyer of silver. This made matters worse, because she thereby increased the supply of silver just as she diminished the demand. Several small countries in Northern Europe, who were economic satellites of Germany to a considerable extent, changed from silver to gold at about the same time, with similar consequences. The American demonetization of silver in 1873 severely restricted American demand for silver and made it legally impossible for the United States to contribute to patching the parachute. Demand for silver by India, previously called "the sink of the world's silver," dropped after 1873 as a result of famine and a suspension of railroad-building there. And all of this took place just at the time of vast new silver discoveries, together with the mining and transportation technology needed to make the new silver quickly marketable, in the American West. The supply-demand ratios of the preceding several decades were a shambles. The secular trend of silver values, relative to gold, for the whole closing third of the nineteenth century was downward, matching, incidentally, the downward trend in farm prices and the rise in concern with the money question.[4]

The unstated major premise in this situation, the premise accepted widely and unreflectingly by most policy-makers and non-governmental economic leaders, is that gold is more real, monetarily, than silver. Very rarely did it occur to anyone in a policy making position that gold might be priced in terms of silver, or that gold might be appreciating in value; instead, silver was said to be depreciating, its price falling. *In terms of gold,* people should have said; but they did not. In a truly bimetallic situation, gold and silver would have been equally measurable in terms of each other. In a purely abstract sense, falling silver prices equalled rising gold prices. This was more than an abstraction in the seventies: while silver demand did drop in Germany, the United States, India, and elsewhere, demand for gold in some of these countries simultaneously rose, to a degree not matched by increased gold production. So pervasive was the assumption, in America and Europe, that gold was the "normal" monetary standard, that the possibility of a gold rise, rather than a silver decline, was hardly mentioned until well into the decade. Silverites who raised the point were almost never met with any answer more substantial than that gold had "intrinsic value."

The device of wholesale price indexes were not totally unknown at the time; Soetbeer in Germany, Jevons in England, and members of the growing "mathematical school" of economics were formulating them. But to measure values, to say nothing of gold or silver, in terms of commodity price levels, was a thing of the future. Economists as well as businessmen could not conceive of an economic system without some fixed point for the measurement of values, and this point was gold. Gold, to their minds, did not have a price; other things (including silver) had prices in relation to gold. American silverites and greenbackers, who broke through these notions far enough to suggest by 1876 that perhaps gold was rising instead of silver falling, thereby put themselves beyond the pale of economic orthodoxy. A universe, even an economic universe, without a fixed, central, stable point to which everything else, all quantities and forces, could be referred, was for most people of that time beyond understanding.

In these circumstances, bimetallism progressed slightly in the middle and late seventies not from the superiority of cosmological arguments for relativism or social Darwinism over those for mechanism or social Newtonism, but from the force of economic events. Monometallism trembled like a great tree in a storm. But it was not uprooted, and amid the general crisis, its ruffled supporters clung to it more desperately than ever.

The British, who in the late sixties were urging the whole world to adopt gold monometallism, began to recognize that the parlous state of the Indian economy, and British trade with India, dictated an acceptance of bimetallism—not for Britain herself, but for the British Empire. Britons holding Indian debts payable in silver, and merchants with a stake in the India trade, were facing trouble as India's ability to buy gold, with her depreciating silver, declined. If the silver decline were not stopped, there would occur (according to an American bimetallist) "a social and industrial revolution of India, which no English statesman could contemplate without dismay." Some British groups, including elements within the British Government and the Government of India, and the Chambers of Commerce of Liverpool and a few other cities, suggested a conference or other means to fix a ratio between the (silver) rupee and the (gold) pound. Not everyone agreed; William Stanley Jevons urged *laisser faire* and opined that "The English Government might perhaps conquer Afghanistan, or exterminate the Zulus, but . . . would not succeed in overcoming the rupee." The British sat tight; but they quietly accepted the necessity of "imperial bimetallism."[5]

For France, the economic crisis forced a suspension of silver coinage to a degree that all the bustling pressure of Esquirou de Parieu and other monometallists had not been able to do just before the Franco-Prussian War. Esquirou left the Government with the end of the Second Empire; bimetallists like Louis Wolowski, previously out of power, entered active politics, and the bimetallist Léon Say became Finance Minister in early 1875. French problems were peculiar, because of the upheaval of the German defeat. By 1873 the leaders of the young Third Republic had forged a policy uniquely combining liberalism with tariff protectionism (they repudiated their free-trade treaty with England) and bimetallism. By the close of 1873, however, pressure against silver within the Latin Union, which France still led, was great. The Swiss and the Belgians wanted silver abolished entirely as a standard. Léon Say and the Government, committed to bimetallism, resisted such an abolition, but only at the cost of "suspending" France's coinage of silver. Say was forced to present the Senate with a brief bill early in 1876 stating that "The fabrication of pieces of five francs in silver, for private account, may be limited or suspended by decree." The bill became law, despite the total-abolition demands of monometallists, on August 5, 1876, just as silver remonetization was being debated in the American Congress, as silver prices dropped to their lowest point, and about three weeks after the Liverpool Chamber of Commerce declared for "imperial" bimetallism. Silver was worse off economically, but stronger politically, than it had been for over a decade in France.[6]

The changes in German policy after 1873 were the most abrupt and remarkable. Where the "German Manchesterdom" had reigned supreme, where silver monometallism had just been replaced by the single gold standard, and where free trade had governed commercial policy, there appeared an end to silver sales, tariff protectionism, and a decided shift to *Nationalökono-*

mie. From 1873 into 1875, Bismarck withdrew the silver coinages of the *Länder,* and by mid-October, 1875, they had nearly all disappeared, with the significant exception of the Prussian thaler, whose conversion into gold involved about $150-million. Just then an article appeared in the German press, signed "S," which the London *Economist* identified as Soetbeer, explaining the difficulties in converting the thaler. A full year later, the silver thaler still had not been converted. Germany had not yet achieved the single gold standard she had legalized three years before, and showed no signs of doing so. The depression, meanwhile, brought large segments of agriculture, and certain manufacturers, out of the free-trade coalition and over to protectionism. This was most apparent among large landed families and the *Centralverein deutscher Industrieller,* an important manufacturers' organization acquainted with the economic theories of Henry C. Carey. During 1874 and 1875, these people made clear their increasing disenchantment with liberalism, political or ideological.

Bismarck responded to these group pressures, which were augmented by the depression and by political problems. In May 1876 he dismissed Delbrück, his Liberal Finance Minister; Ludwig Bamberger and other Liberal ideologues were increasingly isolated thereafter; and the Government of the Reich moved toward protection and halted the drive toward the gold standard by suspending the sale of silver and the demonetization of the silver thaler.[7]

Thus the depression years brought policy changes not dreamt of in 1870. Britain recognized the need for silver within the Empire, France had to suspend much of her silver coinage but staunchly reaffirmed bimetallism, and Germany so turned her back on liberalism as to drop free trade and retain important elements of her silver coinage. American developments were not greatly different. Behind these policy changes, especially in America, the old liberal-mechanistic rhetoric had spent its force or had gone, snarling and cornered, on the defensive.

To a limited extent, these changes had already begun by 1873, and a very able prophet might have foreseen that some of the embryonic group tensions existing in America and elsewhere would be catalyzed by a severe crisis, such as a major depression, into unsuspected new patterns. The nations, assuredly, had looked after their individual interests throughout the period, even at the euphoric conference table at Paris in 1867. Economic nationalism was not wholly new. But until 1873, these tensions and potential rifts were in the shadows; the whole period was characterized by tranquillity, and at least verbally, by unity of liberal purpose. After the middle of 1873 this was no longer the case. The old rhetoric was fragmenting, new economic coalitions were forming, ideology grew harsh, policy changed. The prognosis was neither pleasant nor promising.

15

IDEOLOGY: THE EMERGENCE OF

INTERNATIONAL BIMETALLISM

AND FREE SILVER

Thank heaven, John Sherman told the Senate on January 16, 1874, that the world understood political economy. Of its certain and axiomatic truths,

The most obvious . . . is that a specie standard is the best and the only true standard of all values, recognized as such by all civilized nations of our generation, and established as such by the experience of all commercial nations that have existed from the earliest period of recorded time. . . . This axiom is as immutable as the law of gravitation or the laws of the planetary system, and every device to evade it or avoid it has, by its failure, only demonstrated the universal law that specie measures all values as certainly as the surface of the ocean measures the level of the earth. It is idle for us to try to discuss with intelligence the currency

question until we are impressed with the truth, the universality, and the immutability, of this axiom.

For all the change that had taken place in his rhetoric,
Sherman might as well have been back at the Hotel of the
Tuileries Gardens in the summer of 1867, writing to Samuel
Bulkley Ruggles that the gold standard should be adopted all
over the world. Nor was Sherman alone in this. Much of the
rhetoric of civilization, law, and producerism that was evident on
every monetary issue during the period of tranquillity survived
the Panic of 1873 and the subsequent depression. In 1876 John
Stuart Mill and Adam Smith still topped the political-economic
best-seller list. American academic political economy did not
discard the "axiomatic" policies of free trade and gold monometallism after 1873, but rather, if anything, embraced them all
the more fiercely.

The different thing about the new period was the growing disparity between rhetorical certitudes and the possibilities of actual-
izing them. Rhetorical terms that earlier provided common
ground among groups seemed to take on narrower meanings,
which narrowed their usefulness as social bonds. By the time the
period of stress closed, the value and interest systems of the pre-
1873 period had disappeared forever. The seeds of the new arrangement lay in the crevasses of the earlier one, but it took the
depression, together with the crisis in silver, to nourish these
seeds to bitter and stunted fruit.[1]

In the 1865–73 period the terms "civilization," "law," and
"producer" provided a rhetorical ground acceptable to many
ideological, economic, and other interest groups. With differing
emphasis, these terms appeared in the phraseology of gold monometallists and greenback advocates alike. Although greenbackers
spoke of "the laws of political economy" less often than they
talked of the "producing classes," and although gold monometallists harped more on natural law, both sides shared those terms,
as well as others such as "harmony," "science," "progress," and
"civilization." After 1873, differences in emphasis became differences in dogma. Terms formerly shared tended to become one

group's exclusive property: "law," for example, became more
and more identified with classical and liberal economics and was
appropriated by bullionists, while "producer" came more and
more to mean "farmer."

"Civilization" occasionally appeared in paper money ideology,
particularly among advocates of Henry C. Carey's principle of
association. But Careyism itself lost much support after 1873,
especially among manufacturers, as Carey, William D. Kelley,
and others of the school took a more radical monetary position.
While Carey considered the greenback and the silver dollar to be
"instruments of association" and therefore aids to a good society,
James A. Garfield thought civilization could not exist without
hard money. Paper-money men deny the universality of economic
science, said Garfield; they say each nation has a unique political
economy; they claim foolishly that a government stamp can
confer value. To the future President and to the majority of
other people who used the rhetoric of "civilization," such views
were absurd. (Careyites in turn accused Garfield of inflicting "unparalleled sufferings" by his hard-money policy.) At the Paris
Conference of 1867, delegates connected gold with civilized (especially Christian) nations, silver with barbarous (especially Asiatic)
ones. They continued to do so after 1873. The silver dollar was
scientifically degenerate, in the opinion of gold monometallists.
Although bimetallists, even of the most conservative kind, tried
to relieve silver of the stigma of "barbarism," they could neither
do so nor convince groups raised on *laissez faire* liberalism that
governments could play a legitimate role in monetary policy.[2]

"Law" and "civilization" were becoming the property of a party,
liberal and bullionist, which crossed national boundaries. Scientific and governmental agencies still worked toward a worldwide
metric agreement, but in spite of its "simplicity and perfection,"
some Americans thought it of "doubtful expediency" to separate
from the "English-speaking peoples in this matter." This was
hardly the spirit of 1867.

Meanwhile, as "civilization" and "law" became simply the
shrill slogans of rigorous bullionists, a greenback-labor spokesman
excommunicated manufacturers from the "producing classes." On

both sides of the money question, people no longer sought harmony on common rhetorical ground, but were laying exclusive claims to terminological weapons.[3]

The period after 1873 brought changes not only to rhetoric, but also to monetary ideology. The major change was that bimetallism came to America. It was curious who accepted it, and how.

The ideology of gold monometallism did not change in theory very much from the pre-1873 to the post-1873 period, but it did undergo significant shifts in emphasis, acceptance, and relation to other ideologies. Under the impact of the economic crisis, its adherents grew fewer. Those who continued to maintain it tended either to regard bimetallism (but not paper money) more benignly or else to cling to their monometallism more rigidly and exclusively than ever. No longer were they optimistic about their ideas being adopted by all the world's monetary policy-makers; during the depression, even the staunchest monometallist realized that their doctrine had become inopportune.

Gold monometallism, of course, was one particular type of bullionism. In the sixties, especially in Britain, Germany, and the United States, it was virtually the only type. Silver seemed less "civilized," subject to fluctuation, impossible to keep in circulation, less noble, and less intrinsically valuable than gold. After 1873, some monometallists began to admit that silver might possibly have some valid monetary functions. This new attitude was particularly noticeable among British monometallists, who were beginning to doubt the desirability of a universal gold standard. In 1877, Professor Jevons still looked forward to international coinage unification on a gold basis, and still disliked the idea of an international bimetallic agreement on the usual grounds that to return to silver was uncivilized and unprogressive, that there was plenty of gold in the world for international coinage, and that silver would continue to cheapen. But Jevons did admit to one bimetallist argument, urged by Louis Wolowski and Henri Cernuschi, that the double standard spread fluctuations of supply and demand over a larger area. For such a deep-dyed monometallist, this was a noteworthy admission. Monometallists were seldom able to break free of the notion that two standards meant two fluctuating value levels, a situation economically anomalous and commercially inadmissible, so it seemed. As Congressman Samuel Hooper had said in 1872 of Ernest Seyd's *idée fixe,* "As for the principle of the double valuation, I do not understand it." After 1873, some monometallists retreated from the position that gold was the only adequate standard, everywhere and eternally. Walter Bagehot never swerved from his belief that monometallism was the best system in theory and the best one for England, but even he, in September 1876, realized that "there may be some difficulty in getting the gold for so many [nations] very rapidly," and he then viewed with equanimity the reversion of the United States to a silver standard.[4]

In America, however, certain prominent gold monometallists simply restated their commitment more unequivocally than ever after 1873, in an attempt to club some sense into a refractory and benighted public. Simon Newcomb wrote testily in 1878, that "Every man of intelligence knows that the coined money of all nations is worth only the gold which is in it. . . . The stamp of Government goes for absolutely nothing, except as a certificate of the weight and quality of the metal." Newcomb condemned silver and any form of "depreciated currency" with a host of arguments, just as he had in the mid-sixties: the silver dollar had not been used for forty years; "to revive it would be simply taking the cast-off money of Germany"; gold was "immensely better" and silver "too cumbrous" for large transactions; cheaper currency violated contracts; it enriched speculators; it fostered extravagance; it worsened the evils it was meant to prevent, by raising interest rates; it meant government interference with value, because "it is not the party which issues, but [money's] *quantity,* and the prospect of its *redemption,* which determines its value." Albert S. Bolles did not want any mere government to undertake the "delicate duty" of setting a bimetallic ratio, and the *Banker's Magazine* called the silver demonetization of 1873 a liberal measure, since it restored one more power to "nature" that had been usurped by interfering governments.[5]

Liberalism was becoming crabbed. Appropriated more and more by bullionists, especially gold-monometallist bullionists, it was beginning to be expressed in language redolent of what a later day would call arch-conservatism. Government interference was bad, *laissez faire* (in trade and money) was good, natural laws were ineluctable. The familiar late nineteenth-century amalgam of classical economics (at its gloomiest), rigorous morality, and mechanistic determinism was emerging clearly in the pronouncements of the liberal monometallist group in the late seventies, in tones quite different from its internationalistic and progressive emphasis of a few years before. Very unfortunately, what now seems so obviously a narrow, blinkered, class-derived system of social analysis and policy successfully attached to itself the sanctions of social responsibility. Because of that attachment, to overthrow the policy (which happened early in the twentieth century) meant threatening to overthrow its social matrix as well.

The mixture of gold monometallism, liberalism, and class preservation was very clear in the writings of David A. Wells and Edward Atkinson, two New Englanders whose epistolary tirelessness was matched only by the rigor of their social and financial outlook and the aura of respectability with which they surrounded it. To judge from the surviving manuscript collections, no public figure of any stature escaped a correspondence with these two liberal crusaders. As Congressman Abram Hewitt once said in the late seventies while chairing a hearing, "Mr. Wells is an authority whom we all read." Wells hated high protective tariffs and inconvertible paper currency. Cobden was a master thinker, Henry C. Carey a charlatan. The United States must, he exhorted, return quickly to "that fundamental principle of every truly free government, namely—non-interference to the greatest extent possible with the freedom of the individual." As for money, righteousness was obvious:

> If man refuses to produce the metal best adapted to his wants, and persists in producing another, ill-adapted to his wants, by an artificial, bi-metallic standard, he makes warfare upon the beneficence of the Almighty. Therefore the conclusion:—that the adoption of a bi-metallic standard is a violation of the natural laws of supply and demand, and an attempt to provide for the survival of the unfittest.

Edward Atkinson agreed, and called the prevailing legislative interference, which kept the country from the natural and efficient gold coin basis, socially criminal. The attempt "to reconstruct society by statute methods, under the assumption that a higher power has not so ordained the laws by which society itself exists," among which was gold monometallism, was the chief cause of conflict between labor and capital, the two forces that combined in the productive process. Atkinson's version of "producerism" was very similar terminologically to that of the National Labor Reform party, but his inclusion of Vanderbilt, the railroad builder, among "producers," a man reviled elsewhere as a monopolist of the worst sort, is a measure of the flaccidity of producerism. In Henry Varnum Poor, who was so far to the right as to consider Ricardo, Adam Smith, and J. S. Mill soft on greenbacks, monometallism reached the brink of ideological insanity. But monometallism nevertheless remained respectable and influential, not only among policy-makers but also among "orthodox" commentators.[6]

The great change after 1873 regarding monetary ideologies in America was the advent and spread of bimetallism. Newcomb, Wells, Atkinson and others clung stubbornly to monometallism, but many people used silver's bullion basis as a bridge to a less rigid position. By 1879, a considerable number of Americans, some as respectable as any monometallist, had espoused bimetallism and offered it as the only safe, scientific, suitable solution to the monetary difficulties of America and the world.

Since bimetallism placed the source of money and value in precious metals, it could utilize the same bullionist arguments that supported gold monometallism, which made it much tougher than greenbackism to attack successfully. Whatever was said in favor of the gold standard about "intrinsic value," tradition, universal acceptability, and indestructability could be said also for the double valuation, and in the version known as "international bimetallism" it could even claim to resist inflation and stabilize values as well as gold.

The bimetallist rubric, however, covered two ideologies that were very different. One, "free silver," attracted greenbackers. The other, "international bimetallism," attracted monometallists.

It held that the monetary standard of the world ought to consist of both gold and silver, but the ratio between the two metals had to be stabilized by an international agreement. While the world would thus avoid destroying "half its money stock" through demonetization, it would also avoid, through the internationally-agreed-upon ratio, serious fluctuations between the two metals (specifically, the falling price of silver in terms of gold) that had become a plague in the seventies. The international bimetallists in effect admitted that uncontrolled drops in silver prices wrecked trade and existing contracts so long as the silver price was uncontrolled, but at the same time they believed that demonetizing silver and thus raising gold values and benefiting creditors immensely was a worse evil.

The great objection to international bimetallism, from the *laissez faire* gold-standard point of view, was that it involved "legislative interference"; the pegging of silver by means of a gold-silver ratio set not by "natural forces" but by a treaty. The bimetallist answer to this was that silver demonetization was itself a legislative infringement with the traditional, natural monetary order.

Europe had listened for years to international bimetallist pleas, both from politicians and financiers, and from men like Louis Wolowski in France and Ernest Seyd in England who were involved in practical finance and who also leapt frequently into print. Seyd was the outstanding, and almost the only, bimetallist writing in English, but he made up in quantity what he lacked in companionship. After 1873, as Seyd watched silver fall and depression spread, he believed that all his jeremiads of earlier years were being borne out. In a spate of pamphlets and books published through the middle and late seventies, he hammered home the bimetallist gospel again and again. Seyd believed that "The true cause of the abnormal depression of trade is the contraction of the metallic currency by 'human' law, the so-called 'demonetization of silver.'"

Speaking from nineteenth-century liberal premises, Seyd said that gold monometallism defied natural law, since it upset the forces of nature by "an actual law in the legislative sense, which forcibly restricts the use or demand, and deliberately deteriorates the quality, of silver coin." Speaking in tones reminiscent of American inflationists, he accused "a large party in the United States," whose influence on government was sizable, of deliberately manipulating the money stock to speculate and realize "prodigious fortunes" on fixed contracts. These capitalists, however, would eventually "suffer enormous losses" as debtors were forced to default. Seyd pointed out, as few American inflationists had the wit to do, that a creditor frequently lent money more than once, and if a creditor received lower-valued money in one transaction he was perfectly free to lend it again on the same terms on which a debtor repaid him. Bimetallism was not only natural, but to ignore it was "fatalism and fanaticism," destructive of civilization.

Nevertheless, Seyd admitted, any attempt by a single nation, even one as large as the United States, to adopt bimetallism without an international stabilizing agreement, would be a failure. He was no free-silverite. Seyd wrote the United States Monetary Commission in 1876 that if such agreement could not be had, America for her own protection should "adopt the gold valuation," through regrettable necessity.[7]

Seyd argued the international-bimetallist case, and refuted monometallism, brilliantly. The bullion basis of money; the social necessity of a large quantity of money; the benefit to civilization and all social groups, creditor and debtor alike; the correspondence with natural law, free from legislative interference; the absolute necessity of an international agreement on a bimetallic ratio: this was Seyd's, and many international bimetallists', creed.

After 1873 the sect began to grow. The Belgian economist Emile Laveleye, who in 1867 had said that "the double standard is a counter-truth, it is unceasingly demented by the nature of things," and who then lauded the search for international gold coinage on the gold basis as a reform equivalent in progressiveness to the railroad and the telegraph, by the mid-seventies was just as avidly calling for international bimetallism. Laveleye suspected, however, as Seyd certainly did not, that political economy was not an exact science. Laveleye was almost unique for that day in his denial of natural laws and in his criticism of Walras, Jevons, and other economists of the "mathematical school," together with classical economists from Smith to Bastiat, who "have remained in subjection to the ideas of physiocratic optimism" prevailing in late eighteenth-century France and England. For Laveleye, bimetallism was sufficiently justifiable in that its expansion of the quantity of money was extremely desirable socially. The productive enterprise of debtors was always to be preferred to the unproductive accumulation of the creditor class; "The adoption of gold as the exclusive money is . . . an anti-democratic and an anti-economic measure, since it favors the bondholder at the expense of labor, idle capital at the expense of active capital." An increased quantity of money would lower interest rates much faster than it would raise prices, and this was socially good.

Not suprisingly, Laveleye found much to praise in the speeches of William D. Kelley. Between the social philosophy of the Belgian bimetallist and that of Henry C. Carey, and indeed perhaps even the *Workingman's Advocate,* there was not much to choose. Yet Laveleye was not a greenbacker, and in policy matters he was no more "radical," i.e., shaky about bullionism, than Seyd.[8]

Seyd rested his bimetallism on a heavily classical-economic rationale, while Laveleye's doctrines had much in common with the burgeoning "historical school" of political economy then growing up particularly in Germany but which corresponded at many points with American Careyism. Perhaps bimetallism's attractiveness in the seventies, and in later decades when it became increasingly popular, derived from this ability to draw upon more than one system of political economy. At any rate, the emergence in the seventies of alternatives to classicism, and the persistent popularity in America of Carey's teachings together with Carey's own silverite-greenback proclivities in the years preceding his death in 1879, helped to spread bimetallism in both the international and the free-silver versions. Louis Wolowski, in spite of his classical leanings, translated into French the *Principles of Political Economy* of Wilhelm Roscher, the leader of the historical school in Germany, and a bimetallist. William D. Kelley visited Bismarck in 1879 and found the Iron Chancellor (by then) a sympathetic listener to Careyite doctrines. Kelley reported that Carey and his disciples were having great influence in Germany, Italy, and Austria. In those countries, Kelley snorted, to be a bimetallist and protectionist did not suffice, as it did at home, to tar him with the same brush as "inflationists, swindlers, and repudiators." Bimetallism seemed to be gaining in Britain and Holland, notably among commercial and manufacturing groups. Gold monometallism was losing ground all over Europe to this new viewpoint which appeared to be so socially and economically supportable.[9]

In the United States, international bimetallism began to appear as a serious alternative to gold monometallism shortly after the post-1873 crisis began. There, it was principally the classical rather than the historical version that seemed to attract a following, probably because classical economics was so deeply imbedded in academia, in the press, and in the minds of policy-makers. The historical version, insofar as it existed in America, too easily slipped over into free-silver advocacy or even greenbackism and ceased to be "international" in any significant way. There were positions on the left of international bimetallism in the United States, but in Europe there were not, except for certain radicalisms.

The remarkable thing about American international bimetallism, in fact, was its conservatism. Its political-economic roots were classical, very much like those of gold monometallism. On policy questions its adherents demanded an international bimetallic agreement as a *sine qua non* of silver remonetization, and carefully separated themselves from free-silverites or greenbackers who wanted to expand the currency "irresponsibly." It gradually attracted the kind of support that a few years before would have gone to gold monometallism—liberal, often Northeastern, theory-susceptible people—who by the mid-seventies found straight gold monometallism too rigorous and harsh.

This was probably the major ideological development on the hard-money side of the money question over a thirty-year period: international bimetallism was beginning to replace gold monometallism as the "responsibly conservative" monetary ideology in the United States. The shift occurred between 1873 and 1879.

After that, it was fixed. The Republican platform on which William McKinley ran for President in 1896 was to be international-bimetallist, not monometallist.

The most able systematic expressions of international bimetallism in the United States came from S. Dana Horton, a son of an anti-greenback Civil-War Congressman from Ohio, and Francis Amasa Walker of Massachusetts, a kinsman of the author of the *Science of Wealth,* a Civil War officer, civil servant, and later President of the Massachusetts Institute of Techonology. Horton thought that "real money" "must be a commodity . . . like all other commodities, subject to fluctuations of supply and demand," and Walker believed that the best money "is a money the supply of which is determined by the cost of its production." This let out paper, and let in silver. For both men the demonetization of silver unfairly changed the terms of all existing contracts, to the undeserved benefit of creditor interests and the discouragement of productive enterprise. Like Ernest Seyd and French conservative bimetallists such as Wolowski and Henri Cernuschi, Horton and Walker looked upon inflation of a very moderate sort as acceptable, deflation a thorough evil, and stability in monetary values the ideal: deflation resulting from gold monometallism penalized production; rapid inflation resulting from depreciated paper money "bewilders the economic sense of the community, generates a morbid appetite for further issues, excites speculation, discourages steady industry, and leads ultimately to misery and shame"; but "a moderate and gradual metallic inflation," the product of bimetallism, was good. Walker even found support for his position in utterances of Jevons, Bagehot, Chevalier, and David Hume, and Horton backed his case with Walras, Soetbeer, and Esquirou de Parieu as well—so transferable were bullionist premises.

Both Horton and Walker saw an international agreement on the gold-silver parity ratio as absolutely essential. Locke, Adam Smith, and Ricardo had rejected bimetallism because in their days such an agreement was out of the question, but today, Horton and Walker said, it was not only possible but necessary. In France, Wolowski and Cernuschi advocated it, in Belgium Malou and Laveleye, in England Seyd and "the Liverpool writers" (some connected with the Liverpool Chamber of Commerce), and in the United States, themselves, B. F. Nourse, and George Walker. Francis Walker might also have mentioned Congressman W. S. Groesbeck of Ohio and a Virginia federal judge named Robert W. Hughes, "a follower of Cernuschi and Leon Say, and not of Mr. Bland and Senator Jones," and a growing horde of pamphleteers and journalists to whom the bimetallic standard sanctioned by international agreement was the safe and sure road to monetary stability.[10]

International bimetallism achieved its cachet of respectability when the *Banker's Magazine* opened its columns to it from mid-1876 onward. For more than a year, the *Magazine* published articles on both sides of the issue, from Cernuschi, Laveleye, Wilhelm Roscher, Jevons, and the Anglo-German liberal, Prince-Smith, and its editorial position and the prominent display it gave to bimetallist articles by George M. Weston and George Walker leave no doubt of its bimetallist sympathies. Silver, said Weston, was a "beneficence of nature"; a writer signing himself "Argonaut" warned that to reduce silver to a mere commodity "double[d] the power of capital, a power that already is uncontrollable"; silver was the standard of the Constitution. George Walker, a Massachusetts country banker who a decade earlier had praised McCulloch for contracting the greenbacks, advocated international bimetallism as the steadiest basis for money, since "natural law . . . tends to restore the equilibrium [between the metals], whenever it is anywhere disturbed." The gold monometallism advocated by the American Association for the Advancement of Science was unsound, because in concentrating on the putative fall in the value of silver, it ignored the rise in the value of gold. The *Banker's Magazine* was one of the very few places where this idea was mentioned, other than in the speeches of inflationist politicians.

The international bimetallist legions grew in 1877 and 1878. A prominent geologist avowed in the *Atlantic Monthly* that mining technology demanded that gold never be "trusted out of the company of its steadier-gaited companion," and a New York merchant told a Congressional committee that silver as well as gold was "God's money" and that "the harmony of the social universe cannot be maintained without both." By that time the bimetallist throng included the Boston Board of Trade, which memorialized Congress to institute an international conference to maintain silver.

Even Samuel Bulkley Ruggles and John Sherman were talking like bimetallists. Ruggles still thought bimetallism was a "logical absurdity," but he understood himself to be in agreement with Cernuschi in calling for an international conference to place the gold-silver parity ratio closer to the market ratio. (He had thundered against that same idea in 1867.) Sherman began to advocate what he called "limited bimetallism," a policy whereby silver would be coined in small amounts under strict supervision, if possible at an internationally-agreed-upon-ratio. With such recruits as these, and in view of the justification given bimetallism by Horton, Francis Walker, and the *Banker's Magazine,* international bimetallism was clearly becoming the "new conservatism" of the late seventies. Some contemporary observers recognized this, and suspected it.

By mid-1877, it seemed to George Weston that the proposal of an international conference to set a bimetallic ratio was simply a device to prevent any kind of bimetallic threat to the gold standard from ever occurring. Cernuschi had visited the United States shortly before, and the gold monometallists embraced him; "Public bodies, including Chambers of Commerce of great cities, fresh from denunciations of silver as a robbery of creditors, warmed up with a safe zeal to remonetize it in concert with European nations, which were only too well known to be opposed to it." Was this true? It can never be known how many "international bimetallists" were simply the shrewder wing of the gold-standard group. It is extremely unlikely that Horton and Walker used bimetallism as a blind, and practically inconceivable that Seyd or Wolowski did. But any truck with bimetallism from Ruggles and Sherman was startling. In the final analysis, however, aside from the mental or moral acrobatics in which its adherents involved themselves, the ideology of international bimetallism to a very large extent provided nervous monometallists with a more comfortable and slightly novel, but otherwise not very radical, ground to occupy.[11]

"Free silver," the other kind of bimetallism, was an entirely different matter. Though it was hard to justify theoretically, and was far less conscious of monetary considerations that were other than immediate and domestic, free silver gained a huge following. While international bimetallism was replacing gold monometallism as the chief right-wing stance on the money question, free silver began to replace greenbackism as the new leftism.

Free silver meant simply the reinstatement of the silver standard in America, specifically by authorizing again the coinage, without statutory limit on amount (hence "free") and with full legal-tender power, of the old silver dollar of 412½ grains. Like greenbackism, free silver was an inflationary monetary device, but it was more attractive than greenbackism to many people who could not conceive of money not having a bullion basis. Conversely it was more frightening to gold monometallists and international bimetallists than greenbacks ever could be, because, since it was already specie, it could never be restored through a specie resumption to a parity with gold. Free silver nullified the resumption of specie payments, and therefore the whole structure of American financial policy since the Civil War, far more crushingly than greenbacks. Without international agreement on a bimetallic ratio, and to some minds, regardless of any such agreement, silver freely coined would drive gold out of circulation as long as silver's market price remained considerably below the legal ratio. The country would in practice go on the silver standard, and would thereby place itself at the mercy of foreign creditors who demanded payment in gold, while domestic creditors would be forced to accept payment in currency of less value than that which they had lent.

To its advocates, however, the practical need for more currency more than justified risking these theoretical ills. Probably, they said, remonetizing silver would actually create sufficient new demand to raise the silver price back to par. Many of them argued that it had been legislative interference, through demonetization, that had wreaked such havoc with silver prices to begin with; restore the traditional standard, and values would take care of themselves.

A full-blown ideology of free silver, comparable in analytic formality to gold monometallism or international bimetallism, did not really exist. But the absence of a Chevalier or a Newcomb, a Seyd or a Horton, who would construct a logical political-economic theory of free silver, handicapped the spread of the doctrine not at all. One of its great advantages, in fact, was its ability to draw on classical themes in support of its bullionism, on tradition in support of the double standard, and on Careyite producerism in support of its inflationary tendencies and its economic nationalism. Thus it could go international bimetallism one better since it could restore silver and revive the economy without waiting interminably for an international agreement, and on the other hand it could claim, as greenbackism could not, that it was a traditional and "American" system, resting on a metallic base as good money really should.

Another of free silver's advantages was its ability to attach to itself the quality of emotion and crusade. Not only did it share with other monetary ideologies deep-running currents connecting monetary policy, political economy, and moral philosophy; it also aroused moral indignation, stemming from the shock and anger that gushed forth when people suddenly grasped that America's traditional bimetallism had been quietly done away with in the Coinage Act of 1873. That Act was hardly a secret to monetary experts or to those directly concerned with the making of monetary policy. To the mass of people, however, ostensibly including legislators who took part in it such as Kelley and Senator Stewart of Nevada, the implications of the standards change only became visible after silver fell in price and rose in availability. Since Sherman, Hooper, Knox, and the others most responsible for the Act had not taken great pains to point out what would happen if and when silver fell, the Coinage Act of 1873 very easily became the "Crime of '73." On top of all this, economic distress did its usual work of fraying tempers and provoking anxiety. It seemed obvious to many people that the way to cure depression was a strong, quick dose of inflationary medicine. Resistance to some sort of inflation, and insistence on specie resumption, struck them as mad. Just when the country most needed monetary relaxation, it had apparently been gypped of its traditional silver standard. This, to an age that believed the quantity of money to be the axis of economic values anyway, made it almost inevitable that free silver would become the great weapon of a holy war.

The battle became most intensely joined between free silverites and conservative bullionists (mono- or bimetallist) over the issue of creditor-debtor relations. Free silver, more than greenbackism, flaunted inflationism like a red flag at ideological groups which had been insisting for many years, since long before the Public Credit Act, that the most sacred moral obligation of government and private persons was the repayment of creditors in full, i.e., in gold. The free silverites and greenbackers were perfectly willing to agree that creditors should receive their just due, but they objected strenuously that this meant payment on the gold standard. As in so many aspects of the money question, principle and morality were not in question, but rather the application of them. Gold monometallists and conservative bimetallists insisted even more frantically than they had in 1868–69 that to pay public debts other than in gold was to change the terms of bond contracts to the benefit of debtors and to the defrauding of creditors. Either greenback or silver payment meant payment in money of lesser value than that which had been lent. Free silverites, precisely to the contrary, claimed that payment according to a monetary standard different from that which obtained at the time of the contract (and of course the 1873 Act had indeed changed the legal standard) meant changing the contract to the benefit of creditors and the defrauding of the tax-paying debtors.

There was some truth on both sides. The Funding Act of 1870 made coin payment of bonds the letter of the law, and the Coinage Act of 1873 translated "coin" into "gold"; despite the wailing of silverites, these two laws were irreversible historical facts, and the post-1870 bondholder, at least, would have some grounds for for complaint if the country reverted to bimetallism. But the silverites argued that if the monetary standard could be changed by a law, then another law could change it back again, and if debtors could not complain the first time around, creditors could not validly complain the second time.

The impasse could only be solved by a negotiated compromise or by completely changing the terms of the controversy away from the centrality of the monetary standard. But the ideology of free silver, because it helped to perpetuate the notion that money had to have a metallic base, made the latter alternative less likely.

Paper money still had its advocates in the 1873–79 period, and at certain moments they seemed closer to triumph than ever before. In the form of national bank notes, of course, paper money had an assured future; no one considered them a bar to specie resumption. The Currency Act of 1870 and the Free Banking Act of 1874 had regularized them and made them more flexible, and they constituted roughly half of the nation's circulating currency. An extremist such as Henry Varnum Poor might wish them abolished, but by the late seventies the banks and their note issues were not widely objected to, except by doctrinaire greenbackers.

But their objection was profound. Greenbackers and national bank-note advocates shared almost nothing aside from the belief that paper was an acceptable physical material for currency. Bank note people believed their kind of paper was superior to greenbacks for the very crucial reason that the bank notes were secured and would become convertible into gold at par when specie payments were resumed; they had, in effect, an "intrinsic value." Greenbackers, however, insisted that money was definable not by its form, but by its function: it was pointless, positively bad, to back it up with specie. It was the servant of commerce, not the master, and its form did not matter as long as it performed well as a standard of payment and medium of exchange. Theoretical greenbackism, because it divorced money from any metallic base, was the only really radical monetary doctrine of the time, differing from free silver as much as from gold monometallism.

In the late seventies the Carey school, certain vocal manufacturers such as Peter Cooper, and the greenback-labor group, propagated the idea of separating the form and function of money. One of its clearest statements came from a Grand Rapids furniture manufacturer named William A. Berkey, a self-acknowledged pupil of Carey, Baird, Peter Cooper, and Kelley, and a thoroughgoing exponent of the producer philosophy. Berkey pronounced the separation of greenbacks from any form of bullionism in the most definite terms. "If money possesses an intrinsic, as well as a representative value," he said, "it is then a commodity, as well as money, and is subject to two different and often antagonistic sets of laws." But money, to serve its proper functions, needed no "intrinsic or commercial value" at all. "Those who desire to fully understand the money question can only hope to do so by always keeping in view the fact that the great object of commerce and trade is the exchange of property and products, and that money is designed to be simply a tool to accomplish that end." Greenbacks served that end best. They properly lacked intrinsic value and thus avoided the confusion to which commodity money was always subject, and they had the great advantage over bank note currency of being government issue, not the controlled issue of corporations. They were subject, therefore, only to the public good and the "natural laws which govern trade." The greenbacker dislike of bank issue derived in part from Jacksonian tradition, but it also rested on a principle: the complete separation they believed essential between the function of money and its metallic form, a property hardly true of bank notes.[12]

One of the great misfortunes of the time was that political and economic pressure obscured this greenbacker insight. Immediate and intense demand for inflation pushed the greenbackers into coalition with the free silverites, and thereby into practical acceptance of a bullion basis for money, at the very time that greenback theory of the separation of the form of money from its function was emerging most clearly. Carey, Kelley, Peter Cooper, and Berkey all applauded the advance of free-silver sentiment, and the ease with which they did so derived from the very fact that production, in their view, was a more basic economic consideration than money. To insist factiously that money should not have a bullion form was far less important than to insist, in company with free silverites, that money in any form should be abundant. When the practical opportunity arose in the late seventies to create an inflationist, producerite coalition, they were perfectly willing to join forces with the free silverites, and to overlook silverite dogmatism such as that of Senator Jones of Nevada, who bluntly demanded that money must have "intrinsic value." The greenback-laborite scheme of a 3.65 per cent government bond interconvertible with greenbacks, and the low-interest philosophy that lay behind it, was also soft-pedalled just as it was spreading to the more orthodox manufacturer-protectionist wing of the greenback group. The bond plan may not have been a very serious loss. But at least it had been fresh and novel, and as more and more greenbackers gave tactical support to free silver in the late seventies, less and less was to be heard of it or of the insight that money need not, in fact ought not, be metallic in order to serve society most efficiently. When this happened, the possibility dwindled that Careyism and producerism could be revamped, and that greenbackism could serve as a bridge in political economy and social self-understanding between nineteenth and twentieth century America.[13]

During the period of tranquillity there were, for practical purposes, two ideological groups in America, the gold monometallists and the greenback paper-money advocates. During the period of stress beginning in 1873, there were four: gold monometallists, international bimetallists, free silverites, and greenbackers. On the right, monometallism lost ground to international bimetallism; greenbackism, on the left, slipped toward free silver. From a strictly theoretical standpoint the struggle thus moved from both extremes toward the center. In practical terms, however, the trend was not toward compromise, but to hand-to-hand combat.

16

THE REALIGNMENT

OF

ECONOMIC GROUPS

The post-1873 depression wrought changes in the positions and relations of economic groups that practically destroyed the feeling of inter-group harmony that prevailed earlier. As these changes revealed, the depression of the seventies was America's first depression under conditions of modern industrialism. During it, economic groups took positions on policy questions, and positions vis-à-vis each other, typical not of their behavior in pre-Civil War times, but of modern times. American economic society had turned a corner.

Even the least changed groups, the bankers and people in commerce and transportation, modified their pre-1873 positions significantly. The commercial group, which had been the hardest of hard-money groups before 1873, still contained within its ranks the most intractable people still talking; the Boston Board of Trade, for example, managed to push through the 1876 convention of the National Board of Trade a resolution calling for contraction of the greenbacks, *à la* McCulloch. In doing so, however, they almost destroyed the National Board. At the 1877 meeting, international bimetallism was supported widely, and a resolution for the remonetization of the old standard silver dollar —a resolution, in other words, for free silver—missed passage by only two votes. The Northeast split evenly on the free-silver resolution, but Midwestern delegates voted for it *en masse*. Obviously the hard-money element that controlled the Executive Committee of the National Board of Trade did not represent commercial people throughout the country. The Cincinnati Chamber of Commerce actually passed a free-silver resolution in 1877, and called for the repeal of the Specie Resumption Act of 1875. The only distinct characteristic of the commercial group through these years was not hard money, nor moderate soft money, but turmoil and disagreement. The 1877 vote of the National Board of Trade on financial questions was cast by only 27 delegates from 14 commercial organizations, a drastic diminution from the 53 delegates from 26 organizations who had voted at the 1870 meeting. The National Board did not even meet in 1878; the business community was clearly disenchanted with it. Trade organizations, by and large, still leaned toward harder money than toward softer, but there was little uniformity among them after 1873.[1]

Transportation interests shared with other segments of the commercial group a dislike of "government interference," did not like tariff protection (among other things, it made railroad iron more expensive), and had leaned toward hard money more than most people. After 1873, however, railroad spokesmen were conscious of a connection between retarded monetary circulation and retarded trade, and they became willing to consider policies that a Boston import merchant would have thought unsound. The *Railway World,* probably transportation's leading trade journal, staunchly opposed the greenbackism of "Judge [William D.] Kelley and that school," but it gradually accepted the idea of some form of bimetallism in 1875 and 1876. To remonetize silver would restore silver's former value, and would bring the country closer to specie resumption, said the *World;* if bondholders received silver instead of gold, "It would certainly be no breach of good faith, unless the contract states specifically [sic] that the principal and interest are payable in gold coin."[2]

On the social aspects of the money question, the commercial group shifted more substantially, and in a sniffish direction. Before 1873 the commercial press had spoken often of the natural harmony of the social clauses. Labor, capital, everyone, progressed hand in hand toward the good society. After 1873 the idea of a harmonious multiplicity of groups crumbled. Replacing it was an increasingly bi-polar labor-versus-capital analysis of events and society, which became progressively more shrill as "labor unrest" kept occupying headlines during the depression. The *Commercial and Financial Chronicle* criticized Granger legislation in 1874 as interferences with contracts, and at the time of the Great Strike of 1877 it coupled labor violence and greenbackism as malign obstacles to progress. Laborites who adopted greenbackism were "embracing their worst enemy"; "It is the universal testimony of experience, as well as the doctrine of economists founded on the nature of things, that an irredeemable currency robs and defrauds those who work for a day's wages worse than any other class." Soon after, the *Chronicle* condemned "socialistic, Communistic, or, as they are sometimes called, International workingmen's societies in the midst of us," which propagated notions "subversive of law and order, and destructive of society." The *Chronicle* reassured its readers that such organizations were politically powerless, but in another editorial it felt called upon to defend the morals of Wall Street and the New York Stock Exchange—a revealing defensiveness, virtually unthinkable a decade earlier, that was another indication of how far "social harmony" had declined. The commercial group, at least in the Northeast, was getting sour. Around the country, some of its members were entertaining bimetallist notions. But as a whole, the group remained highly conservative on monetary policy and social relations alike.[3]

Bankers, as before 1873, entertained a wider variety of alternatives on monetary policy than commercial people did, at least organized Eastern commercial people, but their social attitudes shifted in a similar way. Well-established large bankers hewed to monometallism, while many in the currency-hungry West and South favored large-scale expansion of national bank-note issues, and very few agreed with certain vocal men of commerce that currency contraction was a good idea. But bankers were not pro-greenback. The *Banker's Magazine,* the major organ of the group, took Henry C. Carey to task in late 1874 for his greenbackism:

> We regret to see that Mr. Carey, in this matter, is no more than an experimentist. The age is beyond this. . . . The Universe does not move by experiment, but by law; and so must move all its parts. If Mr. Carey's long devotion to scientific economy winds up at least without a single authoritative maxim of law running through this preeminently great and grand theme of social organization, we may well despair of any valuable results from the bureaus at Washington.

Currency and bonds were without substantial value unless they were convertible into precious-metal money. But which precious metal? Not necessarily gold, said the *Banker's Magazine;* some people "who have intelligently held to the theory of the gold standard, have begun to ask themselves whether gold is fit to be the sole standard," it wrote in mid-1876. From that point on, the leading voice of American banking became a consistent advocate of international bimetallism. Its editor testified before the United States Monetary Commission, a congressionally-appointed investigatory body, that gold had risen just as surely as silver had fallen. Society needed an internationally-established ratio between gold and silver, for its own good.

The *Banker's Magazine,* in fact, was deeply worried about what was happening to society. Harmony, the mark of the tranquil pre-depression days, was evaporating; society was polarizing; by 1878, it was claiming that the organization of capital into banks and corporations resulted from a "resistless law" with which one "might as well quarrel [as] with the law of gravitation," and which was criticized only by "ignorant demagogues" and "well-meaning persons misled by error and prejudice." Labor organizations had fallen "into bad hands. Ambitious men, greedy of power, set up for leaders and taught their ignorant and credulous followers to believe that war was the normal relation between the master and the men."

The *Magazine* was no doubt sincere in seeing social polarization as regrettable and deplorable. But it never asked why the "resistless law" of organization did not apply to labor if it applied to capital. The crumbling of social harmony was evidently regrettable most of all because it meant a slipping away of social control. In monetary policy, bankers could espouse international bimetallism, because it was meliorative, did not demand any rejection of basic liberal-mechanistic principles, and did not threaten established social order. By 1879, the president of a large national bank in Chicago told a Congressional committee investigating the cause of the depression that "I have always found that those who are willing to work can get work." The old rhetoric of social harmony was gone; the new rhetoric of American capitalistic conservatism had been born.[4]

A third group shared with the bankers and commercial people a degree of change that was only moderate. Labor, after 1873, embraced bimetallism to a considerable extent, and watched with alarm the growing hostility among social groups. In these characteristics, labor underwent changes similar to those affecting bankers and the commercial group. In content, of course, labor's views were thoroughly different. Bimetallism, for the labor group, meant free silver, not the international bimetallism of the bankers. With its long soft-money tradition, labor was able to adopt free silver along with greenbacks as a money productive of social good. Sometimes the embrace was agonized: the *Workingman's Advocate* noted in mid-1876 that the "bonanza kings" were trying to revive "the double standard," and "of course their only aim is to make a market for silver. Nevertheless we hope they will succeed, unless the greenback can be substituted as the permanent currency of the country." Again, "if we cannot have greenbacks interchangeable with bonds, give us the double standard. We could possibly bear the strain of a return to specie payments on this double basis." Other labor spokesmen agreed that greenbacks were the perfect currency, but that silver would serve, in the circumstances, to thwart the "gold-bugs." Only the Socialist-laborites of New York and Chicago refused to take the money question seriously; they believed that monetary reform of any kind simply perpetuated the "legalized robbery" of the profit system. But they were a tiny faction. To the extent that the labor interest in America had a unified voice during these years, that voice spoke for greenbacks together with free silver.

The laborite currency position rested, as it had earlier, on producerism and a hostility to monopolies (and it so classified the national banking system). These underpinnings had been shared in the past by farmers and, often, by manufacturers, and in the past, labor could easily look upon itself as part of a harmonious coalition of interests. The post-1873 depression did much to destroy that view. Often mistrusted by the farmers, increasingly suspicious of manufacturers and capitalists in general, laborites maintained their soft-money harmonistic attitude under heavy stress. The old producerism lost much of its viability in the post-1873 period, as a series of labor disputes occurred, of which the bloody rioting accompanying the Great Strike of 1877 was only the most shattering. In such circumstances, Carey's optimistic principle of association, or indeed any harmonistic view of social relations, appeared increasingly anachronistic. As the pre-1873 "harmony," such as it had been, became a casualty of economic stringency and social strife, labor began to think of itself as part of a growing army of the dispossessed.[5]

The most sudden and pervasive shift made by any group after 1873 was that of the farmers, and it developed in such a way as to increase disharmony among groups and make coalitions by the farmers, even with labor, very difficult for years to come. The farmers' silence before 1873 on nearly every aspect of the money question had been deafening. On the rare occasions when agricultural spokesmen mentioned money, it was usually in bullionist, hard-money terms. Even then, however, they held two attitudes which they easily made the basis of a vehement soft-money stance after the economic crisis began. One was their insistent and exclusivistic producerism; the other was anti-monopoly, which they had used notably in the Midwest during the heyday of Grangerism to attack railroad and warehousing combinations. Under the stress of the depression, producerism led them to damn "manipulators" of the money supply, and anti-monopoly directed their attack toward national banks as their special enemy. Taken together, producerism and anti-monopoly laid them open to currency expansionism either in the free-silver or greenback versions, whichever was more easily available. Producerism and anti-monopoly prevailed among laborites, but farmers so often thought of themselves as the *only*, or the most basic, producers, that farmer-labor coalition was seriously hampered from the start. Farmers, taken by surprise after 1873 by the existence and possibly greater power of other economic groups in America, reacted defensively.

Such farm agitation as there was before 1873 focussed on the regulation of railroads and was led by members of the Grange, the Patrons of Husbandry. Granger publications seldom discussed national policy questions, except anti-monopoly, and the National Grange, as late as its 1873 meeting, avoided the money question almost entirely. But only two years later the National Grange dealt with resolutions to repeal the Specie Resumption Act, to make greenbacks full legal tender for import duties, to create the 3.65 per cent interconvertible bond that greenback-laborites wanted, and to abolish all national banks and their notes. These resolutions were ruled "political" and hence not proper Grange business, but individual Grangers proceeded to support them. The direct-agitation methods of Grangerism seemed as suited to handle monetary reform as they had been to battle railroad monopolies.[6]

Agricultural publications, even Western ones, took low-tariff, anti-monopoly, producerite attitudes well into 1873, and until then made it clear that the nearest group to the farmers, in interest, was not labor but commercial people interested in cheap transportation and low tariffs. In the summer of 1873, the *Industrial Age*, a leading farm journal published in Chicago, referred frequently to the good work of the New York Cheap Transportation Association, a mercantile group, quoted from the New York *American Grocer*, a marketing trade journal, and wrapped themselves and their mercantile friends within the common banner of producerism.

Very suddenly, this changed. The *Industrial Age*, in response to the unfavorable business cycle and more immediate pressures, started talking about money within ten days after the Panic of 1873. Friendship toward mercantile people withered away and had quite disappeared by late 1875, taking with it a secondary theme of cordiality toward eastern labor. Meanwhile, its affections shifted in favor of industrial labor, who were fellow producers being "crushed" by Wall Street and big capitalists. Money replaced railroad regulation as the "number one" question by December, 1874, greenbacks became "the only safe currency we ever had in the West," and national banks were the worst evil in the country. From concern with railroad monopolies, low tariffs, and a felt coalition of interest with eastern commerce and labor, the *Industrial Age* and other farm voices moved within two years after the depression began to an emphasis on the money question, sympathy with industrial labor, and a very candid sectionalism. The bridges which the farmers used to cross from the earlier position to the later one were producerism and anti-monopoly. Economic pressure had operated on a pre-existing rhetoric to make agricultural feeling on the money question as raucous in the late seventies as it had been quiet or nonexistent a few years before. Farmers responded vigorously to economic change as to nothing else, and insisted more shrilly on their moral rectitude than did any other group.[7]

Manufacturers, manwhile, moved just as rapidly in the opposite direction. Before 1873, the manufacturing group contained pockets of hard-money sentiment, especially in industries such as cotton textiles that were competitively established and technologically stable, but most of the group favored soft money and protective tariffs. Industries growing dynamically were hardly anxious for foreign competition or a scarcity of money needed for capital expansion, and through the late sixties and early seventies, they were happy to watch contraction end, greenbacks and national bank notes stabilized, and resumption day postponed and evaded. Believing not only in the policies favored by Henry C. Carey but his principle of association as well, manufacturers looked at society as a collection of their own, the laborite, and other groups, whose harmony was threatened only by a few grasping and speculating financiers. To the extent before

1873 that manufacturers felt themselves aligned with other groups, their kinship was with other "producers," especially labor.

All this changed, gradually but profoundly, after 1873. Carey continued to impress many manufacturers, most of them were even less in a hurry for specie resumption on the gold basis than they had formerly been, and a good many were straight-out free-silverites and greenbackers. But a sizeable minority were enough awed by classical doctrines to seek speedy resumption as the surest road out of the depression; and others not quite so rigoristic much preferred "free banking" as an expansion device to free silver or the interconvertible bond idea. Manufacturers were still favorable toward some kind of soft-money much more than merchants or bankers, but the inflationist dependability of the manufacturing group was nevertheless lessening.

With this unease went a shift in social attitude. In a rather abrupt fashion, many manufacturers ceased to identify primarily with the "producing classes" and began to think of themselves more naturally as "capitalists," more like bankers or merchants, less like farmers and laborers. The *Iron Age,* in the issue which appeared on the day of the Panic of 1873, criticized trade associations that combined to set prices or to act in a manner "unfavorable to the public interest." By the following April, however, it was deploring strikes and asserting that "The masters must combine for their own protection, and when the struggle is that of combined labor against combined capital, the masters will only need to keep faith with each other to break the unions and emancipate the workingmen from the tyrannous rule to which they have so long submitted." Frankly advocating the blacklist, the ironmasters' journal that this "violent remedy" was justified as the only way "to save the iron trade from utter demoralization."

The ambivalence between obsolescent self-images and pressing realities appeared most vividly in *Manufacturer and Builder.* That journal's producerism was still strong enough in 1874 to allow it to commend the Grange as an organization which might free farmers from "bondholders and moneylenders," and to hope that the 1873 Crash might end speculation and "give the manufacturers and merchants relief from the oppressive rates of interest for capital." But by late 1874, it saw combination differently:

> Labor is a drug to be had in any quantity and on reasonable terms, without liability to dictation from outside parties on any pretence whatever of trade combinations, which have wrought incalculable mischief in forcing rates to an unnatural level. Their power is gone, and capital and labor may now 'reason together.' . . . The severe depression in the building trades dates its origin from the labor strikes of 1872–73.

At the depth of the depression, the New England textile manufacturer and sometime historian William B. Weeden, complaining of strikes and organized labor unrest, talked of "contract, that mystic sacrament of civilization," and from that point the manufacturing group mouthed a conservative capitalistic rhetoric little different from the bankers'.

By no means all American manufacturers switched just then from producer-identification to capitalist-identification; not all of them were producer-minded to begin with, and of those who were, some were more greenbackish than ever. But the shift was common among Pennsylvanians and others whose enterprises were growing palpably too large for producerism to remain a tenable frame of reference.

Several things caused the shift; size was one. Technology was doubtless another, especially as it involved capital investment in new equipment and some dislocations of labor. Change in size and technology must have had a profound effect on, for example, steelmen; U.S. output of steel ingots and castings was under twenty thousand tons in 1867, but was over 935,000 tons in 1879; moreover, nearly all of the new production was by the Bessemer method just being introduced. Another reason was manufacturing spokesmen's complaint about state regulation, and threatened federal regulation, of transportation. Also, as commercial elements modified their hostility to protective tariffs in the hope that the federal government would grant ship subsidies, it became easier for manufacturing and commercial people to ally.

But above all, after 1873, manufacturers could not abide the manifest hostility of labor. The depression following the Panic of 1873 brought to America its first real experience with industrial labor unrest, climaxed with the Great Strike of 1877. Strikes and bloodshed were obviously subversive of the existing social order, and under their hammer-blows the Careyite theme of association, and vaguer notions of social class harmony, were smashed to pieces. Manufacturers woke up in shock after 1873 to find themselves no longer the friends, but the enemies, of the producing classes. Perhaps the idea of social harmony had been a delusion in the first place, and was simply too absurd to be maintained in the face of events after 1873; but as far as the manufacturing interest understood the situation, it had changed, and they changed in response to it. Neither strikes nor protection nor regulation were new, but the massiveness of labor trouble, which arose so suddenly and sweepingly after 1873, made manufacturers' visions of social harmonies look rather silly. The grounds for this notion may have been eroding for years, but while this could be overlooked in the tranquil years, the flood of trouble after 1873 swamped it. Suddenly deprived of their producerism, a great many manufacturers saw no other ideological alternative than the slogans of free enterprise, sanctity of contract, and all the others that soon became familiar.[8]

For manufacturers, as well as for merchants, bankers, laboring men, and farmers, the world seemed to change during the seventies. The old alignments and self-images were never coming back.

17

THE REVIVAL

OF

MONETARY SECTIONALISM

The crisis of the post-1873 years also reawakened and intensified sectional cleavages. Sectional strains had manifested themselves in Congress in 1870, and did so again from 1874 onward. As the depression deepened and free silver began to take its place alongside greenbackism as a popular soft-money position, sectional divisions became more important than they had been since the Civil War itself. While economic groups were shifting away from a felt mutual harmony toward a capital-labor polarity, sectional groups began to reorient themselves according to another and similar polarity, that of creditors versus debtors.

In the population mass of the Northeast, every conceivable monetary position was represented somewhere. But opinion leaders and the more powerful social elements were almost as one in upholding hard money, regardless of what anyone else thought. Pennsylvania, as usual, was not nearly as devoted to monetary rigor as New York and New England were, but in those latter

[216]

regions, old-line gold monometallism, or the increasingly fashionable international bimetallism, were the general rule. Journals such as *Scribner's Monthly*, Henry Ward Beecher's *Christian Union*, the *North American Review*, the *Nation*, the *Popular Science Monthly*, and *Harpers' Weekly*, roundly blasted free silver and greenbackism. New York and New England party platforms and state legislatures, as well as trade organizations and "citizens' associations," called for the gold standard or for bimetallism subject to international agreement. Bank notes were acceptable to the *New York Times*, but the threat of their replacement by greenbacks was "of course, only another step in the miserable programme of repudiation" of the 1878 Congress. In Pennsylvania, meanwhile, both parties found it wise to leave a little room for soft money, either in the form of greenbacks or free silver (as with the Democrats) or at least by free banking (as with the Republicans), but in the rest of the Northeast, silver agitation nearly always took the international-bimetallist form, often in very conservative versions. The Northeast, moreover, had a keen sense of its sectional identity, and its spokesmen often disparaged the South and West as the home of "repudiating debtors."[1]

The Far West was as devoted to specie as the Northeast, but for different reasons and in different ways. In the two Western metropolises of Denver and San Francisco, daily newspapers hesitatingly approved limited silver coinage as long as it did not disturb gold values, and in 1878 the San Francisco Chamber of Commerce remonstrated against restoring full legal-tender power to the silver dollar. But the *Territorial Enterprise* of Virginia City, Nevada, was a wide-open free-silver sheet. Although the tendency was not universal in the Far West, which like other capital-short sections of the country contained a good measure of greenbackism, its sectional representatives seldom quibbled with almost any monetary system which made use of the gold and silver bullion it produced. Its gold monometallists generally shifted after 1873 to one version or another of international bimetallism, while soft-money elements took more than usual care to distinguish between "depreciated" greenbacks and "intrinsically valuable" free silver.[2]

The South changed its monetary attitudes remarkably after

the early seventies. As it crawled to its feet in the postwar years, much of its old orientation toward international commerce remained; but the hard-money stand that this involved—harder sometimes than anywhere else in the country—subsided gradually in favor of greenbacks and free silver. The Northeast, the Republicans, the national banks, were highly suspect; what the South needed, some spokesmen said, was an alliance with the West, paper and abundant coin money, the union of producers, repeal of the "notorious fraud" of silver demonetization, and a postponement of specie resumption. Southern monetary ideology was very consciously sectional, opposed to the "money and bond-holding power of the East." In language that was to become increasingly familiar from that time into the Populist days of the nineties, Southerners damned gold monometallism under which "the civilized world must inevitably fall absolutely under the power of banks, bondholders, and gold rings."[3]

The Midwest contained plenty of inflationist sentiment, some of it for free banking, some for free silver, some for greenbackism. In spite of the anti-greenback, anti-"repudiator," anti-silver positions of certain major Western newspapers, such as the *Chicago Times* and the Cincinnati *Commercial,* greenbacks had the support of many agrarian and political groups and many newspapers, large and small. Midwestern Congressmen vigorously supported free banking in 1874, and considerable sentiment in the West moved toward free silver and greenbackism in subsequent years when free banking had not relieved western currency shortages as its backers had hoped. There, as in the South, a sectional self-consciousness spread as the West began to think of itself as a debtor region with fundamentally different economic interests from the creditor Northeast. "Debtor" was becoming equivalent to producer, and creditor to manipulator. Although neither the debtor-creditor rhetoric nor the policies of soft money ever captured the full support of the Midwest, a great deal of the strength of both the greenback and free-silver movements sprang from the debtor consciousness of that section.[4]

The old order was passing. The events of 1874 to 1879 were to rearrange the terms of argument of the money question, and with it American's self-understanding and self-images into new and grotesque forms.

Narratives, 1873–1879

The Return of Silver

and the Rhetorics

of Social Combat

PART FIVE

Narratives, 1878–1879

The Return of Silver

and the Rhetorics

of Social Combat

18

THE SEARCH

FOR COMPROMISE,

1873–76

Public policy on money, in America from 1873 to 1876, consisted largely of hardy attempts by Republican leaders to keep their party together and to save what they could. The legislative settlements of 1870–73 collapsed after the Panic of 1873, and for well over a year following, Congress felt pressure from many sources to put more currency in circulation, either in the form of greenbacks or national bank notes. Congress responded early in 1874 with a "free banking" bill, which would have made national banks easier to establish and thus would have engendered more of their notes, and an "inflation bill," putting more greenbacks in circulation. In 1875 it passed the Specie Resumption Act. Considered together, these bills represent an attempt, led principally by Senator John Sherman, to maintain the stability which was achieved during the previous period and which was capped by the Coinage Act of February, 1873. The attempt succeeded only partially and temporarily.

Just as soon as the Coinage Act safely cleared Congress, Sherman attempted to create machinery to bring off the last great postwar reform, which had eluded him: the resumption of specie payments. On February 11, 1873, within hours after the Coinage Act left Capitol Hill, Sherman wrote to President Grant, "I am so strongly impressed with the pressing importance at this session to take some step towards the resumption of specie payments that I feel justified in appealing to you to give your aid," and he asked Grant to call publicly for resumption. "We are committed in every way," Sherman pointed out, "to a specie standard and free Banking. There is no safety except in combining them in one measure."[1]

Many of Sherman's difficulties over the following year and a half stemmed from his failure to take his own advice, and keep currency expansion and specie resumption paired. Through 1873 he pushed for a measure that would have resumed specie payments on January 1, 1874. Even hard-money journals blanched at that, while Republican moderates shunned it completely and prevented its passage. Then came the Panic in September, and within weeks the general demand was not for rapid resumption of specie payments, but for expansion of the currency to relieve monetary stringency. The change in the direction of pressure had a dizzying, almost disastrous, effect on the Republican party. Sherman finally recalled in late 1874 his own advice to keep currency expansion and specie resumption tied together in the same measure—something for the left, something for the right—but in the meantime the Republicans were in disarray.

In the final quarter of 1873, after the Panic, spokesmen for economic groups leapt on the money question and rode off in all directions. The *Banker's Magazine* insisted that the government not "interfere" with free banking, and Midwesterners especially favored the idea; many people, particularly those in sections with slender currency resources, could not accept greenbackism but embraced free banking (the removal of limits on the number of national banks that could be chartered and the raising of the limit on total banknote circulation) because it would bring currency expansion while not affecting the amount of currency that would have to be redeemed when resumption finally arrived. Manufacturers also supported free banking, on the grounds that the country needed laws to protect the honest merchant and manufacturer from being forced into bankruptcy. Some manufacturers preferred simply to authorize the Secretary of the Treasury to issue more greenbacks. Left-wing labor agreed; for them, the national banks were "simply a new edition of the state 'wild cat' under national authority"; free banking was unacceptable; greenbacks were the only answer. At the other extreme, the *Commercial and Financial Chronicle* castigated any form of "inflation" whatever, free-banking or greenbackish. Panic or no, said the *Chronicle,* the government had no business expanding or reducing the currency in circulation, because such action affected the standard of value. Congress' main job was to "pass no act, nor keep up any discussion which, without any sure advantage prevents the recuperative moment of returning animation."[2]

Congress, and Sherman, had their work cut out for them. In the session of early 1874, they debated free banking and greenback expansion at length. The Republican leadership favored free banking, but could not prevent the House from taking up greenback expansion first. On March 23, by a more than two-to-one margin, the House voted to raise the legal limit on greenback currency by $44-million, to a total of $400-million. The vote was more sectional than partisan. Westerners and Southerners, both Democrats and Republicans, voted in favor; but a number of Northeastern Democrats and Republicans of prominence voted against.

In the Senate, Sherman substituted for the "inflation bill," as it got dubbed, another measure keeping the greenback total at the existing limit of $382-million, the amount actually circulating. Sherman beat down a right-wing amendment to reduce the amount to $356-million, but could not prevent an amendment from the other side to raise it to the $400-million level of the House bill. After a long and acrimonious debate, the "inflation bill" passed the Senate on April 6, on a 29–24 vote that was quite sectional. The House accepted the Senate version several days later and added an authorization of $46-million in new bank notes. The "inflation bill," as it went to the White House, thus increased both greenbacks and bank notes moderately. (The "inflation," of course, amounted to around 5 per cent of the greenbacks then circulating, and a much smaller percentage of the total money supply. It is inconceivable that Congress and much of the press in the country could have been so excited about a few drops in the bucket—unless one remembers how deeply they believed in the prevailing monetary ideology and rhetoric.)

While the Senate debated the "inflation bill," the Republican leadership in the House managed to bring its free banking bill to the floor. Group pressures were confusing: petitioning against any "further" inflation were many commercial and Northeastern groups, including the Baltimore Board of Trade, the New York Importers' and Grocers' Board of Trade, the New York state assembly, the Portland (Maine) Board of Trade, the Chicago Merchant's Exchange; petitioning for a currency increase were the American Iron and Steel Association, a group of Chicago iron manufacturers, the Peoria Board of Trade, and the Iowa legislature.[3] Perhaps because outside pressures so conflicted, the long House debate on the free banking bill was highly ideological and revealingly sectional. Monetary ideology crystallized, as Republicans such as William D. Kelley and Ben Butler insisted that government and law, not "intrinsic value," created money, while others, many of them Republicans too, staunchly denied that governments had anything to do with fixing values. The ideas were not new, but their candid, even insistent, statement in Congress was new. Congress, for the first time in years, was actually debating the money question instead of agreeing generally on a single ideological attitude. In the final House vote, moderate Republicans (many of them Midwesterners) led the passage of the free-banking bill against an assortment of Democrats and Republicans of both the extreme left and the extreme right. The sectional and ideological divisions were not perfectly black and white, but they were certainly clear enough to show that the ideological and sectional harmony of earlier years had ended.[4]

The House debates on both bills took place almost simultaneously. In the debates, and in the voting, it became clear that free banking served as a kind of way-station for Representatives who could not accept the idea of inconvertible paper currency, yet who wanted specie resumption postponed, perhaps indefinitely. Many Midwesterners were in this category. Hardly anyone thought the "inflation bill" was ideal, but since its final version provided bank-note increases and tighter reserve requirements for national banks, as well as more greenbacks, enough free-banking supporters were mollified so that it passed. Grant's signature was expected.

Jove instead sent a thunderbolt. Apparently the arguments of right-wing deflationism had sunk into the old soldier's mind, and he sent back the inflation bill to Congress on April 22 with his veto. Inflation, as contemplated in the bill, was hardly the road to resumption; as long as more paper circulated than there was gold to back it, resumption was impossible. The quantity of paper money determined the chances of successful resumption, he rumbled; "the balance of trade has nothing to do with the question." Grant, sympathetic neither to the producerite argument for easier money nor to sectional arguments for free banking, rejected the "inflation bill" on grounds certain to infuriate large elements in the Republican party. With a single veto message, the President smashed most of what was left of Sherman's patient effort since 1869 to create Republican harmony on the money question. The Senate failed to override the veto, and the inflation bill died.[5]

Three weeks later, Sherman bravely brought the free-banking bill to the Senate floor. The bill was aimed to satisfy one party wing by expanding the bank-note issue, and the other party wing by "safeguarding" the redeemability of the notes. But nobody was very happy. The bill passed, heavily amended, and a House-Senate conference attached an upper limit of $382-million for the greenbacks, with gradual contraction to $300-million as more bank notes were issued. Grant signed the bill in late June. But the session had been very destructive of Republican unity. Sectionalism in the press as in Congress was so rampant, economic groups so split, monetary rhetoric so powerless to bind groups together any longer, that the Republicans faced the congressional elections in the fall of 1874 deeply divided and often demoralized. The Democrats, for the first time since before the Civil War, captured control of the House of Representatives.[6]

The monetary harmony of 1870–73 was a wreck; the money question was dividing Americans as it was dividing people in Britain, France, and Germany. Sensing this, Sherman and other Republican leaders made a final effort, in the lame-duck session of Congress in late 1874 and early 1875, to retrieve the situation. Sherman recalled his advice to Grant of early 1873, to tie free banking and specie resumption together on the same measure, and in so doing, he achieved a considerable, if temporary, success.

Republican disunity was stronger than ever, after the 1874 fall elections. President Grant and Treasury Secretary Benjamin Bristow called for deflationary legislation, powerful House Republicans such as William D. Kelley pleaded for more greenbacks. Sherman met them all with a compromise measure, and using forces of persuasion which will probably never be fully known, secured its adoption by the Senate Republican caucus. It was to become the Specie Resumption Act of 1875.

Sherman's bill was the most rigorous that inflationists would support, and the most inflationary that the right wing would support; it was, as Sherman said of so many of his bills, the best that could be had. Sherman's best argument, no doubt, was that without it the party would probably lose the Presidency in 1876 as they had lost the House in 1874. In any event, it was a measure designed to unite warring sectional and economic groups within the Republican party, and was in no way the creature of a single hard-money group.[7]

The first section of the bill would redeem fractional paper currency in silver; the second section repealed the .2 per cent charge for coining gold. These provisions were obviously designed to prevent any disaffection from Congressmen responsive to Western gold or silver interests.

The third section, the heart of the bill, appealed to free-banking supporters by removing all limits, sectional as well as aggregate, on bank note issues; it appealed to greenback supporters by setting an absolute lower limit on greenbacks at $300-million, no matter how many new bank notes were issued; and it appealed to the right wing by pledging that specie payments would be resumed on January 1, 1879. The bill provided no machinery whatever for achieving resumption, but the resumption-day pledge, together with Sherman's shrewd use of it to entitle the bill (officially it was "an act to provide for the resumption of specie payments," though a more accurate title would have been "an act to provide for free banking, and for other purposes"), satisfied the hard-money element.

Sherman moved this adroit compromise speedily through the Senate. In a single evening, December 22, 1874, Sherman brought up the bill, desultorily presented a few arguments for each section, ignored Democratic complaints that the Republicans had hammered it out in their party caucus and pledged themselves to it, and watched it pass on almost straight party lines. Representative Horace Maynard of Tennessee presented it to the House on January 7 under a rule preventing amendment, and it sailed through, 136–98, without one Democrat voting in favor and only a scattering of Republicans of the far left and far right voting against. Grant signed it on January 14.[8]

Press and group reaction was diverse and vehement. Commercial and banking papers shrugged off the resumption-day pledge, and one called Sherman's speech "much less sound in principle and much less accurate in statement than might have been supposed." But a National Board of Trade leader saw the Specie Resumption Act for what it was: "This measure was conceded by its friends to be the result of compromise, and like all compromises is not entirely satisfactory to any of its supporters; but . . . we may regard it as an omen for good." The laborite *Workingman's Advocate* did not like it; because of the Act, the people would "be robbed and plundered at wholesale." A Midwestern farm journal called it "the result of a corrupt combination between the Republican bullionists and Republican bankers, who have united up on this financial monstrosity for the purpose of saving the Republican party from destruction." But the displeasure of economic groups, though ominous, was not matched by displeasure in the metropolitan press around the country. Though few major newspapers were delighted with the Act, it apparently had scotched sectionalism.[9]

Sherman and his colleagues had tried, with some success in late 1874 after the disaster of early 1874, to reduce sectional tension and reunite the Republican party on money. Economic groups, despite the work of these Republican leaders, remained split. The money question was emerging again as a political and social concern. Groups were dividing, rhetoric was fragmenting; soon the currency and banking disputes of 1874 and 1875 would take place as minor skirmishes, as the battle over the monetary standard became fully joined in 1876.

19

MAKING A PLACE

FOR SILVER,

1876–77

From early 1876 to late 1877, as silver touched bottom and as the depression showed no signs of ending, legislators and other Americans entered on a great debate over whether, and in what ways, silver ought to have a more prominent place in the monetary system. The issue was explosive. The Republican and Democratic parties were both deeply split on it, and party leaders managed to squelch it during the 1876 presidential campaign, because the electoral effects of a battle over monetary standards were too uncertain. Among policy-makers, however, the money question—what to do about silver, and whether to repeal the Specie Resumption Act—concerned people intensely.

In 1876 the Senate was still safely Republican, and Senators would presumably still be responsive to the caucus whip that Sherman had cracked in order to pass the Specie Resumption Act. But the House of Representatives had a Democratic majority. It became the cockpit of monetary revisionism. But there were three kinds of revisionists: greenbackers, mainly interested in repealing the Specie Resumption pledge and expanding the greenback issue; free-silverites, who were amenable to resumption repeal but whose chief interest was remonetizing the old standard silver dollar; and people who simply wanted more silver used in coinage, because they had some economic interest in it. Conservative Republicans and Democrats hoped to attach the third "revisionist" group to themselves, in order to preserve the gold standard and the Specie Resumption Act.

Here is where international bimetallism, or lip service to it, became a stalking horse for monetary conservatism (i.e., keeping the gold standard intact). Conservatives recognized that some use had to be made of silver beyond that provided in the Coinage Act of 1873. By widening the nonstandard uses of silver, the conservative leadership would separate the third group of "revisionists" from the greenbackers and free-silverites, thwart the latter two groups, and preserve resumption and the gold standard. During the first eight months of 1876, this strategy worked.

The need to provide a place in the coinage system for silver was recognized by the makers of the 1873 Coinage Act when they created the "trade dollar" of 420 grains. It quickly became clear that the trade dollar was not doing the job, and policy-makers continued to seek ways to "take care" of silver without threatening the gold standard. In October and November of 1873, Secretary of the Treasury Richardson, with Linderman's backing, paid out subsidiary silver for greenbacks as silver dropped just then to par with greenbacks. The Specie Resumption Act authorized the replacement of fractional paper by subsidiary silver in early 1875, and later that year a Senate resolution sent Linderman on a trip through the Midwest to find a location for a new Mint branch to be devoted to coining silver. Also in 1875, Linderman recommended that the domestic legal-tender power of the trade dollar be raised to ten dollars. Early in 1876, bills came before the House and the Senate to raise the legal-tender power of the trade dollar further, and to direct the Secretary of the Treasury to go ahead and replace fractional paper with subsidiary silver according to the Specie Resumption Act. Such a bill passed in April 1876, after Sherman suggested—so much had times changed—the coinage of a new 412.8-grain (exactly 1:16) silver dollar with a legal-tender limit of twenty dollars. This long series of attempts to utilize silver culminated in a joint resolution of July 22, 1876, directing the Secretary of the Treasury to sell subsidiary silver for greenbacks up to a limit of $10-million, and to continue redeeming fractional paper with silver to another $40-million. Policy-makers much preferred silver to greenbacks. But they kept the gold standard intact; the July 22 resolution also abolished completely the domestic legal-tender power of the trade dollar.

Despite all this, silverite pressure mounted. Sherman tried to relieve it in additional ways. He tried to resuscitate the idea of international coinage unification, in such a way as to include a silver agreement, and in June 1876, he presented the Senate with a bill to coin the old standard silver dollar with limited legal-tender powers. Sherman had come over to a very cautious kind of international bimetallism. He obviously thought free silver was an extremely serious threat, and was proposing limited international bimetallism as a way of preserving the old gold monometallism with a face-lift.

"It is perfectly obvious," Sherman told the Senate as he presented his silver-dollar bill in 1876, "that if we could in some way prevent gold and silver from fluctuating in their relations to each other the double standard is the best, as giving the largest store of the precious metals to draw upon, and it is now proposed by international treaties to bring this about." Until these treaties existed, however, "it is far wiser for us to stand by the composite system in force in the United States since 1853 [!]." Remonetizing the old silver dollar with limited tender power (which prevented its use for large private payments or government bonds) "provided for an immediate resumption of specie payments in silver coin." It also meant driving out greenbacks, but Sherman preferred not to stress that point; he declared instead that his proposal "is in exact accordance with existing law, and leaves the silver dollar, as now, a subsidiary coin." Sherman's bill did not get to a vote before the session ended. But it typified the strategy of detaching the people interested only in expanding the use of silver from the greenback and free-silver inflationists, and showed that limited international bimetallism had become the tactical stance of many gold-standard supporters.[1]

As Sherman was proposing limited international bimetallism as a means of providing for silver but frustrating the free-silverites, conservative Democrats in the House settled on a very different device to achieve the same purpose: repeal of the Specie Resumption Act. Free-silver and greenback sentiment was very strong in the House, and demanded a stronger antidote than Sherman suggested in the Senate. To repeal the Specie Resumption Act, or parts of it, would supposedly satisfy monetary moderates, and create a middle path (somewhat analogous to the place of free banking two years earlier) between the deflationary possibilities of specie resumption on the right, and the uncertain inflationary perils of free silver or greenbackism on the left. Moreover, many Democrats were still unhappy about the partisan character of the Specie Resumption Act, and some Congressmen were disenchanted with the Act for its lack of machinery to bring resumption about. Many Congressmen supported both resumption repeal and free silver, to be sure, but others put resumption repeal forward as a lightning rod against "inflation."

Free silver and resumption repeal bills poured into the House hopper in early 1876. With both political parties thoroughly divided on both measures, House debates grew labyrinthine as the season went into its final weeks in June and July. Early in May, Representative Richard P. Bland, a Missouri Democrat, reported from committee a free-silver bill. Before it was debated, however, William D. Kelley reported a free-silver bill of his own on July 18. Bland offered his bill again on July 19. In the meantime, another Democrat, John L. Vance of Ohio, tried and failed to bring to the floor a resolution repealing the Specie Resumption Act. Kelley won the race. On July 24, before Bland or Vance could get the House to consider their measures, Kelley moved to suspend the rules and pass his bill, which was a terse measure providing for the free coinage of the 412½-grain silver dollar with full legal-tender power. The vote was 119 in favor, 66 against, and 99 not voting. But since the suspension of the rules required a two-thirds majority, Kelley's bill failed to pass.

Still, free silver seemed to own a clear majority. Bland and Vance voted for Kelley's bill, as did many prominent Democrats, labor-greenback leader Alexander Campbell of Illinois, and a contingent of Midwestern Republicans. Nevertheless, when Bland's free-silver bill finally reached the floor on August 1, it was during the "morning hour" rather than as part of the regular order of business, and its opponents stalled it from day to day. Bland could never get it to a vote. Obviously the free-silverites had yet to win over the Democratic leadership which controlled the calendar.

On August 5, the months-long debate came to a head. S. S. "Sunset" Cox, a conservative Democrat from New York, reported a committee-approved bill to repeal the Specie Resumption Act, and moved that it be passed. Cox also announced that he also intended to introduce a bill to create a joint commission to investigate the "silver question." Until that commission's full report was available, free-silver bills should lie on the table.

A few minutes later, future Republican Speaker Joseph G. Cannon of Illinois, then a soft-money man, warned that the Kelley or Bland free-silver bills were not going to pass during that session unless they were tacked on to Cox's resumption repeal bill. But Cox refused to accept any amendments. The real enemy, Cannon retorted, was Abram Hewitt, "chairman of the national central committee and Tilden's right-bower," like Cox a New Yorker. (Samuel J. Tilden had just been nominated for the Presidency by the Democratic party.) Hewitt heatedly denounced resumption repeal in his own name and Tilden's in a long speech inserted in the *Record*. "Against this bill [free silver] I am charged by the Chamber of Commerce of the City of New York, the jealous guardians of commercial honor," to remonstrate, Hewitt announced. He and the Chamber believed that free silver "proposes to despoil the desolate widows and the helpless orphans of $360,000,000," and would wreck the savings banks which contained "the scanty earnings of the poor. Upon the day-laborer, upon the industrious servant girl, upon the frugal mechanic, therefore, will fall this unparalleled and incredible loss of the means accumulated against a rainy day. . . . It is the old story of the poor sacrificed to the demands of the needy [sic!] speculator and the grasping adventurer." Hewitt moved a resolution creating an investigatory commission on resumption repeal, but his motion lost, creating the spectacle of the overwhelming majority of House Democrats voting against their party's National Chairman.

The debate was quickly shifting away from resumption repeal to the hotter question of free silver. Republicans James A. Garfield of Ohio and Washington Townsend of Pennsylvania cursed the Bland bill as "disastrous," "corrupt," "the most fatal blow which ever was struck at the credit of the nation," which would defraud the laborer of the true value of his wages, give the "bonanza silver miners four or five million dollars a year of additional profit," and constitute a 15 per cent knock-down of government obligations. The worst of it, moaned Townsend, was that it would be "a long step backward in financial economy." Bland rebutted these "arguments" just as vehemently. The free-silver leader damned the "corrupt legislation . . . full of rascalities . . . that has gone on here for the last sixteen years in the interest of the moneyed lords . . . by the party that [has] perpetrated these injustices and brought corruption, fraud, infamy, and dishonor upon the country. . . . if we are to undertake resumption with the gold standard alone, the money sharks will foreclose the mortgages they have upon the people, sell them out of houses and homes, and turn millions of hard-working and industrious people into beggars." Compromise, even communication, was unlikely in such an atmosphere of rancor and sloganeering.

Cox's resumption repeal bill then passed the House, 106–86. Most Democrats and a few Republicans (mostly Midwestern) voted in favor; more Republicans and a number of Democrats, led by Hewitt, opposed it. The House also passed a concurrent resolution establishing a monetary commission. But, as the session closed, Bland's free-silver bill remained mired in the "morning hour" and the resumption-repeal bill disappeared into the maw of the Senate Finance Committee. With the presidential election only weeks away, the Democrats were split. But the Republicans were hardly more united, and to all appearances the gold standard would not survive another Congress.[2]

The election was unusually bitter. The Democratic congressional victory in 1874 had thoroughly frightened the Republicans, and neither the campaign nor its results did anything to relieve tension over the money question or to make victory easy for either side. Both presidential nominees were monetarily very conservative, but both led tickets whose other members often were not. The results were disastrous for the third-party Greenback ticket led by Peter Cooper, which almost totally failed to win any national offices. The presidential contest between Hayes and Tilden was not settled until a few hours before the inauguration when a mixed commission gave the intensely disputed victory to Hayes. The Republicans found their Senate majority narrowed to one, and the Democrats lost about thirty seats in the House. Nevertheless, the resumption repeal and free-silver coalitions had been so powerful in the previous Congress that the chances of some sort of soft-money victory seemed entirely likely.

In the lame-duck session of the Forty-fourth Congress, from December 1876 to early March 1877, Bland's free-silver bill reappeared before the House, while the resumption-repeal bill languished in Sherman's Senate Finance Committee. On December 12, 1876, Bland finally got the floor, and presented a substitute bill practically the same as Kelley's brief proposal of the preceding session, providing simply for the free coinage of full tender 412.8-grain silver dollars. Bland and Kelley had got together, and on December 13, after about two hours' debate during which Bland spoke of the blunder, or worse, of 1873, and Garfield and Hewitt offered bipartisan opposition, the Bland-Kelley free-silver bill passed by a margin of more than three to one, 167–53.

Immediately the pressure was on the Senate. Sherman was quite aware that free silver was far more than the fantasy of picaresque radicals, that it had the support of congressional greenbackers, western silverites, business groups such as the St. Paul Chamber of Commerce, and the legislatures of Wisconsin and Minnesota. On January 16, 1877, he brought the Bland-Kelley bill out of the Senate Finance Committee, but recommended no action to the Senate. Sherman had not wavered in the slightest from the limited bimetallism he had adopted earlier.

Writing to an anxious Hugh McCulloch just before Christmas, 1876, he agreed that the reinstatement of full legal-tender silver dollars "would not only impair the public credit but would lead to great derangement of business and practically establish the single standard of silver." But, said Sherman, free silver was not likely to pass.

> The use of silver ought to be largely encouraged and the silver dollar might well be restored to the coinage of the country. I am in favor of issuing it and a very large sum of subsidiary coins and with them reducing the greenback circulation, making the silver dollar a legal tender to the same extent that U.S. notes are now a legal tender, but excepting expressly customs duties and the public debt. . . . This letter is written for yourself and not for public use, as I will in a short time state in a thorough way the position I intend to occupy on this silver question.

The Senate did not take up the free-silver bill after Sherman presented it so negatively, and the free-silver and resumption-repeal bills died as the Forty-fourth Congress passed into history without acting on them.[3]

Outside of Congress, the monetary debate went on, as the investigatory commission ordered by the joint resolution of August 15, 1876, opened hearings. This body, called the United States Monetary Commission, did help to keep the money question muted during the 1876 campaign, as some of its backers intended. But it developed into much more than the delaying device against free-silver legislation that Congressman Abram Hewitt and others originally sought. It became, in fact, the forum for candid and wide-ranging discussion of the money question. Its hearings and its two-volume report produced in 1877 and 1879 were a rhetorical event, an American parallel to the great French and British investigations into the money question that had appeared from time to time over the preceding ten years.

Chaired by Senator John P. Jones of Nevada, a free-silver and anti-greenback Republican, the Commission leaned toward the silverite side. Senators Lewis Bogy, Democrat of Missouri, and former Treasury Secretary George Boutwell of Massachusetts, and

Representatives Randall Gibson, a "redeemer" Louisiana Democrat, Republican George Willard of Michigan, and "Silver Dick" Bland, were joined by two noncongressional experts, William S. Groesbeck of Ohio, a bimetallist, and the academic monometallist, Francis Bowen of Massachusetts.

The Commission worked hard. They solicited oral and written testimony from bankers, publicists, and monetary experts in America and in Europe, and within a few months produced the first of two massive volumes including a majority report, minority dissents, and over five hundred pages of documentation on the world monetary and coinage situation. The report revealed clearly, for the first time in the United States, that a definite shift in official concern had taken place, from creditors to debtors; that the "producer philosophy" had become identified with the debtor viewpoint; and that the underdog debtor mentality had become rather exclusively the property of farmer-labor groups and was by then rare among manufacturers and other formerly producer-oriented businessmen.

Coming when it did, the Commission's report is evidence that the post-1873 crisis had, within four years, heightened class distinctions and fragmented rhetoric into the slogans of economic groups. Still, though the Commission leaned toward free silver, its tone and manner both in its hearings and its report were reasonable, more reasonable in fact than the attitude of many of the conservative witnesses it heard. It listened to steadfast monometallists, international bimetallists, and a few free-silverites. With them the Commissioners discussed not only the monetary standard but several other matters.

These elicited responses more substantial than the usual assertions that the gold standard served civilization and resulted from natural selection, and that silver was a breach of faith; or that the double standard best upheld producer interests, and so forth; such statements had almost become conditioned reflexes by that time. In the first place, the Commission probed deeply into why silver had fallen. Rather surprisingly, many of the witnesses, even some of the monometallists and limited bimetallists, thought the German demonetization had been a more potent factor than the new Nevada production. Very few people seemed willing to appear hostile to an important domestic industry, even though this forced them to suggest that some governmental policy, rather than "natural causes," had provoked the silver decline.

The Commission also raised the basic question of whether a decline in silver had taken place at all, and suggested that perhaps gold might have appreciated. Edward Atkinson, on the witness stand, simply could not grasp this, since it involved the idea that gold might not be absolutely fixed in value. But some witnesses, to whom the point never seemed to have occurred before, at least admitted the possibility when they were questioned closely. The Commission itself (like the Government of India just at that time) seemed convinced that gold had appreciated. While the Commissioners quite agreed with their conservative witnesses that the ideal monetary standard was a stable one, that neither deflated nor inflated, they parted company with the conservatives on how that ideal could be realized.

The Commission also devoted considerable energy to discovering the social effects of fluctuations in metallic standards. Had the shift from bimetallism to gold unfairly rewarded creditors to the detriment of debtors? Would the remonetization of silver in turn restore a just situation, or would it defraud creditors? Here, of course, was the crux. No one spoke in favor of sin, everyone agreed that contracts such as public debts were inviolable, but agreement vanished upon where true justice lay. Should bondholders receive gold payment, which they evidently expected and which was a prerequisite of investor confidence? Or should they be paid in either gold or silver, both of which were legal standards at the time of any pre-1873 bond purchases? Would remonetization hurt farmers and laboring men, as conservatives claimed it would, by threatening to pay for produce and wages in silver dollars worth 15 per cent less than gold dollars, or would it help farmers and laborers by relieving them of the extra taxes needed to pay a public debt whose gold value was appreciating, and by raising product prices? No one denied the principle that the bondholders should in equity be paid just what they had lent. But as doubts multiplied as to what monetary standard best represented unchanging values, these questions became practically insoluble.

The Monetary Commission divided over the answers. Senator Boutwell, in a minority report, concerned himself with the effect of changes in the monetary standard on the public credit. Dissociating himself from theoretical monometallists, Boutwell nevertheless pointed out that as long as the United States hoped to do business abroad, or borrow money abroad, she would have to deal on the gold standard. Free silver would drive out gold and was therefore unfortunately, but totally, impractical. It was "useless to inquire," the ex-Secretary said, whether gold had risen or silver had fallen, because the fact remained that "Gold being the only universal standard or measure of value, all other articles are tested by it, and however the standard may change, yet so long as it is accepted as the standard, the relation which other articles, including silver, bear to it is one of fact, and all theories in regard to values must conform to the fact." Boutwell was begging all the significant questions. Stating that it was "not now expedient" for the United States to remonetize the old silver dollar, he called for an international conference to discuss an international bimetallic standard and parity ratio, and recommended that in the meantime the United States continue her present policy moving toward specie resumption. Thus the man who as Secretary of the Treasury oversaw the demonetization of silver, and who was still basically a monometallist, advocated international bimetallism. Why not? It left existing arrangements intact.

Professor Bowen and Congressman Gibson presented a longer and even more conservative minority report than Boutwell's, but the other five Commissioners opted for the "double standard," which to them meant free silver. The majority took care to minimize any unpleasant effects remonetization might have, but the fascinating aspect of their report was the way in which they squarely faced the direst monometallist objections to silver, accepted them, but showed them to be harmless. The monometallists argued that under a bimetallic system the cheaper metal would always be the practical standard. What of it? "A rise in the value of money and a fall in general prices are the greatest evils which can befall the world." The monometallists feared a fall in the value of money. What of that? "In the whole history of the human race not a single instance can be pointed out of a fall in the value of either or both of the metals which has not proved a benefaction to mankind," while on the other hand, rises in the value of metallic money have in every case "been attended by financial, industrial, political, and social disaster."

Wouldn't bimetallism allow debtors to settle in cheaper metal? Yes, but creditors always lent in a cheaper standard (national banks, for instance, lent paper notes, not gold), and therefore it was an inequity to force debtors to repay in a dearer metal. The majority rested this, of course, on their conclusion that silver had not fallen as much as gold had risen. But even if silver had fallen, even if the decline had been in relation to goods as well as to gold—and here the majority made a point from which most bimetallic apologists held back—history nevertheless showed that "no fall in the value of metallic money nor a resulting rise in prices have ever proved other than a blessing to the world." The same held for paper money, and the majority report left room for "inconvertible paper" as well as for silver.

Bullionists and "fiat money" advocates differed fundamentally in their conceptions of value, the majority recognized: the former believed money had to have "intrinsic value," the latter insisted, with Bishop Berkeley, that money was not wealth but simply a set of counters for computing and exchanging wealth. This distinction may have made Senator Jones restless, since it did not tally with anti-greenback statements he had made elsewhere, but the majority proceeded with a terse and reasoned statement of the fiat money position, again facing frankly the chief monometallist objections. Granted, paper money was easy to over-issue, and past societies had had disastrous experiences with it. But those societies had been divided between "the governing and the producing classes," and there had been no democratic checks on the governors. In modern democratic societies such as the United States, with "free, stable, and constitutional governments and advanced systems of jurisprudence," over-issues were unlikely, and the control of the monetary system was in the hands of the people, where it belonged. The majority recommended the re-monetization of the silver dollar and the discontinuance of the trade dollar, with an international bimetallic conference welcome but not essential.

With the report of the Monetary Commission, free silver came into its own as a monetary ideology. The hearings of the Commission had produced a confrontation between the gold monometallists and conservative bimetallists on the one hand, and the free-silverites and greenbackers on the other, and if anybody dodged the major issues, it was not the inflationists. Monetary conservatism had at last met headon opposition, in open forum under official auspices, and in the language of current political economy. For both sides, the experience was a turning point. From this time onward, monometallism and conservative bimetallism became defensive rhetorically, as they had already become politically; no longer was the gold standard the creed of social optimists as it had been ten years before. Free silver, on the other hand, not only had for the first time been upheld by an official body, but it had begun to take on the egalitarian and democratic tone that so strongly permeated the rhetoric of the Populists a decade and a half later.

In the United States, the liberalism of the late sixties was rapidly becoming the new conservatism of the late seventies, and conservative it was to remain for two or more generations. Simultaneously, the seed of latter-day American liberalism, which was to sprout in Populism and bloom in the twentieth century (if after much twig bending), was beginning to germinate. Unfortunately the acid of the money question was not the ideal fertilizer.[4]

The Great Strike of the summer of 1877 also revealed, as discussion of the money question was doing, that rhetoric had almost totally broken down and that hostility between groups was stronger, perhaps, than it had ever been. Wage cuts and double-timing on the Baltimore & Ohio and other railroads provoked widespread strikes in cities as far apart as Toledo, Louisville, Chicago, St. Louis, and San Francisco. In Pittsburgh, the strike turned into a bloody riot when nervous National Guardsmen fired on a crowd; one reporter counted 53 killed and 109 hurt. Press reactions deplored the rioting and property destruction, but allocated blame very differently: to some, the strikers were "far more honest than the majority of railroad managers" and were the victims of "financial charlatans" who by demanding resumption and contraction had brought about "vicious legislation in the interest of the rich and the disregard of the producing classes." But others called the strikers highwaymen, and damned this "insurrection against the lawful order and the commercial interest of society which [had to be] put down promptly and effectively, by whatever exercise of force may be necessary."[5]

The Great Strike was frightening evidence of drastic and uncomprehended social change. It was becoming harder and harder for people to communicate with each other. Such harmony as had existed in the pre-1873 world was obviously gone, as society polarized into capital versus labor, creditors versus debtors, rich versus poor.

20

SILVER REMONETIZATION

AND SPECIE RESUMPTION,

1877–78

By the end of October, 1877, Americans had already produced ample evidence of social malaise. The depression continued, the presidential election dispute ended in a way that enraged Democrats, the Monetary Commission and the Great Strike, in their different ways, showed how divided society really was. The Forty-fifth Congress convened on October 13, 1877, to begin two back-to-back sessions that did not end until late June, 1878. In these sessions, Congress eked out a solution (if solution is the word) to the silver problem.

The House passed both a free-silver bill and a bill repealing the key parts of the Specie Resumption Act within six weeks after it convened. Congressman Richard P. Bland drew up and presented the free-silver bill, which simply authorized unlimited coinage of the old 412½-grain standard silver dollar with full legal-tender power, and equalized the terms by which the Mint would buy silver with the terms on which it bought gold. The debate was perfunctory, the vote was overwhelming. Republicans and Democrats combined, 164–34, to send the Bland bill to the Senate on November 5.

Two weeks later, House Democrats, with the help of many Midwestern and Pennsylvania Republicans, passed the bill to repeal the free-banking, greenback retirement, and resumption-day clauses in the Specie Resumption Act. The free-banking and greenback advocates in both parties combined to do this, and together they were irresistible—but barely so. The vote was 133–120, much less decisive than the free-silver vote. Soft-money opinion had changed significantly in the eighteen months since early 1876; the new Congress, elected in 1876, was decidedly "softer" than the previous one. While resumption repeal passed the House by a larger margin in 1876 than in 1877, and was candidly understood in 1876 to be a way of dodging free silver, the free-silverites meanwhile increased substantially. Greenbackism was declining, as was free banking; free silver continued to rise in popularity.[1]

Neither resumption repeal nor free silver were to find such warm welcomes in the Senate. Time, of course, was on the side of resumption; delay brought resumption day, January 1, 1879, steadily closer. John Sherman, who earlier in 1877 had left the Senate to become President Hayes' Secretary of the Treasury, was selling 4 per cent bonds as rapidly as he could to accumulate a gold reserve to meet the demands of resumption day. Aided mightily by a favorable balance of payments, Sherman and other resumptionists were beginning to see light at the end of the tunnel. If the Republican majority in the Senate stalled the resumption repeal bill long enough, events would obviate it.[2]

As for free silver, Senate Republicans and monetary conservatives around the country planned to cure that epidemic with the homeopathic medicine of limited, international bimetallism. The National Board of Trade, at its annual meeting in August 1877, revealed that strategy clearly. In a debate over a free-silver resolution offered by the Cincinnati Chamber of Commerce and an international-bimetallist resolution urged by the Chicago Board of Trade, remarkable correspondences appeared: delegates who had argued currency contraction in former years had become international bimetallists in 1877, and those who had earlier wanted specie resumption postponed had become free-silverites. The new conservatism was bluntly expressed by Joseph Ropes of Boston, who before then had been among the most cogent and consistent gold monometallists and contractionists:

> I think this proposition [an international conference to set a gold-silver ratio] contains just the remedy which is needed. If we undertake to say there shall be no silver, except for subsidiary coinage, in this country, I think we shall be beaten by the inflationists. I think, on the contrary, that if we are willing to adopt this proposition, which is advocated by some of the most intelligent students of political economy here and elsewhere, that we may hope to beat back the far more dangerous proposition which is sure to come.

Free silver, Ropes warned, would be "a very great disaster to the country, an irremediable calamity," but an international treaty "to put gold and silver on a substantial equilibrium" was "by no means impossible." Gone was Ropes' monometallist doctrine that legislatures and treaties should have nothing to do with monetary standards or values. Gone was the conviction that a treaty-set gold-silver ratio was chimerical. The Board passed the international-bimetallist resolution. It almost passed the free-silver resolution too—a delegate from Trenton probably stated what was in many other delegates' minds when he confessed that he had been greatly disturbed by social upheavals; though he was no "repudiationist," he saw no reason why people should "have their industries paralyzed by doing more than what is promised to be done in the [government] bond." Depression and riots were too high a price for over-paying public creditors. International bimetallism, however, was the more popular answer.

Certain powerful voices still called for pristine gold monometallism. Henry Linderman remained skeptical of any use of silver as a standard, even by international agreement, and the *Railway World* and the *Commercial and Financial Chronicle* extolled the gold standard and called the paying of bonds in silver nothing but the 1868 "Ohio idea" of greenback payment "silvered over." August Belmont, the investment banker and Democratic leader, wrote Sherman that free silver would be a catastrophe for the credit of the United States in Europe. East-coast national bankers petitioned Congress not to restore silver; if it had not been demonetized in 1873, "the gravest disasters would have overtaken the nation." Monometallism was far from dead.

But free silver petitions piled up in the Senate. They came from all over the country, from "citizens' groups," from state legislatures, from chambers of commerce. Clearly, a compromise had to be worked out, and international bimetallism was the indicated way.[3]

Senator William B. Allison, an Iowa Republican, brought the Bland free-silver bill out of the Senate Finance Committee with two amendments which, in a minimum of words, channelled it safely into a measure for limited international bimetallism. The first amendment got rid of the "free" part of the Bland bill by instructing the Treasury to buy only two to four million dollars' worth of silver at the market per month, to be coined into 412½-grain dollars, instead of any and all silver presented to the Mint. This limited the bill's bimetallism. Secondly, the Allison version called for an international conference to discuss and if possible agree on a worldwide bimetallic ratio, after which the limit on silver purchases could be removed and the United States could safely undertake free-silver coinage without having its gold stocks exhausted or its credit undermined.

Before the Senate could act on Allison's bill, however, the free-silverites counter-attacked with a concurrent resolution authorizing payment of the public bonds in silver dollars—a device to neutralize Allison's plan. Senator Stanley Matthews of Ohio, a Republican and, ironically, the man who took John Sherman's seat when Sherman joined Hayes' Cabinet, presented the resolution, which observed that silver was "coin" at the time of the Public Credit Act of 1869, and the Funding Act of 1870, and on that basis asserted that "to restore to coinage such silver coins as legal tender in payment of said bonds [referred to in those acts], principal and interest, is not in violation of the public faith, nor in derogation of the rights of the public creditor." The Matthews

Resolution passed the Senate easily, 43–22, on January 25, 1878. New York and New England Senators were unanimously against it, but some steadfast conservatives such as Eli Saulsbury of Delaware, convinced that silver was indeed a standard in 1870 and that law and equity supported Matthews' point, joined the free-silverites to help it pass. Three days later the House concurred, 189–79.

But the Matthews Resolution did not solve all of the free-silverites' problems. It declared the public debt payable in silver dollars, but if there were no silver dollars coined, or only a few, it would be nugatory. The Senate vote and debate showed, moreover, that free silver would probably not pass the Senate, and if it did, by a margin insufficient to override the veto that President Hayes would doubtless give it. Allison's compromise still lived.

As the Senate began to debate Allison's bill in late January, it quickly became obvious that it would pass substantially as Allison presented it, over the opposition of die-hard gold monometallists and wrathful free-silverites alike. The arguments were heated, but quite predictable, and by February 18, the Senate had passed the Bland bill with Allison's crucial amendments. Three days later the House concurred in the Senate version, to the relief of conservatives and the disgust of its many free-silverites.

The Bland-Allison bill next came under the baleful scrutiny of Rutherford B. Hayes. The President had made it clear, in his address to Congress three months earlier, that he would not sign a free-silver bill. His diary entries for early February, while the Senate debate raged, show that he neither changed his mind nor troubled to educate it. Seeing no particular difference between the bill before him and a true free-silver measure, failing to understand the crucial changes made by Allison and the Senate Republicans, Hayes sent the bill back to Congress with a veto message that was orthodox, blunt, blind in its monometallism, and confused in the few phrases where it mentioned silver sympathetically. Compared to the analyses of the money question that Sherman and many other financial experts had been making for years, the veto message was crude and jejune. It still stopped the bill, to the delight of monometallic experts around the country, and free-silverites who knew that the Allison amendments had seriously damaged their cause. Moderates, who had worked hard for limited and international bimetallism as the only way to turn aside free silver, or perhaps an ugly social conflict, were aghast. Hayes did not understand what was going on, or if he did could not inch his conscience over the short distance from rigorous monometallism to the limited international bimetallism contained in the Bland-Allison bill.

On February 28, as soon as the Senate received Hayes' veto, it flung it back at him by a vote of 46 to 19, and the House did the same, 196 to 73. The Bland-Allison Act became law. America remonetized silver, within strict limits. It did so in a way that pleased no one, but that anesthetized free silver for years to come.[4]

The bill to repeal the Specie Resumption Act still confronted the Senate. After the Bland-Allison Act had been passed, resumption repeal had little point, either to prevent resumption in silver or extend greenback "inflation," because silver no longer threatened to inundate the country on resumption day, while the new silver dollars promised to loosen the currency tightness somewhat. The gold premium, moreover, was dropping all the time; when the Senate finally took up resumption repeal, resumption day was only seven months away and the premium was very low. Yet the repeal bill came within a hairsbreadth of passing.

There was plenty of public support for it. As the London *Times* quaked in fear of American "repudiation" of debts either through free silver or resumption repeal, petitions—not only from greenback clubs but from the Kentucky legislature, the Savannah Cotton Exchange, the Charleston (S. C.) Chamber of Commerce, and others, urged repeal. Even a few metropolitan bankers, such as George Opdyke and Henry A. Heiser of New York, disliked the Specie Resumption Act; Heiser called it "pernicious." Henry Carey Baird testified, predictably, that the greenback regime ought to be perpetuated. Most bankers, however, seemed to learn longingly for resumption, and opposed repeal. John Sherman certainly did; the Secretary, as he testified to a House Committee, was building up Treasury gold reserves; while the Bland-Allison silver bill had hurt his policy "because they have got the impression in Europe that this silver bill is going to derange matters, and that belief brought back upon us . . .

seventy-five millions of bonds," Sherman thought confidence was increasing that the United States would really resume specie payments on the first of January, 1879, as promised. Sherman could afford to appear confident. The balance of payments was still running strongly in America's favor, and the gold premium was, by late spring of 1878, less than one per cent.

But resumption repeal, for all that, nearly passed the Senate in May and June. In that period, another of the interminable series of congressional compromises emerged, saving the Specie Resumption Act, but at the same time stabilizing and preserving the greenbacks. The repeal bill that reached the Senate floor, early in May, was not the same bill that the House had passed the previous autumn. Repeal of the resumption day clause, the major object of revisionists for two years, had been stricken. On the other hand, the greenbacks had ostensibly been strengthened by making them receivable for customs duties after October 1, 1878, and for 4 per cent resumption bonds immediately. Senator Thomas W. Ferry of Michigan, a Republican moderate who presented this amended version, argued that these changes would hurry and assure specie resumption, but would block currency contraction permanently, and might even cause some currency expansion. The Senate bill, in fact, was designed to satisfy the resumptionists, while dangling carrots before the greenbackers.

The debate on the Ferry version lasted several weeks, and was punctuated by attempts to amend it either rightward or leftward. But the only successful amendment of consequence prohibited the Secretary of the Treasury from retiring any more greenbacks as new national bank notes came into circulation, thus fixing (for eighty years, as it turned out) the total greenback circulation at $346-million, rather than the $300-million specified in the 1875 Resumption Act. Daniel Voorhees, an Indiana Democrat, made a last-ditch attempt to amend the bill by striking the resumption-day clause, but this was defeated, 29–32. Thereupon the Ferry bill passed easily. After all that argument, the House never got around to agreeing to the amendments, and resumption repeal died of inanition as the Forty-fifth Congress adjourned *sine die*.[5]

The old monometallist policy had been badly dented and bruised between early 1876 and early 1878. But it was still essentially intact. Silver was still not a monetary standard, the green-backs were on their way to par with gold, and the government was going to repay its bonds at par in gold. In some ways, soft-money had been crushingly defeated. Not only had the concept of irredeemable paper currency been discarded, along with the greenbacker insight that money's form should have nothing to do with its function, but, in addition, silver politics (either free-silverite or international bimetallist) had only confirmed the United States in its commitment to a metallic standard for its money.

Even so, the United States had entertained, in the context of the trans-Atlantic community, heretical notions. Americans would discover this at the international bimetallic conference to which the Bland-Allison Act committed them, and which the government proceeded to arrange in the spring and summer of 1878. International coinage unification, comatose since the early seventies, was about to revive under American therapy. But other countries were to regard the project as quackery.

21

THE INTERNATIONAL

MONETARY CONFERENCE

AT PARIS, 1878

On May 4, 1878, the *Commercial and Financial Chronicle* greeted its readers with an account of the opening of the Paris Universal Exposition of 1878. "The most beautiful of cities, the gayest of capitals, put on its best attire," enthused the watchdog of monetary sobriety; such occasions "cannot be too often repeated, if they shall hasten the reign of universal brotherhood." Expensive though they may be, the cost "will not be grudged, if they help to secure for us . . . the poet's dream—'The parliament of Man. the federation of the world'."

Despite the devastations of war and depression, Republican France was giving the world an even more glorious Exposition than Imperial France had done eleven years before. The intervening years had left their mark—the Tuileries Palace had largely disappeared, and the Communards had burned down the Ministry of Finance—but the Hotel of the Tuileries Gardens on the

Rue de Rivoli, where Sherman stayed in 1867, still ranked as a first-class hotel, better in Baedeker's opinion than the Meurice or the Windsor, and the new Exposition covered not only all the space occupied by the old one, but sprawled across the Pont d'Iena as far as the Place du Trocadero on the *rive droite*. There a grand new Exposition building, the present Palais de Chaillot, accommodated a full twenty per cent more exhibitors than Napoléon III's last Exposition. The French recovery had been incredible, discomfiting the Germans and amazing everyone else. The trumpets of the Third Republic were blowing louder and more firmly than those that had sounded the thrilling imperial fanfares of 1867, and for the edification of the serious-minded, the French were even playing host to another International Monetary Conference.

But history was not easily reversed. The glitter of the Exposition could not entirely wipe away recent memories, and the only euphoria that was to pervade the Monetary Conference of 1878 came not on the wings of Parisian summer breezes, but was imported by the American delegation in their diplomatic baggage. It did not travel well.[1]

The United States had not allowed the international coinage unification idea to languish entirely during the seventies, and from time to time Sherman and others made efforts in the direction of unification, particularly with the British. But even these abortive moves had a crabbed quality. Sherman seemed to have rejected the universalism of the old Ruggles plan in favor of an Anglo-Saxonist idea, according to which "the English-speaking races are to become predominant in civilized society throughout the world, while the Latin peoples, to whom mainly the franc basis is confined, are stationary." The preliminary arrangements for the 1878 Conference did not even consider the idea of an international coinage unit, the major aim of the 1867 Conference, until the British said it was the only ground upon which they could attend. The United States, anxious to settle upon an international bimetallic ratio, was the instigator of the 1878 Conference, and the only country optimistic about it. Nearly everyone else had serious misgivings. Britain and the Scandinavian countries gave no sign of budging from gold monometallism, the

Latin Union was disenchanted with silver, and the Germans saw no reason to attend at all. Months before the Conference began, Americans, bristling with defensiveness, were protesting that they sought a bimetallic ratio to help the whole world, not just to get the Bland bill through Congress.[2]

The major European monetary powers were going their separate ways, none of which were America's. Britain had adopted a practical policy of "imperial bimetallism"—gold for herself, silver for India—and if British delegates could attend an International Monetary Conference without giving the impression that Albion would change her domestic standard, attend they would. The British minister in Washington had warned the Foreign Office that British holders of United States government bonds might suffer if the Bland bill passed, but the Foreign Office felt that this was none of their official business; accommodating the India Office, on the other hand, was. The India Office wanted Britain to participate in the "Conference on the subject of a Bimetallic Currency," so British delegates went to Paris. From the start, however, they had no intention of formalizing a bimetallic treaty.[3]

Germany would not even go that far. Bismarck was too busy playing the "honest broker" to become involved in any monetary tinkering with *Nationalökonomie*, and with a sizable stock of silver still to dispose of, he preferred to stay clear of a Conference or treaties that might limit his freedom of action.[4]

In France, Esquirou de Parieu and other monometallists were battling as vehemently as ever against the "retrograde" and evil system of bimetallism. Government policy, however, was not in their hands. The conservative bimetallist, Léon Say, was directing French public finance with the same firmness under the newly elected Gambetta that he had done under MacMahon, and Say considered that the condition of the Latin Monetary Union and of silver itself was too shaky to permit any sudden moves on his part. Anti-silver sentiment was stronger in the Latin Union than it had ever been, and with the Latin Union Treaty up for renewal in late 1878, Say judged a vigorous stand for bimetallism to be inopportune. On January 28, 1878, the same day that the

United States House of Representatives passed the Matthews Resolution declaring public bonds payable in silver dollars, Say asked the Chamber of Deputies to suspend the coinage of five-franc silver pieces for another fourteen months. Say made it perfectly clear, as he had in 1876 and 1874, that the silver suspension did not mean a permanent hostility toward silver; France was still committed to bimetallism in principle. But it was inexpedient, he said, to coin silver until events showed clearly whether silver had a viable future as a monetary standard. The Chamber and Senate gave Say the further suspension he wanted.[5]

The United States was without allies from the very beginning. Nevertheless, the Hayes Administration proceeded to bring people to the conference table, as the Bland-Allison Act directed. The Germans declined the invitation flatly, and the British accepted with the discouraging comment that "H.M. Government are unable to hold out the slightest prospect that England will depart from the policy in respect to currency questions which she has pursued for sixty years," but since the situation was otherwise in some of H.M.'s other dominions, there might be some profit in discussing the silver question. Hayes got an appropriation from Congress and sent three American Commissioners and a secretary trudging bravely off to Paris.

The Commissioners found Paris a lonelier place by far than Samuel Ruggles and John Sherman had found it in 1867. They undoubtedly expected this even before they left, since the press clearly did. The *Commercial and Financial Chronicle* did not expect that the results of the Conference, even if there were any, would be acceptable to the United States, while the *Nation* remarked resignedly that "Our only escape from silver depreciation and silver monometallism is international bimetallism." The *New York Times* misapprehended the situation completely, running an editorial entitled "Promoting the Federation of the World," in which it seemed to think that the Conference was about to agree on an international gold metric coinage unit, which would be a good thing, benefiting all trading nations and helping inculcate "true notions of the nature and purposes of money." The editor of the Topeka *Commonwealth,* who was planning a junket to the Paris Exposition and was so excited about it that he filled dozens of columns with advice on "How to Get to Paris," perhaps made the wisest, if most innocent, comment when he advised American tourists not to bring silver to Paris. Europeans "won't touch it," he warned; "they know it is not what it purports to be on its face." The American Commissioners were soon to find out how true that was.[6]

Even Ernest Seyd was not sanguine about the Conference, and gloomily warned Francis Walker that if Britain would not guarantee the future of the silver standard in India, "both France and the United States would do better to abandon silver." The fact of the matter was that as the International Monetary Conference of 1878 opened, the American proposal of a treaty to establish a worldwide gold-silver ratio had no support and no real hope of success. The major nations simply had different problems and different policies than they had in 1867. The United States was pleading for international bimetallism, not the universal gold standard. Germany, having switched from silver to gold, would not even attend. Britain no longer urged the rest of the world to adopt gold monometallism but would not commit herself in a treaty to the "imperial bimetallism" she was practicing. France had cast down the monometallists from their seats of power, but could do no more for silver than "wait and see." The other nations, like the United States in its domestic affairs, had moved away from gold toward silver, but they could not, or would not, give silver full monetary status. Economic nationalism, not the optimistic, liberal internationalism of 1867, was the order of the day.[7]

The Americans were hopelessly isolated from the first moments of the Conference, as it opened at the French Ministry of Foreign Affairs on August 10. Incompetent in the French language, unprepared with concrete proposals and documentation on coinage and silver developments, burdened with the palpable fact that a resuscitation of silver was in the American national interest but hardly anyone else's, the American Commissioners got nowhere. Charles Feer-Herzog of Switzerland and George J. Göschen of Britain led the Conference in a thorough squelching of bimetallism, and Léon Say, in the chair, did nothing to stop them, or to ease the Americans' discomfiture. Say did give the Americans a chance to save face by offering to entertain a "factual discussion" on bullion and coinage practices around the world, but the Americans stuck with their request for a bimetallic ratio, thereby choosing death to dishonor. This was unwise. As Feer-Herzog and Göschen leapt on every fuzzy statement and weak argument that the Americans presented, and Fenton and Groesbeck in particular presented many, the Americans and their proposal went down in a blaze of ignominy. The Belgian and Swedish delegates, among others, reverted to the slogans of gold monometallism— "Gold alone responds to the needs of an active circulation and of an advanced civilization"; "Silver remains exclusively the Money of peoples which are backward or stationary"—and the only faintly serious disagreement among the Europeans was whether Germany or somebody else was responsible for the fall in silver prices. Francis Walker and Horton did acquit themselves respectably in a long verbal slugging match with Feer-Herzog, Göschen, and a few of their satellites at the fourth session, on August 22, but no one's position changed.

Groesbeck and Horton made a final effort at the fifth session to rejuvenate the Conference by lengthy set-pieces on the virtues of international bimetallism. Groesbeck even produced a letter from John Sherman, written in July, in which Sherman ruefully admitted that although he had supported gold at the 1867 Conference, "At that time the wisest among us did not anticipate the sudden fall of Silver or the rise of Gold [!] that has occurred." The economic dangers of dropping silver, Sherman claimed, outweighed "all theoretical objections" to bimetallism, and he hoped the Conference would set a gold-silver ratio. But either Groesbeck was no Ruggles, or the world was not prepared; Sherman's letter was not the bombshell that his 1867 letter had been. The Europeans were not moved.

Finally, on August 28, Léon Say observed that discussion on the American proposal seemed to have ended, and he recessed the meeting for forty-five minutes "in order that the Delegates of the other States might agree among themselves as to the collective answer which they might wish to make." The Americans were utterly alone. The European delegates returned with a blank refusal to consider an international gold-silver ratio; each nation had to set its own monetary standard according to its "special situation." Complete failure. Fenton replied formally that, as for monetary standards, "We remain upon ours; the European states upon theirs."[8]

The Swiss and British official reports were even less friendly than the Conference discussions themselves. Feer-Herzog called the whole affair an attempt by the United States to secure international approbation for the policies of the repudiationist majority that had taken over the country. Silver was nothing but a device to escape paying government bonds at full value. American greenbackism was no better than German socialism. The British report, one-twentieth as long as the British report on the 1867 Conference, dealt summarily and sarcastically with the American proposal; the Americans were simply interested in protecting their domestic silver product.

Horton's report to the United States Congress put a very different face on the Conference, and laid blame for its admitted failure on "the delicate relations, political and financial, of the Latin Union." But this was of little help. As the *Commercial and Financial Chronicle* remarked, "The International Monetary Conference has met and adjourned. What else it has accomplished it would be quite difficult to state."[9]

Practically its only accomplishment, in fact, was to provide a yardstick on the progress of economic nationalism since 1867. Nations in a common civilization, a common money market, and with common monetary ideologies, had fragmented just as economic, ideological, and sectional groups were fragmenting within the United States. Whatever else might be said about the Monetary Conference of eleven years earlier, it at least demonstrated some unity of purpose among the major nations. By 1878, such unity, and the notion of international amity, hardly received so much as lip service. The post-1873 depression had had effects on international relations that were no happier than its effects on intergroup relations within the United States.

There, tensions continued despite the imminence of specie resumption and the lifting of the depression. A House committee began hearings in the late summer of 1878 to discover why the "labor and productive interests of the country, [who are the] source of all wealth," were so badly depressed. The election campaign of 1878 brought organized greenbackism, in the form of the National party, more support at the polls than it had ever enjoyed, and more than a dozen greenback Congressmen were elected to the next Congress with soft-money business, farmer, and labor votes.[10]

But the soft-money people were too late to stop specie resumption. John Sherman resolutely continued to accumulate a gold reserve at the Treasury through surplus revenue and the sale of bonds, and when resumption day came, the Treasury's reserve equalled almost 40 per cent of the outstanding greenbacks. The peculiar character of the post-1873 depression in America, which brought a favorable trade balance and increased manufacturing, would have made specie resumption likely regardless of what Sherman did, but in any event, the gold premium disappeared on December 17, 1878, to the rejoicing of the financial community and much of the general press. A labor journal carped that specie payments would not last, and suspension would again occur, to the great embarrassment of the whole country. But nothing of the sort happened. The United States, after seventeen years' experience with inconvertible paper currency, returned to the "fixed standard" and "universal law of value."[11]

Sixteen silver bills faced the final session of the stormy Forty-fifth Congress, but every one of them died. So did the bill to repeal the Specie Resumption Act, snuffed out belatedly in the House on February 22, 1879, on a tabling motion by James A. Garfield, the next President of the United States. The new Congress convened in March. It killed the trade dollar, and the House passed a free-silver bill in May; but the Senate let it lie. The struggle over the money question in America was jerking to a stop.

Prosperity started to return in early 1879, and with it came a semblance of the social tranquillity of pre-1873 days. But events had happened that the country could not forget; the clock would not turn back. The *Banker's Magazine* explained its support of international bimetallism as "an antidote to the poison of 'Greenback' paper theories and . . . one of the defenses of the National-bank system," and with this announcement, international bimetallism had clearly taken the place of gold monometallism as the ideology of American monetary conservatives. Free silver, on the other hand, was replacing greenbackism on the left. At the same time, the old sectional and economic divisions within American society, instead of disappearing, had rearranged themselves into new and ominous dualisms pitting capital against labor, debtors against creditors, haves against have-nots.

Abroad, the Latin Union renewed itself for another six years at a conference in Paris in the fall of 1878, but it stopped coining silver almost completely. In May 1879, Bismarck suspended Germany's silver sales. France and the United States jointly convoked another International Monetary Conference at Paris in 1881, to protect silver; Germany and India managed to attend; but the results were no better than in 1878. International coinage, the universal adoption of the metric system, and international monetary harmony, those noble dreams of 1867, had disappeared as surely and finally as the inconvertible greenback, intergroup harmony, the silver standard, and the old liberalism in America. America and the West were backing their way toward the twentieth century.[12]

PART SIX

Postscript

The historian must doubt the possibility of having capitalism without gold fetishism in some form or other.

NORMAN O. BROWN, *Life Against Death*

22

THE MONEY QUESTION

AS A

SOCIAL AND MORAL CUL-DE-SAC

The history of the money question in the West in the 1860's and seventies is a tale fraught with portents and ironies. Now that we know the events of the succeeding fifty years, we can see how the period had a tragic aura not sensed by its participants.

The contrasts between the International Monetary Conferences of 1867 and 1878 were sharp, unpleasant, and discouraging. The internationalistic liberalism of 1867 led not into a golden age of accomplished progress, but into suspicious economic nationalism. The sheen of early Victorian optimism tarnished, the liberal-mechanistic world-view no longer dominated. Trends within the United States paralleled these trends among the nations, and above them all, in America, stood the shift from the rhetoric of social harmony in the first half of the period to the rhetoric of social combat in the second. The reversal was not absolute. Yet a subtle change distinctly took place, with 1873 the year of passage. Obviously the development of the money question in those days cannot fully explain World War I, the Depression of the 1930's, or the continuing failure to come to terms rationally with the international trends of urbanization and industrialization. Obviously too, the rhetoric of harmony still had its spokesmen long after the fragmentations of the seventies.[1] But in this period, with regard to money, the men of the West failed to comprehend and resolve a problem of crucial significance. In this period they began to lose the opportunity to create for themselves, by rational choice, individual and collective self-images adequate to their changing environment.

The money question in America, where the issue was in many ways most vividly joined, developed as it did in large part because of chance, ignorance, and changing rhetoric. There was a large element of the fortuitous in the history of the question from 1865 to 1879, and one wonders whether it would have become as pressing if, for example, India had not had a famine in 1874 which lowered her demand for silver; or if Jay Cooke had not become over-involved in Northern Pacific bonds; or if Bismarck had decided to fight German particularism by some device other than gold monometallism; or if gold and silver had been discovered simultaneously rather than consecutively in Western America. A host of unrelated personal decisions, from California to Berlin, in fact, everywhere that an American voter helped send to Congress someone slightly more convinced of the need to protect investor confidence and the public credit than to promote liquidity, converged to create the history of the money question. Examples of contributing forces abound. Free choice and circumstance created individual decisions; but chance governed their confluence.

As for ignorance, there are plenty of examples of that too. What one hard-money man believed in as "the magistral economic science of the day" has now been consigned in bulk to the ash-heap of outworn theories, but in that day it was attractive and powerful. John Sherman did not seem to observe that his sale of resumption bonds made resumption harder, not easier, by raising the demand for gold. Contractionists who in the early seventies laughed at the idea that the trade needs of a growing country might very well absorb any "redundancy" in greenback currency were proved wrong within half a decade. Gold mono-metallists who insisted that deflation was socially better than in-flation, and who claimed that drops in money supply did not affect value since prices and wages dropped also, ignored the ob-vious corollary that if this was true, increases in money supply should not have affected values either. Inconvertible paper and noncurrency money such as checks, deposits, and clearing-house certificates, which were growing in use, if anything made pro-duction easier and lightened the depression burden in the United States and France, compared to specie-paying Britain and Ger-many. Many people ignored the evidence of their own eyes that the greenbacks helped insulate the United States from external fluctuations and stimulated domestic enterprise. Even Edward Atkinson recognized that the United States' separation of its domestic and foreign exchanges might have had great advantages, but his bullionist commitment prevented him from accepting, perhaps from even seeing, this conclusion. People in all sections of the United States consistently refused to recognize that money had long since become something a great deal more than currency alone; yet the South and the West, where the two terms actually did mean much the same thing since noncurrency money was much scarcer there than in the Northeast, were damned as im-moral for suggesting that money ought to be in greater supply.

On the other side, inflationists found it extremely difficult to grasp the importance of investor confidence for an economy whose expansion depended on large importations of foreign capital. People who attributed the fall of silver after 1873 to the inexorable workings of supply and demand refused to admit that government policies had assisted the decline in demand, whereas vast gold increases after 1848 had scarcely affected the parity ratio at all. Both sides were altogether too willing to accept con-spiracy and malevolence as governing motives in the explanation of events. Both were too prone to explain economic phenomena dogmatically.

But the most staggering example of what, in today's view, must be written off as ignorance, was the confusion by so many people of the form of money with its functions. Money, they said, had to be metallic, intrinsically valuable, and universally negotiable. Greenbacks were none of these. Thus they were not money, despite the evidence that stared people in the face that they did function successfully as money in domestic exchanges. If the economist Joseph Schumpeter had announced in 1870, as he was to do in 1939, that the tying of money to any sort of commodity basis, gold or otherwise, was not only unnecessary to its functioning but also harmful, he would have been relegated to the ranks of the radical greenbackers. Only the greenbackers understood what Schumpeter later stated, that money was not subject to supply and demand in anything like the way that commodities were, and that production, not money, really counted. One can only guess how John Sherman might have reacted to President Kennedy talking not of valuing the dollar in terms of gold, but of valuing gold in terms of the dollar. It was a pity that this greenbacker insight was swallowed up in the comparatively retrograde ideology of free silver. It was also an irony that the most vocal claimants to producerism both in the seventies and the nineties made money their chief programmatic reform.[2]

The temptation to blame policy-makers for corruption and economic groups of selfishness, in the face of these anomalies, is great. But no one can know what little acts of intellectual dishonesty or failure of nerve they may have involved. It is beyond belief that none occurred. Yet it is just as absurd to believe that they *always* occurred: it must never be forgotten that each interest, each ideology, each rhetoric, each world-view, had a plausibility and self-consistency that made it altogether possible for large masses of people to proceed (divergently) in what each group believed to be the path of righteousness. When hard-money men accused greenbackers and silverites of attempt to commit fraud, and the latter accused gold monometallists of conspiracy, they all meant it, unfortunately for both of them. All of them, so much the worse for the next two or three generations, were people in the grip of theories, dooming each other to discuss their society, what it meant and where it was going, on the basis of an increasingly irrelevant issue.

Social fragmentation afflicted America, and possibly the other major nations, during those years, as the money question became more and more important. Previously thin cracks among groups widened into major cleavages. For example, what had formerly been slight variations in emphasis with regard to the broadly held producer philosophy became points of departure for exclusive claims, the differences eclipsing the common points. Harmony formerly felt among manufacturing and laboring interests evaporated into a fog of mistrust. A view of society in which several large economic groups were understood to share common goals, and work with each other toward civilized progress, began to polarize into a dualistic social interpretation opposing capital versus labor, and debtors versus creditors, as farmer and labor groups moved toward the debtor side, manufacturers toward the creditor-capitalist side. Careyism became an anachronism, useful only as a weapon. Contention overrode harmony, society was splitting, ugly querulousness impregnated America's view of itself. But when the period ended, no one seemed able to create a new social synthesis. The first one was faulty and weak. But Americans, for lack of a real substitute, caught within the confining walls of the prevailing rhetoric, condemned themselves to repeat their mistakes. They had created a view of society in which the money question was the operative center. This view they found wanting, but they could not throw it aside for a better one.

For reasons such as these, American society was perhaps the most interesting, at least at a good distance, of all the economically powerful Western nations of the time. It was the only one, for example, in which a radically dissident group came near to controlling monetary legislation even briefly, and as a consequence was the only one where the argument about the form and function of money became public.

Another product of the unlovely social changes of the time was the now-familiar "conservative" rhetoric of *laissez faire* and "free enterprise." As Samuel Rezneck has pointed out, such voices as E. L. Godkin, William Graham Sumner, and Abram Hewitt began, just then, to talk of how government assistance reduced the self-reliance of the lower classes, and how these classes had themselves to blame for their troubles because they were extravagant and lacked thrift. Such notions were not wholly new, but wide acceptance of them and their easy replacement of the rhetoric of "harmony" were. Meanwhile, laboring groups, farmers (for the first time), and others created a monetary and social rhetoric of their own which had little in common with "orthodox" opinion, much less than their rhetoric had had in previous years, and which was far more a weapon for change in their own behalf.[3]

The monetary and political arguments of the late sixties and early seventies had little in common with those of the Populist period. But there is much resemblance between the arguments of the middle and late seventies, and those of the Populist period. The shape of the money question in the late nineteenth century —the class antagonisms, the main lines of argument on both sides, the very terminology—crystallized in the period of stress from 1873 into 1879.

Thus by 1879 the society had polarized. On one side were the monometallists, the conservative international bimetallists, the commercial-banking-manufacturing capitalists, situated often in the Northeast or the older Middle West, all of them talking more and more in the new conservative rhetoric whose terms were *laissez faire*, private property, survival of the fittest, sanctity of contract, communist agitator, inflationary madness. On the other were greenbackers and free-silverites, farmers, labor, a dwindling number of manufacturers (usually from the Midwest or South), all crying of the bullying, bloated bondholders, the Crime of '73, the producing classes' need to be eternally vigilant against creditor-capitalist oppression. When the money question subsided in 1879, as prosperity, specie payments, and a modicum of silver returned, the earlier victories of the gold monometallists had been ended, but not reversed, and rhetoric had deteriorated from a system of potential social intercommunication to the reflex slogans of group self-protection. The money question turned Arcadia into a battlefield.

By 1879, the question had exhausted itself of any possibility of providing a productive meeting point upon which groups could attempt to convince each other of their points of view. But because the two sides were almost equally strong, neither could win a clearcut victory, nor would they compromise. Rational decisions did not emerge; hence 1879 brought not peace, but a truce, and America condemned herself to continue the war when the next depression reintroduced campaign conditions. The rhetoric of the second phase of the money question was already available and operative by 1879. It was in the late seventies that terms such as "goldbug" and "money power" first appeared in post-Civil War circumstances, and in 1872 that William D. Kelley gave the country a preview of the Populist spell-binder, Mary Elizabeth Lease, when he railed at British monetary influence, "The powers that ruled us were the monopoly that has made a hell of Ireland, and of India!" Senators William A. Peffer, the Kansas Populist, and Henry Teller, the Colorado Silver Republican, said nothing new in 1893 when they claimed that the "moneyed centers" and not the "productive agencies of this country" wanted silver purchases ended. On the other side, the argument that the silver dollar was a "debased" dollar and a cheat, and that its free coinage "at its intrinsic value" would hurl the country onto silver monometallism, changed in only one detail between the late seventies and 1893: silver had dropped even further in gold prices. Thus William McKinley talked of "fifty-three cent dollars" in the campaign of 1896, when he ran for President on an international-bimetallist platform against the free-silverite William Jennings Bryan.

The conservatism of McKinley's position was already conservative in the late seventies. During the 1896 campaign, the secretary of the London Bimetallic League wrote Francis Amasa Walker that "our Cause—the Cause of International Bimetallism, & of a stable par of exchange,—is best secured by Major McKinley," whom he hoped would not be captured by the "extreme gold monometallists of New York," nor, of course, the country by the free-silverites. "Anarchist" and "communist" were epithets often hurled by monetary conservatives against Populists in the nineties, but they were not new either. In the index to Henry Varnum Poor's book on the money question, published in 1878, there was the entry, "Greenback Party. See Communists." Horace White could still chant the bullionist litany in 1896 with all its old incantations of "natural evolution beneficial to all classes," "progress," the pleasure-pain principle, "the monetary standard of Christendom" (shades of Samuel B. Ruggles!), the creditor and debtor classes.

The issues and the problems of the nineties, of course, were hardly the same as those of the seventies. Industrialization, class relations, the growth of cities, business consolidation, and the perennial concerns of social organization had become knottier. But, more's the pity, rhetoric and group self-images had not shifted accordingly. Consequently, these new difficulties were not likely to be solved, especially in a rhetorical contest that had failed to resolve anything fifteen to twenty years before. In broad terms, a legacy of social interpretation was bequeathed by the Reconstruction period to the rest of the nineteenth century, and here the Civil War and its aftermath laid a dead hand on American society very perduringly.

Very seldom were there signs that these rhetorical sets were breakable. A very occasional commentator could point out common ground between the contending parties, as the editorialist of the *New York Commercial Bulletin* did in 1879 when he showed how inflationists and contractionists alike believed in the quantity theory, or when Willard Fisher in 1896 criticized *both* Coin Harvey and J. Laurence Laughlin for wasting time on how many cubic feet of bullion there were in the world or what the 1792 Coinage Act had said about gold and silver, while they ignored questions such as whether silver had actually depreciated or gold had risen, what the true relation was between prices and money, what effect "money substitutes" had on prices, and so forth.

The last time that questions like these had been asked in a remotely serious way in a politically responsible setting was in the hearings of the Monetary Commission of 1876. By 1879—to say nothing of 1896—serious discussion of them was inadmissible either to the free silver or the international-bimetallist side. Theoretical political economy was even narrower in the nineties than twenty years earlier, when Careyism still claimed some respect. Despite a few forward steps, such as a certain acceptance of the idea that values might be measured in a range of commodities rather than in bullion, the academic and respectable political economists of the nineties talked of free silver and greenbackism as apocalyptic madness.

This by no means ended in 1900. Even today, one occasionally reads of "greenback fallacies" and "soft-money delusions" despite the not very obscure fact that, for decades, the United States and every other major industrial country have used domestic money systems constituted of credit devices and inconvertible paper. They have even done so for many international exchanges as well.[4]

The attachment of people to gold monometallism and its erstwhile *Doppelgänger*, international bimetallism, did not really end until society not only arrived at new political combinations and new economic and financial relationships, but also revised its rhetoric and its patterns of thought. The gold standard had once been a liberal and progressive step in international payments, finance, and the technology of economic activity in general; but its progressiveness did not outlast the mid-nineteenth century. When Ruggles, Sherman, Esquirou de Parieu, the Germans, and the British in 1867 proclaimed universal gold monometallism to be the money of the future and the key to a healthy and harmonious world civilization, their statements were hyperbolic, but still had some connection with reality. With the growth in size of international and internal payments, paralleling growth in industrial output, silver really did become less useful, and as long as it was assumed that money had to be metallic, the use of gold understandably increased. In the mid-nineteenth century, when nonmetallic reserve currencies like the present Euro-dollar and Euro-sterling were undreamt of, the international gold standard could reasonably be interpreted as a forward step for civilization.

The trouble was that when industrial and commercial development progressed still further, demanding wider use of nonmetallic forms of credit and money for large payments, gold was still thought of as progressive. The more that gold monometallism was attacked by men and events, the more tenaciously it was maintained, even in the face of the obvious fact that the total and per-capita money stock of the United States steadily and rapidly rose from 1867 to 1900, while the per-capita stock of metallic money grew not at all. Gold was not up to handling unsupported the monetary needs of the country after the Civil War. Its adoption was once a step forward, a very short one, in the machinery of world finance. Yet hard-money men defended it stoutly, more devotedly even in the nineties, when there was less ground for it, than they had from 1865 to 1879.

The hard-money viewpoint rested at least as much upon a mechanistic and deterministic world-view as it did on the realities of exchange. Attacks only hardened the devotion of the gold monometallists and conservative bimetallists to their belief that economic laws were simple and inexorable. Logically there was a contradiction between this attachment to pre-determined laws like supply and demand on the one hand, and *laissez faire* liberalism with its roots in free-will doctrines on the other, but the contradiction did not trouble these people in practice. The laws were relatively few and very certain, and real freedom consisted in understanding them and staying within the limits they prescribed. There was no freedom in disobeying the laws of Nature. Such was social Newtonism. Darwinian or other evolutionary doctrines should have shaken these verities, and indeed they were to be thus shaken later. But in the third quarter of the century, they provoked very little sense of relativism and change. Instead, at first, they were simply assimilated into the mechanistic view, "evolution" becoming a law of progress very little different *as a kind of law* from the supply-and-demand law or the law of free economic action itself. Only later would evolutionary views threaten such certainties, and not until the certainties had begun to crack under the force of other events.

After McKinley defeated Bryan in 1896, the event which meant the final defeat of free silver by gold monometallism and international bimetallism, the money question lost its fighting edge, its power to draw the country into ideological civil war along its narrow grounds. There are several obvious reasons for this: the end of the depression of the nineties and the resulting reduction in soft-money pressure, as in 1879; the gold discoveries made shortly after 1896; the fact that Bryan's defeat was sufficiently decisive to indicate that free silver was not likely to elect a President; the business consolidations of the late nineties, which helped channel monetary producerism into anti-monopoly producerism; and changes in the structure of social and economic groups through the long-term impact of economic and demographic changes.

Another reason for the demise of the money question was at least as important as any of these: because the defeat of free silver in 1896 seemed to assure the continued existence of the gold standard, i.e., civilization, the compulsive character of the rhetorical debate of the previous quarter-century disappeared with the end of soft-money pressure. The tension was broken, the armies could demobilize, the whole problem could recede to the level of administrative technicality. With the end of the second phase of the post-Civil War money question, the rhetorical battlecries of the seventies and nineties were by then so far from corresponding to pressing needs that the mass of people were not going to respond again. There was not going to be a third phase. Money was a policy problem did indeed continue into the days of the National Monetary Commission, the Pujo Committee investigation of 1911–13, the establishment of the Federal Reserve System under President Wilson, and into the New Deal; in 1932, in the next depression, Winston Churchill could again suggest that money was the most critical of the world's problems.[5] But it was not so believed. After 1896, in America, as late nineteenth-century conditions and arguments crumbled, the rhetorics connected to them ceased to captivate the mass of the people.

While it lasted, however, the money question gripped the country like a vise. There were many reasons why it did. Currency did indeed affect everyone in the society. Also, though not every member of society worried about money as a moral question, talked about it, and considered it crucial, opinion leaders and group elites did. Also, it had been a major issue in the late sixties, and had emerged as the last and most difficult problem of the Civil War, except race (successfully shelved), to solve. Also, panic and depression kept it alive after 1873 and worsened it by putting economic stress on every group. Also, people were intrigued by the drama and mystery, the apparent inevitability, of financial crises. The very fact, so often repeated, that money was crucial, helped to make it so. The money question resulted partly from the growing pains of a society as yet innocent of the process and requirements of industrialization. Money concerned directly all the important groups in the social power structure, like the New Yorkers and New Englanders who expounded the ideology of international liberalism and the gold standard when the needs of their own society lay in a different direction. That such policy helped these elites perpetuate themselves was not a matter of conspiracy or conscious plan, but of ignorance and indifference. Greenbacks were untraditional, "unnormal"; with the exception of Careyism, no reputable economic doctrine existed to gainsay the notion that money had to be tangible, hard, and of "intrinsic value." Nor was any political philosophy practically available which systematically justified the national government's playing a positive role in financial affairs.

But most of all, the money question was so gripping because it engaged the contending world-views of the members of society, bringing them into confrontation on the level of rhetoric in a manner which almost unavoidably loaded them down with the weight of moral systems that could not be compromised. Money was critical because it was moral.

Concentration on the money question from 1868 to 1879 supported and nurtured rhetorics which virtually insured that social conflict would recur on much the same terms whenever another economic crisis arrived. This happened ten to fifteen years later. As the money question evolved in its first phase, it worked great social damage because it made alternative policies, for the whole society, difficult to find. The limited bimetallism of the Bland-Allison Act solved nothing except to relieve a little of the political and sectional pressure against the gold standard. International bimetallism simply could not be achieved, because Britain, Germany, and the Latin Union were adamantly against it for particular nationalist reasons. Even if it had been achieved, its effect on the price of silver would have been very doubtful. Free silver would very probably indeed, as its opponents claimed, have driven gold out of circulation, placed the United States for practical purposes on a single silver standard, and made her liable, like India, to the prices other people set for gold. Whether free silver, on the other hand, would really have stimulated production, is questionable. If the United States had kept the greenback standard domestically, perhaps the economy and society would have benefited despite the harm such a policy might have done to the public credit. There were no easy answers, as there never seem to be with money standards, and it would have been miraculous had the men of the 1870's created a thoroughly efficient and socially viable policy.

What is clear, however, is that the money question as it actually developed made even so much as the consideration of reasonable alternatives extremely unlikely. It congealed the traditional commitment to metallic money for domestic as well as international payments at a time when the separation of the form and functions of money first became a glimmering possibility. It congealed the commitment of hard-money men to *laissez-faire,* the rhetoric of civilization, progress, and natural law, and the world-view of mechanistic determinism, and at the same time forced soft-money groups to seek relief in a carping and outworn producerism and a sense of persecution that reality did not justify. The spawn of the money question were hardened rhetoric, class divisions, social antagonism, and the inability to consider a serious, wide, and realistic range of answers to the social concerns of the time.

For a lack of such alternatives, because it allowed itself to become so profoundly involved with the money question, American society threw away whatever opportunity it had to shift smoothly from the preindustrial past into the emerging industrial future. It failed to shape events, and was instead shaped by them. Thus it doomed itself to repeat its own mistakes.

tical purposes on a single silver standard, and made her liable, like India, to the prices other people set for gold. Whether free silver, on the other hand, would really have stimulated production, is questionable. If the United States had kept the greenback standard domestically, perhaps the economy and money would have benefited despite the harm such a policy might have done to the public credit. There were no easy answers, as there never seem to be with money managed, unfit would have been miscalculations had the men of the 1890s created a thoroughly efficient and socially viable policy.

What is clear, however, is that the money question, as it actually developed made even so much in the consideration of reasonable alternatives as extremely, unlikely, it compelled the traditional commitment to healthy money for domestic as well as international payments at a time when the separation of the form and functions of money first became a glimmering possibility. It congealed the commitment to hard money, men to take a very, the rhetoric of civilization, progress, and material law, and the world-view of monopsonous externalism, and at the same time forced old-money people to seek relief in a carping and outworn provincialism, and, a sense of persuasion that reality did not justify. The spawn of the money question were hardened rhetoric, class divisions, social antagonism, and the inability to consider a serious, wider, and realistic range of answers to the social concerns of the time.

For a lack of such alternatives, because it allowed itself to become so profoundly involved with the money question, American society, there were whatever opportunity it had to shift smoothly from the preindustrial past into the emerging industrial future, to relief to shape events, and was instead shaped by them. Thus it doomed itself to repeat its own mistakes.

Notes

Notes.

NOTES

Notes to Chapter 1 (pp 4-15)

1. Robert P. Sharkey, *Money, Class, and Party: An Economic Study of Civil War and Reconstruction* (Baltimore: Johns Hopkins Press, 1959); Irwin Unger, *The Greenback Era: A Social and Political History of American Finance, 1865-1879* (Princeton: Princeton University Press, 1964). Also, Stanley Coben, "Northeastern Business and Radical Reconstruction: A Re-examination," *Mississippi Valley Historical Review*, XLVI (June 1959), 67-90; Irwin Unger, "Business Men and Specie Resumption," *Political Science Quarterly*, LXXIV (March 1959), 46-70; Unger, "The Business Community and the Origins of the 1875 Resumption Act," *Business History Review*, XXXV (Summer 1961), 247-62.

For the more strictly economic history of the period, see Wesley C. Mitchell, *Gold, Prices, and Wages under the Greenback Standard* (University of California Publications in Economics, I; Berkeley: The University Press, 1908); Willard L. Thorp, *Business Annals* (New York: National Bureau of Economic Research, Inc., 1926); James K. Kindahl, "The Economics of Specie Resumption: The United States, 1865-1879," unpublished Ph.D. dissertation, Department of Economics, University of Chicago, 1958; Milton Friedman and Anna Jacobson Schwartz, *A Monetary History of the United States, 1867-1960* (Princeton: Published by Princeton University Press for the National Bureau of Economic Research, Inc., 1963); Warren M. Persons *et al.*, "Business and Financial Conditions following the Civil War in the United States," *The Review of Economic Statistics*, Supplement, Preliminary Volume 2 (1920), 1-55.

Note to Chapter 3

1. This is not far from the definition given by Joseph La Palombara, *Interest Groups in Italian Politics* (Princeton: Princeton University

Press, 1964), pp. 15–18. Pp. 13–26 of that book contain a very succinct and useful statement of present day interest-group theory.

Notes to Chapter 4

1. London *Economist*, September 15, 1866, p. 1078; Michel Chevalier, "De l'Etablissement d'une Monnaie universelle," *Journal des Economistes*, XII (3d series; November 1868), 210; Wolowski, *L'Or et L'Argent* (Paris: Librairie de Guillaumin et Cie, 1870), pp. 17–18, 33.

2. Wolowski address, *passim*, at the June 5, 1867, meeting of the Paris Société d'Economie Politique, as reported in *Journal des Economistes*, VI (3d series; June 1867); Gamaliel Bradford in *North American Review*, January 1870, 209, 215; Francis Bowen, *American Political Economy: including Strictures on the Management of the Currency and the Finances since 1861* (New York: Charles Scribner's Sons, 1870), pp. iii–iv, 18–21; Edward C. Kirkland, *Business in the Gilded Age: The Conservative's Balance Sheet* (Madison: University of Wisconsin Press, 1952), *passim;* Robert G. McCloskey, *American Conservatism in the Age of Enterprise* (Cambridge: Harvard University Press, 1951), pp. 170–71; Gottfried von Haberler, *The Theory of International Trade* (London: William Hodge & Company, Limited, 1950), p. 26; Joseph Dorfman, *The Economic Mind in American Civilization* (New York: The Viking Press, 1949), iii: 49–50.

3. See for example the statements of David J. King, a Boston manufacturer, and H. H. Bryant, a Boston wholesale merchant, in *HED* 5, 46:2 (November 1879), pp. 396, 399; William A. Berkey (a Michigan manufacturer, and a greenbacker), *The Money Question* (Grand Rapids: W. W. Hard, Steam Book and Job Printer, 1876), p. 345; *Banker's Magazine*, December 1878, 422 (an editorial). Don C. Barrett, writing from as unflinchingly a hard-money position as Hugh McCulloch had done sixty-five years earlier, thought prices and money quantity corresponded remarkably during the "greenback period" (*The Greenbacks and the Resumption of Specie Payments,, 1862–1879* [Cambridge: Harvard University Press, 1931], pp. 104–06). Today the "quantity theory," in its strict formulation according to which changes in prices and money quantity are supposed to relate exactly, is seldom held, but in the vaguer sense that a decrease in money supply leads to some lowering of prices, it is difficult to argue with; see Haberler, *op. cit.*, p. 28. It should be added that it is hardly ever thought of today without three refinements: that the velocity with which money circulates is as important a variable as the quantity itself; that money means not only cur-

rency but various forms of credit such as checks and bank deposits as well; and that since the sources of these are very numerous and their amount is fluid, it is hard to speak of money having a definite "quantity" at all. In the 1860's and 70's, these refinements were seldom understood, and when they were, it was usually by the economically "unorthodox."

Also, New York Daily Commercial Bulletin, *The Money Question: A Series of Editorial Articles published in the New York Daily Commercial Bulletin of March . . . 1879 . . .* (n.p., 1879), pp. 5, 10, 16, 19–20, 23.

4. The term appeared in New Orleans publications of the time, with reference to staple growers. Also, see the dedications in Jonathan Periam, *The Groundswell: A History of the Origin, Aims, and Progress of the Farmers' Movement* (Cincinnati: E. Hannaford & Company, 1874), p. 5, and John G. Wells, *The Grange Illustrated; or Patron's Handbook* (New York: Grange Publishing Co., 1874), p. v; *Commercial and Financial Chronicle,* April 16, 1870.

5. Speech of General S. F. Cary, late in 1868, in *Workingman's Advocate* (Chicago), December 18, 1869; Campbell's call for Labor Reform Party meeting at Bloomington, Illinois, in *ibid.,* January, 12–20, 1872; Sylvis in *ibid.,* May 20, 1871; Chicago *Industrial Age,* August 20, 1873.

6. Kirkland, *Business in the Gilded Age,* p. 51; Hugh McCulloch to Winslow, Lanier & Co., Treasury Department, March 28, 1867, in McCulloch papers, Lilly Library of Indiana University; *Banker's Magazine,* March 1872, 657–58, 663–66; Simon Newcomb, *A Critical Examination of our Financial Policy during the Southern Rebellion* (New York: D. Appleton and Company, 1865), pp. 79–8; Amasa Walker in *Banker's Magazine,* March 1867, 725–38; Poor, *Resumption and the Silver Question* (New York: H. V. and H. W. Poor, 68 Broadway, 1878), p. iii and chapter 1 *passim;* Sharkey, *Money, Class, and Party,* pp. 165–66, 207.

7. *Industrial Age,* October 25, 1873, commenting on the opening of the Chicago meeting of the National Board of Trade; compare with its views of a few months earlier toward business groups. Also, *Senate Report* 703, 44:2, pp. 3–4 (response of Henry C. Carey), 360–63 (testimony of Thurlow Weed).

Notes to Chapter 5

1. See, for example, *Banker's Magazine,* December 1866, 464–65, reprinting from the *Economist* of September 1866.

2. For a discussion of Utilitarian political economy (especially Ricardo, John Stuart Mill, and J. R. MacCulloch), and its links with the

Newtonian outlook, see Elie Halévy, *The Growth of Philosophic Radicalism* (London: Faber & Faber Limited, 1934), pp. 6, 478.

3. Walker, *The Science of Wealth: A Manual of Political Economy, Embracing the Laws of Trade, Currency, and Finance* (Boston: Little, Brown and Company, 1866), p. 131. Also, Simon Newcomb, *Critical Examination,* p. 118.

4. Hugh McCulloch, in *HED* 2, 40:2, pp. ix, xliii; Walker, *op. cit.,* book III, p. 3; Hooper to Charles Sumner, Washington, March 26, 1865, in John Bright papers, Add. Mss. 43390, British Museum.

5. Francis Bowen, *American Political Economy,* pp. 238, 248–49; Samuel Hooper, *Currency or Money* (Boston: Little, Brown and Company, 1855), p. 7; Newcomb, *Critical Examination,* p. 109; Henry R. Linderman (director of the Philadelphia Mint during much of this period, and, as later chapters will show, a key monetary policy-maker), *Money and Legal Tender in the United States* (New York: G. P. Putnam's Sons, 1878), pp. 103–04; M. Richard Leverson, "On the Uses and Functions of Money," *Banker's Magazine,* February 1868, 601–18.

6. Newcomb, *Critical Examination,* p. 118; *Senate Report* 117, 40:2, p.7.

7. McCulloch to Henry C. Carey, Treasury Department, July 6, 1865, and other letters from McCulloch to, e.g., Edward Atkinson, David A. Wells, E. H. Derby, Pliny Freeman, George Opdyke, Joseph Wharton, in McCulloch papers, Lilly Library of Indiana University; Amasa Walker to McCulloch, North Brookfield, Mass., February 4, 1867, in McCulloch papers, Library of Congress; Newcomb in *North American Review,* July 1870, 127, 139, 150, 153, wherein he urged laborers to study Bastiat and learn that society is naturally harmonious; Newcomb, *The ABC of Finance* (New York: Harper & Brothers, Publishers, 1878), pp. 1–36.

8. Henry C. Carey, *Money: a lecture delivered before the New York Geographical and Statistical Society* ("reprinted from the Merchants' Magazine for April 1857"; New York: Press of Hunt's Merchants' Magazine, 1857), pp. 4, 8, 25, 28, and *passim;* A. D. H. Kaplan, *Henry Charles Carey: A Study in American Economic Thought* (Baltimore: The Johns Hopkins Press, 1931), pp. 54–55, 58–62.

9. "Henry Charles Carey, *Dictionary of American Biography,* iii: 487–89; "Henry Carey Baird," *ibid.,* i: 510; Baird, *John Sherman: a Critical Examination of his Claims to Statesmanship* (Philadelphia: Henry Carey Baird & Co., 1907), p. 4; Malcolm R. Eiselen, *The Rise of Pennsylvania Protectionism* (Philadelphia: University of Pennsylvania, 1932), pp. 274, 276; Carey correspondence with James Moore Swank

(of the American Iron and Steel Association) in Swank papers, Pennsylvania Historical Society; Carey to Eugene Dühring, Philadelphia?, June 25, 1872, in H. C. Carey papers in Edward Carey Gardiner collection, Pennsylvania Historical Society; Dorfman, *Economic Mind in American Civilization,* iii: 8, 9; Kaplan, *op. cit.,* pp. 45–46; Arnold W. Green, *Henry Charles Carey: Nineteenth Century Sociologist* (Philadelphia: University of Pennsylvania Press, 1951), pp. 180–82.

10. William D. Kelley, *Speeches, Addresses and Letters on Industrial and Financial Questions* (Philadelphia: Henry Carey Baird, Industrial Publisher, 1872), speech of January 3, 1867, *passim;* Kaplan, *op. cit.,* p. 78; Sidney Fine, *Laissez Faire and the General-Welfare State,* pp. 305–06; Unger, *Greenback Era,* pp. 95–101.

11. John Jay Knox, *A History of Banking in the United States* (New York: Bradford Rhodes & Company, 1900), pp. 132–33; Hooper, *Currency or Money,* pp. 22, 87; Albert S. Bolles, *The Financial History of the United States, from 1861 to 1885* (New York: D. Appleton and Company, 1886), pp. 271–72; McCulloch in *HED* 2, 40:2, p. xvii; McCulloch to George S. Coe, Treasury Department, January 31, 1868, in McCulloch papers, Lilly Library of Indiana University; Walker in *Banker's Magazine,* March 1867, 738.

12. McCulloch to Henry R. Linderman, September 25, 1868, in McCulloch papers, Lilly Library of Indiana University.

13. Walker in *Banker's Magazine,* September 1867, 161–70; Bowen, *American Political Economy,* chap. 16; Newcomb, *Critical Examination,* pp. 203, 222; Samuel Hooper, *An Examination of the Theory and the Effect of Laws Regulating the Amount of Specie in Banks* (Boston: Little, Brown and Company, 1860), p. 3; Hooper to (Secretary of the Treasury) Salmon P. Chase, Washington, May 30, 1864, in NA RG 56, Letters to the Secretary of the Treasury from Congress, box 58; McCulloch, *Our National and Financial Future* (commonly known as "the Fort Wayne Address," October 11, 1865; Fort Wayne, Ind.: n.p., 1865), pp. 12–13; McCulloch, *Men and Measures of Half a Century* (New York: Charles Scribner's Sons, 1888), pp. 179–80.

14. Report of David A. Wells in *SED* 2, 39:2 (January 3, 1867); Hooper, *Currency or Money,* p. 76; Walker, *Science of Wealth,* book III, part 1, *passim; Commercial and Financial Chronicle,* October 20, 1877; Herbert R. Ferleger, *David A. Wells and the American Revenue System 1865–1870* (New York: privately printed, 1942), pp. 36–38; American Free-Trade League, *The League* (after mid-1868, *The Free Trader*), 1867–68 *passim,* but especially October 1867, 46; June 1869, 7; November 1869, 96–98; February 1870, 134.

Notes to Chapter 6

1. Particularly the works of Coben, Sharkey, and Unger, cited above (p. 4n.).

2. It hardly entered any banker's head that the United States would ever have a full-valued silver coinage; a double standard was inconceivable and unworkable. Before the mid-'seventies the *Commercial and Financial Chronicle,* and other journals, hardly mentioned silver coinage. Also, Sharkey, *op. cit.,* p. 299; Fritz Redlich, *The Molding of American Banking: Men and Ideas* (New York: Hafner Publishing Company, 1951), ii: 105–08, 158.

3. *Banker's Magazine,* January 1867, 481–84, August 1867, first two editorials, November 1867, 354 (quoted); *Commercial and Financial Chronicle,* June 22, 1872, February 22, 1873; George Walker to McCulloch, Springfield, Mass., December 4, 1867, E. G. Barkam [?], to McCulloch, New York, October 10, 1867, Levi P. Morton to McCulloch, New York, January 8, 1867, all in McCulloch papers, Library of Congress; McCulloch to George S. Coe, Treasury Department, March 2, 1866, in McCulloch papers, Lilly Library of Indiana University; Barry E. Supple, "A Business Elite: German-Jewish Financiers in Nineteenth-Century New York," *Business History Review,* XXXI (Summer 1957), 157, 176.

4. George Coe testimony, *House Report* 328, 43:2, pp. 63, 73; *Banker's Magazine,* February 1867, 574, November 1867, 345–47, March 1873, 739–40; Jay Cooke to H. Fahnestock, New York, May 23, 1871, in McCulloch papers, Lilly Library; Henrietta M. Larson, *Jay Cooke, Private Banker* (Cambridge: Harvard University Press, 1936), p. 207; Bray Hammond, "The North's Empty Purse, 1861–1862," *American Historical Review,* LXVII (October 1961), 14.

5. *Commercial and Financial Chronicle,* May 28, 1870 (editorial on Illinois Granger constitution, approving its anti-monopoly aspects); Philadelphia Board of Trade, *Thirty-sixth Annual Report* (Philadelphia: J. B. Chandler, 1869), pp. 22, 24.

6. Unger, *Greenback Era,* pp. 144–57; petition from New York State Chamber of Commerce, January 18, 1872, in *SMD* 34, 42:2; *Commercial and Financial Chronicle,* September 11, 1869; National Board of Trade, *Proceedings,* 1868, speech of John Welsh (President of Philadelphia Board of Trade), pp. 4–5, and *Proceedings,* 1870, speech of Joseph Ropes, pp. 215, 219, 222–23; Hugh McCulloch to E. G. Spaulding, December 12, 1868, in McCulloch papers, Lilly Library.

7. Unger, *Greenback Era,* chapter 2 *passim;* Unger, "Business Men and Specie Resumption," 52–60, 69; Sharkey, *op. cit.,* pp. 287–88; *Iron*

Age, June 26, July 31, 1873; American Iron and Steel Association, *Bulletin,* 1873 *passim;* Berkey, *The Money Question,* p. 345; Kelley, *Speeches,* pp. 137–38; Johnstown, Pa., *Industrial Bulletin,* November 1, December 1, 1870, February 1, March 1, June 1, July 1, 1871; *Manufacturer and Builder* (New York), January 1869, pp. 22, 26, November 1869, p. 340, February 1870, pp. 55–56, August 1873, p. 185.

8. Selig Perlman, *A History of Trade Unionism in the United States* (New York: The Macmillan Company, 1922), p. 45; *Locomotive Engineer's Journal,* 1873 *passim;* Gerald N. Grob, *Workers and Utopia: A Study of Ideological Conflict in the American Labor Movement 1865–1900* ([Evanston] Northwestern University Press, 1961), pp. 12, 27–28; Norman J. Ware, *The Labor Movement in the United States 1860–1895: A Study in Democracy* (New York: D. Appleton and Company, 1929), pp. 10–11, chapters 1 and 2 *passim; Workingman's Advocate,* August 11, 1866; Fine, *Laissez Faire and the General-Welfare State,* pp. 318–19.

9. Sharkey, *op. cit.,* chapter 5; Unger, *Greenback Era,* pp. 105–06.

10. Sylvis in *Workingman's Advocate,* May 8, 1869, May 20, 1871; also, *ibid.,* April 24, 1869, January 27, February 3, 1872.

11. *Workingman's Advocate,* April 24, September 25, 1869; January 27, 1872.

12. *Ibid.,* April 21, 1866; January 13–20, 27, 1872; August 2, 1873.

13. *Ibid.,* October 16, 30, November 6, 1869; Pottsville, Pa., *Miners Journal,* February 27, July 31, 1869.

14. Farmers of course varied greatly in economic position; Lee Benson has shown considerable economic differences among farmers even in a single state (*Merchants, Farmers and Railroads: Railroad Regulation and New York Politics, 1850–1887* [Cambridge: Harvard University Press, 1955], p. 81 and *passim*). But muteness on money was general. Also, *Moore's Rural New-Yorker,* January 9, 16, 1869; James Dabney McCabe, *History of the Grange Movement* (Chicago: National Publishing Company, 1874), chapter 21; Solon J. Buck, *The Granger Movement* (Cambridge: Harvard University Press, 1913), pp. 20–21; Henrietta M. Larson, *The Wheat Market and the Farmer in Minnesota, 1858–1900* (New York: Columbia University, 1926), *passim.*

15. O. H. Kelley, *Origin and Progress of the Order of the Patrons of Husbandry* (Philadelphia: J. A. Wagenseller, 1875), pp. 125–26, 256; *Moore's Rural New-Yorker,* January 9, 16, June 12, July 13, August 14, 1869; McCabe, *History of the Grange,* pp. 405–06; John G. Wells, *The Grange Illustrated; or Patron's Hand Book* (New York: Grange Publishing Company, 1874), p. 71.

16. Kelley, *Origin and Progress,* p. 264; Wells, *Grange Illustrated,* p. 71; *Moore's Rural New-Yorker,* February 6, April 10, and *passim,* 1869, January 29, February 12, 1870.

Notes to Chapter 7

1. Examples of group rhetorics criss-crossing party lines are in Charles Sumner (Republican) to John Bright, Washington, August 13, 1868, in Bright papers, Add. Mss. 43390, British Museum; Hugh McCulloch to Henry R. Linderman (both Democrats), September 25, 1868, in McCulloch papers, Lilly Library of Indiana University; Jay Cooke to Sherman (both Republicans), Philadelphia, January 22, 1866, in Sherman papers, Library of Congress; Pottsville, Pa., *Miners Journal,* February 27, 1869. The generalization could be documented indefinitely. On Republican intraparty divisions, for example, see Sharkey, *op. cit., passim* and especially pp. 277–85.

2. Only recently have scholars such as Professors Coben and Sharkey revised that misapprehension. For a clear statement of the inadequacy of the sectional interpretation of Reconstruction, see Coben, *loc. cit.,* 89–90.

3. *Popular Science Monthly,* March 1878, 581; *Nation,* March 5, 1868, February 4, May 20, 1869, July 7, 1870, February 27, 1873; *Harper's Weekly,* January 19, 1867, January 29, 1870; *New York Times,* February 17, 1873; New York *World,* June 3, 10, July 30, 1867, February 1, 4, 1873.

4. *De Bow's Review,* September 1869, 753, October 1869, 838; New Orleans *Price Current,* October 19, December 7, 1870; Coben, *loc. cit.,* 83–84.

5. George L. Anderson, "The South and Problems of Post-Civil War Finance," *Journal of Southern History,* IX (May 1943), 183–216; (Baltimore) *Southern Review,* April 1870, 355, 396, 399–401; *De Bow's Review,* October 1867, 379, June 1868, 537–38, July 1868, 585; New Orleans *Price Current,* October 30, December 1, 11, 1869, January 14, April 15, May 10, 1871, January 15, 18, 22, February 5, 26, April 5, 1873.

6. Edward Atkinson to McCulloch, Boston, November 7, 1867, in McCulloch papers, Library of Congress; Cincinnati *Commercial,* July 3, 6, 1868; George L. Anderson, "Western Attitudes Toward National Banks, 1873–74," *Mississippi Valley Historical Review,* XXIII (September 1936), 208–12; *Indianapolis Sentinel,* October 19, 1868; Redlich, *Molding of American Banking,* ii: 118–20.

7. *Banker's Magazine* quoting San Francisco *Commercial Herald,* August 1873, 138–39; *SMD* 96, 42:2; *HMD* 146, 42:2; petition from Citizens of San Francisco, January 22, 1872, NA LB, Senate Finance Committee records. I found very little comment of any kind on monetary affairs in the *San Francisco Bulletin* or the *Rocky Mountain News* of Denver.

8. Walker to John Bright, North Brookfield, Mass., October 22, 1866, in Bright papers, Add. Mss. 43391, British Museum. See also, same place, Henry Adams to Bright, Washington, February 3, 1869.

9. Jean Dubois, *Le Vocabulaire Politique et Social en France de 1869 à 1872* (Paris: Librairie Larousse [1962]), pp. 51, 67–68, 71, 79; Charles Le Touzé, "De l'Uniformité monétaire et de l'unité d'étalon," *Journal des Economistes,* IX (3d series; March 1868), 420; Wolowski in "Société d'Economie Politique, Réunion du 5 juin 1867; Discussion: La question monétaire," *Journal des Economistes,* VI (3d series; June 1867), 437–38.

10. A. Sartorius von Waltershausen, *Deutsche Wirtschaftsgeschichte, 1815–1914* (Jena: Verlag von Gustav Fischer, 1920), pp. iii, 251–52; Otto Hartwig, *Ludwig Bamberger. Eine Biographische Skizze* (Marburg; Universitäts-Buchdruckerei, C. L. Pfeil, 1900), pp. 34–35 and *passim;* "Adolph Soetbeer," in R. H. I. Palgrave, comp., *Palgrave's Dictionary of Political Economy* (Henry Higgs, ed.; London: Macmillan and Co., Limited, 1926), iii: 440; Ludwig Bamberger, *Zur deutschen Münzgesetzgebung* (Berlin: Lüderitz'sche Verlagsbuchhandlung, 1872), pp. 16, 24, 30; William D. Kelley, *Letters from Europe* (Philadelphia: Porter and Coates [1879]), pp. 21–22.

Notes to Chapter 8

1. *Harper's Magazine,* January 1868, 161.

2. William E. Gladstone to M. [Achille] Fould, July 16, 1866, in Gladstone papers, Add. Mss. 44536, British Museum; Esquirou de Parieu, "La question monétaire en France et à l'Etranger," *Revue Contemporaine,* XLVIII (2d series; December 31, 1865), 722 (italics in original).

3. Edward F. Cox, "The metric system: a quarter-century of acceptance (1851–1876)," *Osiris* (Bruges), XIII (1958), 362–64; Henry B. Russell, *International Monetary Conferences: Their Purposes, Character, and Results* (New York and London: Harper & Brothers Publishers, 1898), pp. 18–20.

4. Russell, *op. cit.,* pp. 21–22; *HED* 266, 41:2, p. 7; "Report of the

Proceedings of the International Statistical Congress held in Berlin
. . .," British Parliamentary Papers, 1864, lviii, p. 737.

5. Henry Russell suggested that Napoleon retained bimetallism in
1865 in order to have something to give away at the 1867 Conference
in return for international acceptance of the franc. This is possible,
but perhaps attributes to Napoleon a cunning and prescience he probably lacked. In any event, Napoleon kept appointing bimetallist Finance
Ministers all through the period. (Russell, *op. cit.*, pp. 25–31). Henry
Parker Willis suggested, more plausibly, pressure from Rothschild and
the Bank of France (*A History of the Latin Monetary Union* [Chicago:
The University of Chicago Press, 1901], pp. 42–60). See also Esquirou
de Parieu, "Les Conférences monétaires internationales de 1867, et leurs
résultats," *Journal des Economistes*, XIII (3d series; February 1869),
254.

6. France, Ministère des Finances et Ministère de l'Agriculture, du
Commerce et des Travaux Publics, *Enquête sur les principes et les
faits généraux qui régissent la circulation monétaire et fiduciaire* (6 vols.;
Paris: Imprimerie Impériale, 1867–69), i: 2–12, vi: 1–79; *HED* 148,
39:1, 1–6; *HED* 5, 39:2, 19–21; British Parliamentary Papers, 1867–68,
xxiii, pp. 1–2 ("Report of the International Conference on Weights,
Measures, and Coins" [C. 4021]); Willis, *op. cit.*, pp. 74–78; Esquirou
de Parieu, "L'Union Monétaire de la France, de l'Italie, de la Belgique
et de la Suisse," *Revue Contemporaine*, LIII (October 31, 1866), 621–
22; *Banker's Magazine*, March 1867, 661–73; American Association for
the Advancement of Science, *Proceedings*, 1868, pp. viii, 122–23.

7. *House Report* 62, 39:1, pp. 2–4; *House Journal*, 39:1, pp. 66, 124,
640; *Congressional Globe*, 39:1, pp. 2653–54, 2665, 2760.

8. Beckwith to Seward, Paris, June 29, 1866, and July 17, 1866, in
SED 5, 39:2, pp. 17–36.

9. *Ibid.*, pp. 37–39.

10. *Dictionary of American Biography*, xvi: 220; Ruggles papers,
New York Public Library; John Jay Knox to Ruggles, Washington,
December 16, 1868, in Ruggles papers, *ibid.*; Hugh McCulloch to Rug-
gles, April 25, 1865, in McCulloch papers, Lilly Library of Indiana
University; National Board of Trade, *Proceedings*, 1868, p. 16. A biog-
raphy of Ruggles is D. G. Brinton Thompson, *Ruggles of New York*
(New York: Columbia University Press, 1946).

11. Ruggles to Seward, July 18, 1867, in *SED* 14, 40:2 (Ruggles'
report on the Paris Conference), p. 17.

12. *HED* 266, 41:2, pp. 7, 15–21; New York State Chamber of Commerce, *Ninth Annual Report . . . 1866–'67* (New York: John W. Amer-

man, Printer, 1867), p. 18. The original copy of the resolution, dated
May 19, 1866, is in the Sherman papers, Library of Congress.

13. National Board of Trade, *Proceedings,* 1870, p. 228.

14. *SED* 5, 39:2, pp. 3–14, 45; *Congressional Globe,* 39:2, pp. 1721,
1782–83, 1789–90.

15. *SED* 14, 40:2, pp. 2–4; "Extracts from the Report of the International Committee on Weights, Measures, and Coins," *SED* 5, 39:2,
pp. 7–9.

16. Russell, *op. cit.,* p. 42, says Chevalier introduced Ruggles to
Esquirou de Parieu.

17. *Dictionary of American Biography,* x: 260; *Congressional Globe,*
39:2, p. 1784 (March 2, 1867). Kasson's biographer says Kasson "ran
into" Sherman aboard the ship, and says little else about Kasson's activity in Paris (Edward Younger, *John A. Kasson* [Iowa City: State
Historical Society of Iowa, 1955], pp. 221–23, 227).

18. For biographical data about Sherman, see Jeanette Nichols, "John
Sherman," *Dictionary of American Biography,* xvii: 84–88; *Biographical
Directory of the Congress, 1774–1949 (House Document 607, 81:2),* p.
1806; James G. Randall, "John Sherman and Reconstruction," *Mississippi Valley Historical Review,* XIX (December 1932), *passim.*

19. John Sherman, *Recollections of Forty Years in the House, Senate
and Cabinet. An Autobiography* (Chicago: The Werner Company,
1895), pp. 396–400. The introduction states that "My hope is that those
who read them will be able to correct the wild delusions of many honest
citizens who became infected with the 'greenback craze', or the 'free
coinage of silver'." (P. iv). Also, Jay Cooke to Sherman, Philadelphia,
April 15, 1867; Samuel Hooper to Sherman, Washington, April 9,
1867; James Yates to Sherman, London, May 3, 1867, all in Sherman
papers, Library of Congress.

20. Sherman, *Recollections,* pp. 400, 406–09; *SED* 14, 40:2, pp. 13–14.

21. Ruggles to Sherman, Paris, May 17, 1867, Sherman papers, Library of Congress. It is reprinted in Ruggles' official report.

22. Sherman to Ruggles, Paris, May 18, 1867, in *SED* 14, 40:2, pp. 9,
107–09. There is a draft, obviously a first draft and in Sherman's
hand, among some undated material in the Sherman papers, Library of
Congress.

23. H. B. Rogers, Jr., to Sherman, Paris, May 21, 1867, in Sherman
papers, Library of Congress; Russell, *op. cit.,* pp. 44–45.

24. *SED* 14, 40:2, p. 6.

25. Kasson stayed in Europe until December to negotiate postal
agreements (Younger, *op. cit.,* p. 228). Sherman's memoirs state that

he left Kasson behind when Sherman went from London to Paris in early May, which is not true. Sherman, *Recollections*, pp. 396, 406; also, Russell, *op. cit.*, pp. 48–51; F. W. Seward to Ruggles, Washington, June 21, 1867, in *SED* 14, 40:2, p. 11; Ruggles to Sherman, Paris, June 20; Committee on Weights, Measures, and Coinage of the International Exposition to Sherman, Paris, June 22; John A. Dix to Sherman, Paris, June 26; LeGrand Lockwood to Sherman, Paris, June 30; J. S. Morgan to Sherman, London, June (?), all 1867, and all in Sherman papers, Library of Congress.

26. This and what follows rests on the English translation of the *procès verbaux* of the Conference, in *SED* 14, 40:2, pp. 25–81.

27. Francis A. Walker, "The Monetary Conferences of 1867 and 1878, and the Future of Silver," *Princeton Review*, January 1879, 33.

28. The British role in the adoption of the gold standard was apparently not great. There was far too much French and American activity in favor of gold to necessitate it. The British no doubt did what they could to prevent the franc from becoming the new international unit, as Ruggles informed Sherman a few months later, but at the same time they were equally undesirous of being isolated from a successful unification scheme. The British delegates' report to Parliament suggests that Ruggles, though he never realized it, had nearly convinced them, if not their Government, of the merits of his 25-franc plan. Sherman, *Recollections*, p. 410; "Report of the Master of the Mint and Mr. Rivers Wilson on the International Monetary Conference . . .," British Parliamentary Papers, 1867–68, xxvii (C. 4021), p. 73.

29. The most immediate result of the Conference was a draft treaty of July 31, 1867, between Austria and France, making the gold Austrian ten-florin and the French gold 25-franc pieces identical. This put France and Austria, and subsequently the whole Latin Union, on a common basis and encouraged gold monometallists everywhere, the moreso since France was bimetallic and Austria was on the silver standard domestically. The obvious diplomatic implication is that this was an anti-Prussian move by the French and Austrians.

30. *HED* 266, 41:2, p. 7 (a supplementary report by Ruggles, made in 1870); Willis, *op. cit.*, pp. 82–83.

31. *SED* 14, 40:2, pp. 81–83, 86–102.

Notes to Chapter 9

1. McCulloch to Greeley, June 13, 1866, in McCulloch papers, Lilly Library of Indiana University.

2. Charles Reemelin to McCulloch, Dent, Ohio, December 4, 1867; Spaulding to McCulloch, Buffalo, December 5, 1867; Edwards Pierrepont to McCulloch, New York, December 6, 1867; Amasa Walker to McCulloch, North Brookfield, Mass., December 8, 1867; Francis Lieber to McCulloch, New York, December 11, 1867, all in McCulloch papers, Library of Congress. Also, *HED* 2, 40:2, pp. ix, xi, xliii.

3. McCulloch to House Speaker Schuyler Colfax, May 28, 1866, and Van Dyck to McCulloch, May 30, 1866, in *Banker's Magazine*, July 1866, 34–38; LeGrand Lockwood to Sherman, New York, March 5, 1866, in Sherman papers, Library of Congress; Chas. Lüling & Co. to Albert Speyer, Louis I. von Hoffmann to Albert Speyer, E. D. Morgan & Co. to Van Dyck, all New York, all May 30, 1866, in McCulloch papers, Library of Congress.

4. W. C. Patterson to Sherman, Philadelphia, March 15, 1866; George Opdyke to Sherman, New York, March 16, 1866; S. P. Townshend to Sherman, New York, March 17, 1866; Jay Cooke to Sherman, Philadelphia, April 20, 1866; all in Sherman papers, Library of Congress. Also, Henrietta M. Larson, *Jay Cooke*, pp. 205–06; Henry Clews to McCulloch, New York, March 9, 1866, in *Banker's Magazine*, May 1867, 822–25; McCulloch to Horace Greeley, June 13, 1866, and to Samuel Hooper, March 26, 1868, in McCulloch papers, Lilly Library; Sharkey, *op. cit.*, pp. 131–32; Coben, *loc. cit.*, 78–80; H. C. Carey to F. A. Conkling, Philadelphia, March 26, 1867, in *Banker's Magazine*, May 1867, 862–63.

5. *HED* 2, 40:2, pp. i, v–vii; McCulloch to Van Dyck, December 20, 1867, and to John Sherman, December 18, 1867, in McCulloch papers, Lilly Library.

6. Kelley, *Speeches*, pp. 111, 114, 133, 223, 226; *Congressional Globe*, 40:2, pp. 69–79, 407–16, 435–41, 500–02, 520–26, 537, 652, 986; *Banker's Magazine*, March 1868, 749. The amendment referred to was offered by Edmunds of Vermont and would have explicitly forbidden the Treasury to increase the amount of circulating greenbacks by releasing any that it had retired. Midwesterners voted 16–4 against; Northeasterners 12–7 for (with both Pennsylvania and both Rhode Island Senators opposed); of the 7 voting Democrats, 6 opposed the bill, thus favoring further contraction; the Democrats, early in 1868, were thus measurably "harder" than the Republicans, quite in contrast to their presidential platform of six months later.

7. George Greenlief Evans, *Illustrated History of the United States Mint* (Philadelphia: George G. Evans, publisher, 1888), pp. 104–05; Pollock to McCulloch, Philadelphia, September 9, 1865, NA RG 104,

to ST; Kelley to Linderman, Washington, June 25, 1868, in NA RG 104, GCM, box 114; McCulloch to Linderman, July 31, 1867, McCulloch to Col. Edward Cooper (at the White House), September 30, 1867, McCulloch to S. S. Cox, October 24, November 22, 1867, all in McCulloch papers, Lilly Library.

8. *HED* 2, 40:2, pp. 326, 329–30; *House Journal*, 42:2, p. 1144; Sherman to McCulloch, Washington, December 23, 1867, in NA RG 56, Incoming letters to the Secretary (Committee correspondence), box 82; Sherman to McCulloch, Washington, December 23, 1867, in NA RG 104, GCM, box 113; McCulloch to Linderman, Washington, December 26, 1867, *ibid.;* Joseph Wharton to Linderman, Philadelphia, December 30, 1867, *ibid.;* Linderman to McCulloch, Philadelphia, November 23, 1867, January 2, 1868, NA RG 104, to ST; McCulloch to Linderman, December 23, 26, 27, 1867, and McCulloch to Joseph Wharton, August 25, 1865, in McCulloch papers, Lilly Library.

9. *Senate Report* 117, 40:2, pp. 1–6; *Senate Journal*, 40:2, pp. 73, 465 (January 6 and June 9, 1868); *Congressional Globe*, 40:2, pp. 318, 2959 (same dates); *Banker's Magazine*, February 1868, 629.

10. Sherman, *Recollections*, especially pp. 396, 400; resolution of New York Chamber of Commerce, authored by Ruggles, thanking Sherman and Kasson for work on metric coinage bill, May 1866, in Sherman papers, Library of Congress; Ruggles, *The Dollar of our Fathers* (New York: Press of the Chamber of Commerce, 1877), pp. 6–7.

11. J. L. Ringwalt to Mint Director James Pollock, Denver, October 17, 1865, in NA RG 104, to ST; Ruggles, *International Statistical Congress at Berlin. Sixth Days Session. September 11th, 1863. Report from the United States of America* (n.p., n.d.; pamphlet found in New York Public Library), *passim; HED* 266, 41:2, p. 7; *Banker's Magazine*, July 1869, 6–11; Russell, *op. cit.*, p. 32.

12. Rodman W. Paul, *Mining Frontiers of the Far West, 1848–1880* (New York: Holt, Rinehart and Winston, 1963), especially plate between pp. 108–09, "Vertical Section of the Comstock Lode," reprinted from George F. Becker, *Geology of the Comstock Lode*, 1882; McCulloch in *HED* 2, 40:2, pp xxxviii–xxxix; McCulloch to J. Ross Browne, Treasury Department, July 16, 1866, in McCulloch papers, Lilly Library; Browne report, *HED* 29, 39:2, especially pp. 7–12, 33–35, 49, 52–53, 72, 84–85; Taylor report, *HED* 92, 39:2; Linderman report for 1866, *HED* 4, 39:2, p. 236; same for 1867, *HED* 2, 40:2, p. 326; Ernest Seyd, *Suggestions in Reference to the Metallic Currency of the United States of America* (London: Trübner & Co., 1871), appendices on bullion refining.

13. As on p. 99, *supra.*

14. *Senate Report* 117, 40:2, pp. 8–16; William D. Kelley to Linderman, Philadelphia, May 30?, 1868, and same to same, June 22, 1868, in NA RG 104, GCM, box 114; *Congressional Globe*, 40:2, p. 2959 (June 9, 1868); *Senate Journal*, 40:2, p. 466 (same day); *Banker's Magazine,* October 1868, 304.

15. Edward F. Cox, "The metric system: a quarter-century of acceptance," *loc. cit., 371–72*; American Academy for the Advancement of Science, *Proceedings,* 1867, p. 167; *Banker's Magazine,* April 1869, 798; *SMD* 28, 40:2, pp. 1–2.

16. *New York Times,* June 12, 1868; Edward McPherson, *The Political History of the United States of America during the Period of Reconstruction* (Washington: James J. Chapman, 1880), pp. 364, 367.

17. Dorfman, *op. cit.,* iii: 22; McCulloch to S. S. Cox, October 24 and November 22, 1867, McCulloch to Linderman, October 11, 1867, McCulloch to Samuel Randall, September 24, 1868, in McCulloch papers, Lilly Library; Cincinnati *Commercial,* September 9, 1868; *Indianapolis Sentinel,* June 20, 1868; *New York Times,* November 2, 1868; McPherson, *Political History,* pp. 478–84.

18. *Commerical and Financial Chronicle,* August 29, November 21, 1868; National Board of Trade, *Proceedings,* 1868, pp. 98, 214–23.

19. *Banker's Magazine,* August 1868, 81–83, and December 1868, 462–65; Sharkey, *op. cit.,* pp. 122–23; McPherson, *Political History,* pp. 387–88, 391–92.

20. McPherson, *Political History,* pp. 354–55, 412–13; *SMD* 12, 40:3; *House Journal,* 40:3, pp. 438–39, 479, 526; *Congressional Globe,* 40:3, pp. 1428–29, 1448, 1470–71, 1534–39, 1650–78, 1834, 1879, 1883, appendix pp. 292–93; *Senate Journal,* 41:1, pp. 25, 34, 45; *House Journal,* 41:1, pp. 34, 80; *Congressional Globe,* 41:1, pp. 48, 53, 60–66, 70; *HED* 2, 40:2; pp. xxiii–xxxii; Max L. Shipley, "The Background and Legal Aspects of the Pendleton Plan," *Mississippi Valley Historical Review,* XXIV (December 1937), 329–39.

Notes to Chapter 10

1. British Parliamentary Papers, 1867–68, xxvii (C. 4021), *passim;* Louis Mallet to Under-Secretary of the Home Office, Board of Trade, March 15, 1867, BT 12/4, no. 176, Public Record Office; British Parliamentary Papers, "Report of the Royal Commission on International Coinage," 1867–68, xxvii (C. 4073), pp. ix–xviii.

2. William E. Gladstone to W. Childers, M.P., in Gladstone pa-

pers, Add. Mss. 44536, British Museum; Michel Chevalier to Gladstone, Paris, July 13, 1868, *ibid.*, Add. Mss. 44127; Asa Briggs, *Victorian People* (London: Odhams Press Limited, 1954), pp. 262, 267, for an illuminating sketch of Lowe; Ernest Seyd, "On International Coinage and the Variations of the Foreign Exchanges during Recent Years," *Journal of the Statistical Society of London*, XXXIII (March 1870), 42 and *passim*, for a bimetallist's view; W. S. Jevons, "On the Condition of the Metallic Currency of the United Kingdom, with Reference to the Question of International Coinage," *ibid.*, XXXI (December 1868), 428 and *passim*; France, *Enquête sur la Question Monétaire*, pp. 209–10, 218, 226; *Speeches, Letters, Articles & C. on the Gold Coinage Controversy of 1869* ("For Private Circulation Only"; London; Printed at the Bank of England, 1870), *passim*; British Parliamentary Papers, 1870, i, pp. 286–93; *ibid.*, 1868–69, xxiii (C. 4186), p. 733; *ibid.*, 1870, xli, p. 206; Louis Mallet to the Secretary of Treasury, Board of Trade, December 16, 1869, BT 12/6, no. 571, Public Record Office.

3. Charles Le Touzé, "De l'Uniformité monétaire et de l'unité d'étalon," *Journal des Economistes*, IX (3d series; March 1868), 415, 419; Esquirou de Parieu, "Situation de la Question Monétaire Internationale," *loc. cit.*, 57; France, Ministère des Finances, *Procès-verbaux et rapport de la Commission Monétaire* (Paris: Imprimerie Impériale, 1869), pp. iii–iv, 1–2.

4. France, Ministère des Finances, *Procès-verbaux et rapport de la Commission Monétaire*, *passim*; the Minister of Finance, M. Magne, was nominal chairman of the Commission. Other members were Senators Dumas, Rouland, Chevalier, Wolowski, and de Lavenay, who with Esquirou gave it a narrow monometallist majority.

5. France, Conseil Supérieur du commerce, de l'agriculture et de l'industrie, *Enquête sur la question monétaire* (Paris: Imprimerie nationale, 1872; 2 vols.), *passim*.

6. Warren M. Persons *et. al.*, "Business and Financial Conditions Following the Civil War in the United States," *Review of Economic Statistics*, Supplement, Preliminary Volume II (1920), 15; Willard L. Thorp, *Business Annals* (New York: National Bureau of Economic Research, Inc., 1926), pp. 189–90; A. L. Dunham, "The Attempt of President Thiers to Restore Protection in France (1871–1873)", *Journal of Economic and Business History*, I (1929), 302–24; London *Economist*, July 17, 1872, 926, and August 24, 1872, 1046; France, *Enquête sur la Question Monétaire* (Paris: Imprimerie Nationale, 1872), p. vii; *La Crise Monétaire en France, Octobre 1871* (Paris: Librairie de E. Dentu, 1871).

7. Esquirou de Parieu, "Situation de la Question Monétaire International," *loc. cit.*, 55–56; W. O. Henderson, *The Zollverein* (Cambridge: At the University Press, 1939), pp. 139–40, 249–52; Deutsche Handelstag, *Zusammenstellung der Erklärungen und Gutachten von 35 Deutschen Handelsvorständen in Betreff der Goldausmünzung in Deutschland* ("Hrsg. vom bleibenden Ausschuss des Deutschen Handelstages im Marz 1865"; Berlin: Stilke & Van Muyden, 1865), *passim*.

8. [A. Gschwendner, ed.] *Zur Allgemeinen Münzeinheit. Die internationale Münzconferenz zu Paris im Jahre 1867. Uebersetzung, Einleitung und Bemerkungen* (Erlangen: Verlag von Ferdinand Enke, 1869), pp. 3, 10, 58–60.

9. "Bericht über die Verhandlungen des neunten Kongresses deutscher Volkswirthe, zu Hamburg am 26., 27., 28. und 29. August 1867," *Vierteljahrschrift für Volkswirthschaft und Kulturgeschichte*, XIX (Berlin; 1867), 183–93.

10. Werner Sombart, *Die deutsche Volkswirtschaft im neunzehnten Jahrhundert, und im Amfang des 20. Jahrhundert; Eine Einführung in die Nationalökonomie* (Berlin: Georg Bondi, 1927), p. 128; Deutsche Handelstag, *Verhandlungen des Vierten Deutschen Handelstages zu Berlin vom 20 bis 23. Oktober 1868* (Berlin: Verlag von Stilke & Van Muyden, 1868), pp. v–viii.

11. Deutsche Handelstag, *Verhandlungen*, 1868, pp. 27–50, 142.

12. *Ibid.*, pp. 38–39, 44; Theodore S. Hamerow, *Restoration, Revolution, Reaction: Economics and Politics in Germany, 1815–1871* (Princeton: Princeton University Press, 1958), p. 253; Ivo Nikolai Lambi, *Free Trade and Protection in Germany, 1868–79* (Beiheft 44, *Vierteljahrschrift für Sozial- und Wirtschaftsgeschichte;* Wiesbaden: Frans Steiner Verlag GmbH, 1963), pp. 1–4.

13. Knies, *Das Geld*, quoted in S. Dana Horton, *Silver and Gold* (Cincinnati: Robert Clarke & Co., 1877), p. 13; Joseph A. Schumpeter, *Business Cycles* (New York: McGraw-Hill Book Company, Inc., 1939), i: 308, 362–63; G. S. Graham, "Cobden's Influence on Bismarck," *Queen's Quarterly* (Kingston, Ontario; Summer 1931), 436–39; Walter Lotz, *Die Ideen der deutschen Handelspolitik* (Leipzig: Verlag von Dunker & Humblot, 1892), pp. 102–19.

14. Germany, *Stenographische Berichte über die Verhandlungen des Reichstages*, 1871, pp. 227–43, 317–18, 337, 489; Ludwig Bamberger, *Zur deutschen Münzgesetzgebung*, pp. 26, 30; Economist, October 7 (1210), November 25 (1430), 1871; (London) *Times*, October 10, 19, 20, 23, November 7, 20, 1871.

15. Germany, *Reichsgesetzblatt*, 1871, Nr 745, pp. 404–406; *Econo-*

mist, October 21, 1871, 1265; H. P. Willis, *A History of the Latin Monetary Union*, p. 112.

16. *Stenographische Berichte über die Verhandlungen des Reichstages*, 1873, i: 521–22, 534–35, 1369, 1384; *Reichsgesetzblatt*, 1873, Nr 953, pp. 233–40; (London) *Times*, April 23, 26, 28, May 7, July 2, 1873; *Economist*, January 6, 1872, 6; March 1 (246), March 8 (278), May 24 (623–24), 1873; Lotz, *op. cit.*, p. 102; Schumpeter, *op. cit.*, i: 363; Werner Sombart, *op. cit.*, p. 128.

17. John Lothrop Motley to Hamilton Fish, London, July 9, 1871, in NA, Diplomatic Correspondence London, dispatch 380; *SED* 16, 42:2; *Economist*, March 1, 1873, 245; Ernest Seyd, "On Currency Laws and their Effect on Pauperism," *Journal of Statistical Society of London*, XXXIV (March 1871), 1–12, 19.

Notes to Chapter 11

1. National Board of Trade, *Proceedings*, 1869, pp. 147–85, 188–205, 265–87, 299–326; *Commercial and Financial Chronicle*, October 2, February 26, 1870; *Free-Trader*, October 1869, 70.

2. H. V. Poor to Edward Atkinson, Washington, July 16, 1868, in Atkinson papers, Massachusetts Historical Society; *Free-Trader*, July 1869, 20–21; McCulloch, *Men and Measures of Half a Century*, p. 348; *Commercial and Financial Chronicle*, April 24, May 1, 22, August 7, December 11, 1869; James A. Garfield to Boutwell, Washington, January 31, 1870, in NA RG 56, to ST, box 75; *Moore's Rural New-Yorker*, March 19, 1870; *Workingman's Advocate*, September 25, 1869; *Banker's Magazine*, March 1870, 671–75.

3. *Workingman's Advocate*, November 27, 1869; Kelley, *Speeches*, p. 393; *Commercial and Financial Chronicle*, January 22, April 23, May 14, 28, 1870; *HED* 2, 41:2 (annual report of the Comptroller of the Currency, 1869), pp. 36–39.

4. Republicans favored it, 37–15; Democrats opposed it, 2–8. Northeastern Senators opposed it, 3–15; Midwesterners favored it, 17–4; Southerners favored it, 15–2; the Far West split, California opposed and Oregon and Nevada in favor. *Congressional Globe*, 41:2, pp. 697–700, 706–07, 729–37, 777–85, 810–12, 901–06, 934–46, 967.

5. *HED* 2, 41:2, p. xvii; *Senate Journal*, 41:2, p. 399; *Workingman's Advocate*, February 12, 1870; *Commercial and Financial Chronicle*, March 19, 1870; *Congressional Globe*, 41:2, debates on S. 380, p. 378 intermittently through p. 1884.

6. *SED* 16, 42:2; O. Ferriss to Linderman, Washington, June 18,

1868, in NA RG 104, GCM, box 114; Elias Harket Derby to McCulloch, Philadelphia, February 9, 1869, in NA RG 104, to ST; McCulloch to E. B. Elliott, Treasury Department, January 2, 1869, NA RG 56, from ST, xxii: 497; William D. Kelley to McCulloch, Washington, NA RG 56, Secretary from Congress, box 60; National Board of Trade, *Proceedings,* 1869, p. 329.

7. John Hewston, Jr., to W. E. DuBois, San Francisco, June 8, 1868, NA RG 104, GCM, box 114; DuBois to Director, August ?, 1868, *ibid.,* box 115; DuBois to Linderman, April 6, 1869, *ibid.,* box 117; Boutwell to Linderman, Treasury Department, October 17, 1869, in NA RG 104, Treasury to Mint; *Banker's Magazine,* September 1869, 161–76; Rossiter W. Raymond (J. Ross Browne's successor as the Treasury's investigator of western mining conditions) report, *HED* 54, 40:3, pp. v, 5, 50–51.

8. John Jay Knox, *A History of Banking in the United States* (revised and edited by Bradford Rhodes and Elmer H. Youngman; New York: Bradford Rhodes & Company, 1900), pp. vii–x; *HED* 4, 39:2, pp. 29, 262–67; Knox to Linderman, two letters, August 1867, in NA RG 104, GCM, box 112; same to same, June 22, 1868, *ibid.,* box 114; Knox to Pollock, November 8, 1869, *ibid.,* box 120; Knox to Pollock, March 8, 1870, *ibid.,* box 121; Linderman to Knox, Philadelphia, October 8 and November 8, 1869, January 7, 1870, NA RG 56, to ST; *SED* 51, 41:2, *passim; HED* 207, 41:2, pp. 95–99, 113; Pollock to Boutwell, February 6, March 7, 1870, NA RG 104, to ST; Pollock to Knox, March 10, 1870, *ibid.;* Linderman to Boutwell, New York, April 26, 1870, *ibid.*

9. Knox's manuscript draft said "The present law can be so construed as to authorize" rather than "consequently authorize"; conscience triumphed as well as style. The letters to Knox from commentators on the draft appear in *HED* 307, 41:2, part "A." Knox's report is Knox to Boutwell, April 25, 1870, *SMD* 132, 41:2, pp. 2–12; the draft of this letter is in NA RG 104, Fair Copies of Letters to Mint, V: 418–38.

10. Boutwell to Linderman, Treasury Department, March 5, 1870, NA RG 104, Fair copies of Incoming Letters; printed version and ms. addendum to H.R. 1113 (Kelley's bill) in NA LB, HR 41A–F5.1; Docket Book and Minute Book, House Committee on Coinage, Weights, and Measures, February–April 1870, in NA LB; Hooper to Pollock, Washington, March 17, 1870, in NA RG 104, GCM, box 121; *HED* 266, 41:2.

11. *Congressional Globe,* 41:2, pp. 4266, 4434, 4478, 4949, 5303; *Commercial and Financial Chronicle,* July 9, August 20, 27, 1870; New

Orleans *Price Current,* June 22, 1870; San Francisco *Daily Bulletin,* July 8, 1870.

12. *Congressional Globe,* 41:2, pp. 5071, 5463–67, 5523, 5531–32; Boutwell to Sherman, July 13, 1870, in Sherman papers, Library of Congress.

13. *HED* 2, 42:2, pp. xvii–xx, 255–57; Sherman to editor of *Cincinnati Commercial,* Washington, March 17, 1870, in Sherman papers, Library of Congress; Larson, *Jay Cooke,* pp. 321–22; *Commercial and Financial Chronicle,* March 18, 1871; Benjamin Moran to Hamilton Fish, London, March 17, 1871, NA, Diplomatic Correspondence London, dispatch 264.

Notes to Chapter 12

1. *House Journal,* 42:2, pp. 20–21, 28 (December 4–5, 1871), 255–56 (February 1, 1872); *House Report* 7, 42:2; *Commercial and Financial Chronicle,* May 27, 1871; *Workingman's Advocate,* July 27, 1872; *HED* 2, 42:2, pp. 29–37.

2. Ms. of speech by Sherman, January 26, 1871, in Sherman papers, Library of Congress; *Commercial and Financial Chronicle,* October 22, 1870, February 11, 1871, May 4, 1872; *Senate Report* 275, 42:3; *HED* 2, 42:2, pp. ix–x; *Senate Journal,* 42:3, p. 107 (January 6, 1872); *HED* 42, 42:3; *Banker's Magazine,* August 1872, 139–40, and November 1872, 386; *SMD* 91, 42:2; *SMD* 109, 42:2; *House Journal,* 42:2, pp. 472, 1014, 1069, 1130 (March 11, May 30, June 7, 8, 1872).

3. *Workingman's Advocate,* November 18, 1871, and February 15, August 9, 1873; *Banker's* Magazine, August 1871, 83, and September 1871, 229–30; Larson, *Jay Cooke,* p. 384; New Orleans *Price Current,* May 24, 1873.

4. National Board of Trade, *Proceedings,* 1870, pp. 214–26; *ibid.,* 1871, pp. 235–81; *ibid.,* 1872, pp. 192–212; *ibid.,* 1875, pp. 13–15; *SMD* 99, 42:2.

5. Edward McPherson, *Hand-Book of Politics for 1872,* pp. 148–71, 204–11; Cyrus W. Field to John Bright, December 10, 1875, in Bright papers, Add. Mss. 43391, British Museum; *New York Times,* November 4, 1872; *North American Review,* October 1872, 402, 419; *HED* 2, 42:3; *Senate Journal,* 42:3, p. 16.

6. *HED* 307, 41:2, part "B."

7. Sherman failed to mention, if he knew it, that Lowe's proposal had sunk without a trace (see above, pp. 112–14), nor did he make two more effective points: Britain really did have a coinage charge in practice, since all coining on private account had to go through the Bank

of England, which made such a charge; also, a seignorage (profit or debasement) was not the same thing as a coinage charge (fee for actual cost of coining).

8. *Congressional Globe*, 41:3, pp. 155, 373–77, 394–99; Louis A. Garnett ("Manager of the San Francisco Assaying and Refining Works"), *The Rapid Decline in the Production of the Precious Metals in the United States. The Refining and Coining of Gold, and the Mint Charge Therefor* (n.p., [1869]), pp. 4–5; *HED* 4, 39:2, pp. 268–69; W. E. DuBois and Jacob Eckfeldt to Pollock, Philadelphia, August 3, 1870, NA RG 104, GCM, box 121; "Assayers of Story and Lyon Counties, Nevada," to Director of Mint (printed circular), early 1871, p. 12, in *ibid.*, box 122; *Commercial and Financial Chronicle*, December 24, 1870; *Banker's Magazine*, July 1870, February 1871; Sherman, *Recollections*, p. 509.

9. *Congressional Globe*, 41:2, pp. 447, 483, 1665; *House Journal*, 42:1, p. 18.

10. Quotations are from Pollock to Boutwell, Philadelphia, February 6, 1872, NA RG 104, to ST; from *HED* 2, 42:2, pp. 432–33; and from *Congressional Record*, XXV, p. 222 (August 8, 1893). Also, Pollock to Boutwell, Mint, February 17, 1872, and Pollock to Acting Secretary W. A. Richardson, Mint, June 19, 1872, NA RG 104, to ST; Raymond Report, *HED* 10, 42:1, p. 93 and *passim;* Mint Director's report for 1871, *HED* 2, 42:2, pp. 427, 440; Mint Director's report for 1872, *HED* 2, 42:3, pp. 430–34, 442; Russell, *International Monetary Conferences*, p. 103. Paul M. O'Leary, in "The Scene of the Crime of 1873 Revisited: A Note," *Journal of Political Economy*, August 1960, 388–92, says that Linderman's demonetization activities were "purposive and deliberate," with which I certainly agree, but rests his view on the contention that Linderman "had his own figures" on silver production and coinage. This would add emphasis to the point, but the figures published openly in Pollock's and Boutwell's reports seem sufficiently convincing.

11. *Dictionary of American Biography*, x: 300; *Biographical Directory of the U.S. Congress*, House Document 607, 81:2, p. 1398; Kelley to Boutwell, Altoona, Pa., November 8, 1871, enclosing letter from C. S. Eyster to Kelley, Denver, November 2, 1871, NA RG 56, to ST from Congress, box 60.

12. Pollock to Boutwell, Mint, October 15, 1869, NA RG 104, GCM. There are many letters in RG 104 between Wharton, Mint, and Treasury officials, and between these officials and other (unsuccessful) nickel bidders. A few other pertinent letters are in the McCulloch papers. See also Carothers, *Fractional Coinage*, pp. 226–28.

13. Minute Books of Committee on Coinage, Weights, and Measures, and of Committee on Banking and Currency, and draft H. R. 5 (substitute S. 859) in Committee papers, 1871, NA LB; *Congressional Globe*, 42:2, p. 308 (January 8, 1872).

14. *Congressional Globe*, 42:2, pp. 322–28, 336–40 (January 9 and 10, 1872); *House Journal*, 42:2, pp. 128–35.

15. *Dictionary of American Biography*, ix: 203; *Biographical Directory of the U.S. Congress, House Document* 607, 81:2, p. 1328.

16. *Congressional Globe*, 42:2, pp. 993–94 (February 13, 1872); Boutwell to Hooper, Treasury Department, February 3, 1872, NA RG 104, Fair Copies of Letters to Mint, v. IV; Hooper to Pollock, Washington, March 13, 1872, NA RG 104, GCM, box 124.

17. Ernest Seyd, *Suggestions in Reference to the Metallic Currency of the United States of America* (London: Trübner & Co., 1871), pp. 2–11, 39–51, 159–60; Seyd, *The Question of Seignorage and Charge for Coining* (London: Effingham Wilson, 1868), *passim;* Seyd, *Bullion and Foreign Exchanges Theoretically and Practically Considered* (London: Effingham Wilson, 1868), pp. 650–56; Seyd to Hooper, London, February 17, 1872, in *SMD* 29, 53:1, pp. 1–13. (a draft copy exists in Treasury records, U.S. Archives, for 1872).

18. H. R. Linderman, *The Free Coinage of Gold* (Philadelphia: n.p., 1872; dated February 22, 1872); Linderman to A. A. Sargent, May 7, 1874, in *SMD* 109, 43:1, pp. 1–2; John Jay Knox in *House Report* 3967, 51:2 (February 23, 1891), p. 454; Linderman in Mint Director's report for 1875, *HED* 2, 44:1, p. 298; Sherman *Recollections*, pp. 465–66.

19. *Congressional Globe*, 42:2, pp. 2304–17, 2343; *HMD* 13, 42:3, p. 59; Minute Book of Banking and Currency Committee, 1871–72, NA LB 42A–F4.1; *House Journal*, 42:2, p. 583 (March 26, 1872); R. W. Tayler, "United States Mint: Report on its Management and Condition by the Comptroller of the Treasury to the Secretary," April 3, 1872, in Clayton McMichael papers, Pennsylvania Historical Society (my thanks to Allen Weinstein for calling this item to my attention); George Eyster to Boutwell, Philadelphia, August 7, October 23, 1871, and January 23, February 20, July 22, November 15, 1872, NA RG 56, to ST, box 30.

20. New York State Chamber of Commerce, *Report of the Committee on Coinage . . . April 4, 1872* (New York: John W. Amerman, 1872), pp. 4–6; Resolution of New York State Chamber of Commerce on coinage, May 6, 1872, presented by Senator Roscoe Conkling, in NA LB, Senate Finance Committee papers; *Senate Journal*, 42:2, pp. 682 (May 8,

1872), 868 (May 28, 1872), 871 (May 29, 1872); *Congressional Globe,* 42:2, p. 3883.

21. *Congressional Globe,* 42:3, p. 203 (December 16, 1872); *Banker's Magazine,* June 1873, 926–27; *New York World,* January 11, 1873; Ruggles to Publishers of *Congressional Globe,* January 21, 1873, in Ruggles papers, New York Public Library; National Board of Trade, *Proceedings,* 1870, p. 327; *ibid.,* 1872, pp. 218–19.

22. *HED* 2, 42:3, p. 417; Thos. C. Acton to Pollock, New York Assay Office, September 11, 1872, NA RG 104, GCM, box 126; *Economist,* November 9, 1872, p. 1365.

23. *HED* 2, 42:3, pp. xi–xii, 432.

24. *Banker's Magazine,* March 1873, 710–12; Linderman, *Money and Legal Tender in the United States* (New York: G. P. Putnam's Sons, 1878), pp. 48–50, 58–60. In this book, Linderman oddly denied on p. 44 that the German demonetization or any other indication of the fall in silver price preceded the planning of the silver dollar demonetization, but on p. 48 he said that the German action was not only known but was taken at the Treasury as a warning signal. Also, Evans, *Illustrated History of the United States Mint,* p. 105; Linderman to Boutwell, Philadelphia, May 21, 1872, NA RG 104, to ST; Boutwell to Sherman, Treasury, December 14, 1872 (enclosing drafts of the trade dollar amendment to the coinage bill), NA RG 104, Fair Copies of Letters to the Mint, vol. V; Knox to Pollock, Washington, January 13, 1873, and Acting Treasury Secretary Richardson to Pollock, January 13, 1873, NA RG 104, GCM, box 127; *House Report* 3967, 51:2 (1891), p. 451; *Senate Report* 703, 44:2 (1876), p. 200.

25. *Congressional* Globe, 42:3, discussion and action on H.R. 2934, *passim* pp. 363–1364 (January 7–February 14, 1873).

Notes to Chapter 13

1. Rep. Richard P. Bland (D-Mo.) in *Congressional Record,* 44:1 (August 5, 1876), pp. 4234, 5236; *Workingman's Advocate,* August 26, 1876; Esquirou de Parieu in *Le Correspondant,* LXXV (new series; May 25, 1878), 722.

2. *Senate Report* 703, 44:2, pp. 89–93; *Congressional Record,* VI (45:1), p. 271 (November 7, 1877).

3. Mrs. Sarah E. V. Emery, *Seven Financial Conspiracies That Shook the World* (East Lansing, Mich.: Robert Smith & Co., 1887), pp. 57–60, 68; *Atchison Times,* September 4, 1890; *Topeka Daily Press,* April 8, 1894; "Island Home," in Populist Party Pamphlets, II, Kansas State

Historical Society; *Congressional Record,* 53:1, p. 561 (August 21, 1893).

4. Stewart in *Congressional Record,* 53:1, pp. 1212–17, 1230–31, 2911; *Proceedings of the First National Silver Convention . . . St. Louis, 1889* (St. Louis: Burton & Skinner Stationery Co.), pp. xiii, 20–23, 57, 111–12, 202; National Executive Silver Committee, *Silver in the Fifty-first Congress, Preceded by a Summary of the Coinage Laws . . . and a History of the Act of 1873. . . .*(Washington: Geo. R. Gray, 1890), pp. 14–30.

5. First National Silver Convention, *Proceedings,* pp. 153, 156; John Davis Scrapbooks, Kansas State Historical Society; *New York Sun,* September 21, 1893; Boutwell to Linderman, several letters, August–October 1871, NA RG 104, Fair Copies of Letters from Treasury to Mint; *Congressional Record,* 53:1, pp. 1059–60, 1870–72 (August 30, September 28, 1893); Knox, *History of Banking,* p. 144; Seyd, *Suggestions,* p. 207.

6. *Congressional Record,* 53:1, pp. 1054–61 (August 30, 1893); Linderman, *Money and Legal Tender,* pp. 44–45; Boutwell, *Reminiscences of Sixty Years in Public Affairs* (New York: McClure, Phillips & Co., 1902), ii: 130, 151.

7. For a discussion, with specific references, of the orthodox legend of the Coinage Act of 1873, see Walter T. K. Nugent, *The Money Question During Reconstruction* (New York: W. W. Norton & Co., 1967), pp. 65–66, 111–15. A similar point with reference to greenbacks was made by Bray Hammond in "The North's Empty Purse, 1861–1862," *American Historical Review,* LXVII (October 1961), 15.

Notes to Chapter 14

1. *Commercial and Financial Chronicle,* October 25, 1873; *Workingman's Advocate,* October 18, November 15, 1873; *Brotherhood of Locomotive Engineers' Weekly Journal,* November 1873, 531.

2. The following sketch of American and other economic conditions in the seventies is based on Thorp, *Business Annals,* pp. 76–79, 94–95, 129–33, 166–68, 188–90, 206–09; Persons *et al.,* "Business and Financial Conditions Following the Civil War in the United States," *loc. cit.,* 9–17; Wesley C. Mitchell, *Gold, Prices, and Wages under the Greenback Standard,* p. 282; O. V. Wells, "The Depression of 1873," *Agricultural History,* XI (July 1937), 238–48; J. T. W. Newbold, "The Beginnings of the World Crisis, 1873–97," *Economic History* (A supplement to the *Economic Journal*), II (1932), 425, 431–32.

3. Adding plausibility to the notion that the country's financial ills rested in its use of inconvertible paper. This unfortunate conclusion ignored certain facts, such as that the Panic occurred in America not during a time of severe greenback fluctuation but three years after the greenback had stabilized at a fairly low level above gold.

4. Seyd, *The Fall in the Price of Silver* (London: Henry S. King & Co., 1876), pp. 63, 81; Francis A. Walker, "The Monetary Conferences of 1867 and 1878, and the Future of Silver," *loc. cit.,* 34–39; Newbold, "Beginnings of the World Crisis," *loc. cit.,* 435.

5. Walter Bagehot, *Some Articles on the Depreciation of Silver and on Topics Connected With It* (London: Henry S. King & Co., 1877), pp. 5–6; Robert Giffen, *Essays in Finance* (London: George Bell and Sons, 1900), pp. 202–03; Ernest Seyd, *Fall in the Price of Silver,* pp. 101–02; Francis A. Walker, "The Monetary Conferences of 1867 and 1878," *loc. cit.,* 40; Russell, *International Monetary Conferences,* pp. 146–48; Samuel Smith, "Three Letters on the Silver Question," appendix to H. Cernuschi, *Nomisma, or, Legal Tender* (New York: D. Appleton and Company, 1877), p. 146; (London) *Times,* July 11, 20, 29, 1876; Stephen Bourne, "On Some Phases of the Silver Question," *Journal of the Statistical Society of London,* XLII (June 1879), 447.

6. Léon Say, *Les Finances de la France sous la Troisième République,* ii: 61–106, iv: 1–2; Willis, *History of the Latin Monetary Union,* chaps. 12, 13; France, Assemblée Nationale, *Annales,* XXXII (June 18, 1874), pp. 255–56; France, Ministère des Finances, *Recueil des Lois de Finances,* 1874, pp. 293–94; 1876, pp. 8–9, 75.

7. *Banker's Magazine,* November 1873, 350; *Economist,* November 15, 1873; May 16, 1874; September 18, October 16, 30, November 20, December 11, 18, 25, 1875; April 22, September 30, November 11, 1876. Also, (London) *Times,* July 6, 1874; July 5, 1875. Also, Stolper, *German Economy,* p. 33; Oswald Schneider, *Bismarcks Finanz- und Wirtschaftspolitik* (Munich and Leipzig: Verlag von Duncker & Humblot, 1912), pp. 50–51; Lambi, *Free Trade and Protection in Germany,* pp. 91–92, chapter 9 *passim;* Bruno Gebhardt, *Handbuch der Deutschen Geschichte* (Stuttgart: Union Verlag, 1960), iii: 403–04; Wilhelm Gerloff, *Die Finanz- und Zollpolitik des Deutschen Reiches* (Jena: Verlag von Gustav Fischer, 1913), p. 120; Horst Kohl, ed., *Die politischen Reden des Fürsten Bismarck* (Stuttgart and Berlin: J. G. Cotta'sche Buchhandlung Nachfolger, 1922), v: 177; Hartwig, *Bamberger,* pp. 53–58; Bamberger, *Reichsgold: Studien über Währung und Wechsel* (Leipzig: F. A. Brockhaus, 1876), *passim.*

Notes to Chapter 15

1. *Congressional Record*, 43:1, p. 698; Dorfman, *Economic Mind in American Civilization*, iii: 81.

2. Henry Carey Baird, *The Silver Dollar* (Philadelphia: Henry Carey Baird & Co., 1883), pp. 3, 10–19, 27; Baird, *John Sherman*, pp. 2–3; James A. Garfield, "The Currency Conflict," *Atlantic Monthly*, February 1876, 223–29; *Popular Science Monthly*, January 1877, 368, and March 1878, 582; *Banker's Magazine*, November 1878, 364; Bagehot, *Physics and Politics*, p. 11; *SED* 58, 45:3, pp. 742–43; H. V. Poor, *Resumption and the Silver Question*, pp. 125–31.

3. *HED* 18, 19, and 20, 45:1; A. A. A. S., *Proceedings*, 1875, pp. 19–25; *Commercial and Financial Chronicle*, July 7, 1877; *House Reports* 53, 64, 136, 45:3; *HMD* 29, 45:3, p. 51.

4. Jevons paper, in American Social Science Association, *The Silver Question* (Boston: A. Williams & Co., 1877), pp. 27–32; Bagehot, *Some Articles on the Depreciation of Silver*, pp. 79–80, 114.

5. Newcomb, *The ABC of Finance*, pp. 38–42, 53–56, 69–72, 96–98; *SMD* 109, 43:1 (May 7, 1874), p. 3; *Banker's Magazine*, June 1874, 940.

6. *HMD* 29, 45:3, p. 173; David A. Wells, *The Recent Financial, Industrial, and Commercial Experiences of the United States* (New York: J. H. and C. M. Godsell, 1872), pp. 44, 59–61; Wells, *The Silver Question* (New York: G. P. Putnam's Sons, 1878), pp. 13, 19, 34, 37, 40; Wells, *Robinson Crusoe's Money* (New York: Harper & Brothers, Publishers, 1879), pp. 31–32, 40, 79–80, 94–98; Henry Varnum Poor, *Resumption and the Silver Question*, pp. 229, 237–39, 241; J. K. Upton, *Money in Politics* (Boston: D. Lothrop Company, 1884), pp. vii, xi; David K. Watson, *History of American Coinage* (New York: G. P. Putnam's Sons, 1899), pp. 142–43.

7. Seyd, *Reform of the Bank of England Note Issue* (London: Harrison and Sons, 1873), p. 111; Seyd, *The Banks of Issue Question* (London: Edward Standford, 1875), p. 78; Seyd, *The Fall in the Price of Silver* (London: Henry S. King & Co., 1876), *passim;* Seyd, *The Decline of Prosperity: Its Insidious Cause and Obvious Remedy* (London: Edward Standford, 1879), *passim; Senate Report* 703, 44:2, pp. 106–11.

8. Emile de Laveleye, "La monnaie internationale, projet de Confédération Monétaire," *Revue des Deux Mondes*, LXVIII (2d series; April 1, 1867), 629, 633, 636; Laveleye article in *ibid.*, July 1875, trans. in *Banker's Magazine*, February 1879, 608–09, March 1879, 698–706, April 1879, 767; Laveleye, *Bi-metallic Money* (trans. George Walker;

New York: The Banker's Magazine and Statistical Register, 1877), *passim.*

9. Dorfman, *Economic Mind*, iii: 83–89; Fine, *Laissez Faire and the General-Welfare State*, pp. 198–200; Russell, *International Monetary Conferences*, pp. 140–45; Wolowski, "Essay on the Historical Method in Political Economy," in Wilhelm Roscher, *Principles of Political Economy* (New York: Henry Holt & Co., 1878), i: 10, 17, 23, 27–34; Roscher, *ibid.*, ii: 123–26; William D. Kelley, *Letters from Europe* (Philadelphia: Porter and Coates [1879]), pp. 21–23, 31; *Banker's Magazine,* February 1878, 581–82; Samuel Smith, *Three Letters on the Silver Question,* pp. 156–57.

10. S. Dana Horton, *Silver and Gold* (Cincinnati: Robert Clarke & Co., 1877), especially pp. 14–15, 36, 52–56, 145–46, 153; Francis A. Walker, *Money in its Relations to Trade and Industry* (New York: Henry Holt and Company, 1889 [1st printing 1879]), especially pp. 67, 78–80, 136, 152, 181–83, 324; Walker, "The Monetary Conferences of 1867 and 1878," *loc. cit.*, 43–44; Walker, *International Bimetallism* (New York: Henry Holt and Company, 1896), pp. iv, 155–62; W. S. Groesbeck, *Gold and Silver* (Cincinnati: Robert Clarke & Co., 1877), *passim;* Robert W. Hughes, *A Popular Treatise on the Currency Question, written from a Southern Point of View* (New York: G. P. Putnam's Sons, 1879), especially pp. iv–v, 29–44, 66, 127–34, 212–13; H. D. Barrows, *Bi-Metalism* (n.p., n.d., signed Los Angeles, May 28, 1876), *passim;* B. F. Nourse letter, *Commercial and Financial Chronicle,* December 14, 1878; Nourse paper in American Social Science Association, *The Silver Question* (Boston: A. Williams & Co., 1877), pp. 6–25.

11. *Banker's Magazine,* March 1867, 674–88, May 1876, 867, July 1876, 56–57, September 1876, 206–07, October 1876, 256–57, August 1877, 132–36, March 1878, 710–11, May 1878, 853, November 1878, 385; George Walker to McCulloch, Springfield, Mass., December 4, 1867, in McCulloch papers, Library of Congress; N. S. Shaler, "The Silver Question Geologically Considered," *Atlantic Monthly,* May 1878, 629; SMD 26, 44:2; HMD 29, 45:3, pp. 364–65; S. B. Ruggles, *Vital Necessity of Preliminary International Monetary Conference for Establishing the Relative Legal Values of Gold and Silver Coin* ("Letter from Samuel B. Ruggles in behalf of the New-York Chamber of Commerce, to the Director of the Mint of the United States, November 28th, 1876"; New York: Press of the Chamber of Commerce, 1877), *passim;* Ruggles, *The Dollar of Our Fathers* (New York: Press of the Chamber of Commerce, 1877), pp. 5–6; Sherman, *Recollections,* p. 546.

12. William A. Berkey, *The Money Question* (Grand Rapids: W. W. Hart, 1876), pp. iii–iv, 30–47, 53, 311, 359; *House Report* 328, 43:2, pp. 2–5; Cooper in *HED* 5, 46:2 (September 1879), pp. 377–78; Henry Carey Baird, "Money and its Substitutes," *Atlantic Monthly*, March 1876, 345, 356–57.

13. Berkey, *op. cit.*, pp. 358, 363–67; Henry Carey Baird, *Criticisms of the Recent Financial Policies of the United States and France* (Philadelphia: Henry Carey Baird & Co., 1875), pp. 3–4, 15; Peter Cooper, *Ideas for a Science of Good Government* (New York: Trow's Printing and Bookbinding Company, 1883), pp. 21, 26, 121, 155, 329, 391; Dorfman, *Economic Mind*, iii: 16–18; *HED* 5, 46:2 (July 1879), pp. 129, 132, 134; Laughlin, *History of Bimetallism*, p. 191*n;* Usher, *The Greenback Movement of 1875–1884*, p. 9.

Notes to Chapter 16

1. National Board of Trade, *Proceedings*, 1875, pp. 130–61, 1876, pp. 43, 69–84, 91–127, 1877, p. 45 and *passim*, 1879 pp. 3–5, 31, 162; National Board of Trade, *The National Board of Trade: Its Past and Its Future* (Boston: James F. Cotter & Co., 1878), pp. 2–7; Cincinnati Chamber of Commerce, *Annual Report*, 1877, p. 23.

2. *Railway World* (Philadelphia), October 23, 30, 1875; February 12, 26, May 13, August 26, December 23, 1876; April 13, 1878.

3. *Commercial and Financial Chronicle*, September 12, 1874; August 11, September 15, 1877; January 19, July 13, 1878.

4. [Presidents of Boston, New York and Philadelphia national banks], *The Silver Question; Memorial to Congress, January 1878* (New York: Arthur & Bonnell, 1878), *passim; Banker's Magazine*, May 1874, 842, 847, November 1874, 372, July 1876, 3–4, August 1876, 82–83, August 1878, 85–86, 117; *Senate Report* 703, 44:2, ii: 433–34; *HED* 5, 46:2, pp. 6–12, 14–20, 52–68.

5. (Pittsburgh) *National Labor Tribune*, May 4, 29, July 3, 1875, January 20, 27, 1877, December 7, 1878; *Workingman's Advocate*, September 27, November 22, December 18, 1873, January 31, February 7, November 14–21, 28, 1874, January 30, May 29, 1875, February 12, March 11, April 8, May 13, 1876; *HED* 5, 46:2, pp. 155–56; (New York) *Socialist*, April 22, May 13, June 10, 1876; (New York) *Labor Standard*, September 2, 1876, March 10, 1878.

6. National Grange, *Proceedings of the Sixth Session* (Washington: Gibson Brothers, 1873); same, *Journal of the Ninth Session* (Louisville: Printed by John P. Morton & Co., 1875), pp. 175–77; *American Agricul-*

turist, November 1873; Jonathan Periam, *The Groundswell* (Cincinnati: E. Hannaford & Company, 1874); Lee Benson, *Merchants, Farmers, and Railroads,* p. 274*n.*

7. *Prairie Farmer,* January 4, 25, May 7, 1873; Stephen R. Smith, *Grains for the Grangers* (Philadelphia: John E. Potter & Company, 1874), pp. 167, 189; (Chicago) *Industrial Age,* August 20, 30, September 6, 20, 27, October 25, 1873, January 3, March 28, April 18, December 26, 1874, January 2, 1875; National Grange, *Journal,* 1875, p. 152.

8. (New York) *Iron Age,* September 18, 1873, March 26, April 9, 16, September 10, 1874; William B. Weeden, "The Functions of Association in its Relation to Labor," *Popular Science Monthly,* March 1876, 586–95; Dorfman, *Economic Mind,* iii: 16–18; Unger, *Greenback Era,* pp. 283–85; *Senate Report* 703, 44:2, pp. 3–15; American Iron and Steel Association, *Bulletin,* November 12, 1873; *HMD* 29, 45:3, pp. 123–24; *HED* 5, 46:2, pp. 172–76; Johnstown (Pa.) *Industrial Bulletin,* May 1873, May 1874; *Manufacturer and Builder,* October 1873, p. 234; February 1874, pp. 39–40; December 1874, p. 275.

Notes to Chapter 17

1. See the periodicals mentioned, *passim* for the years 1874–79, but especially *Scribner's Monthly,* November 1878, 147; *Nation,* April 30, 1874, July 19, 26, August 2, December 6, 13, 1877, February 28, May 9, June 20, August 1, December 26, 1878; *Popular Science Monthly,* March 1878, 587; *Harpers' Weekly,* August 11, December 29, 1877. Also, *New York Times,* January 21, 1875, July 8, 1877, February 21, 1878; *McPherson's Hand-book of Politics,* 1876, pp. 226–33; *SMD* 46, 44:1; *SMD* 47, 44:1; *SMD* 13, 45:2; *SMD* 26, 45:2.

2. *San Francisco Daily Bulletin,* February 1, 2, 5, 7, 23, 1878; (Denver) *Rocky Mountain News,* October 12, 16, 17, 1873, February 17, 24, March 2, December 18, 1878; H. D. Barrows, *Silver and Greenbacks* (Los Angeles: n.p., 1877); Conrad Wiegand, *An Appeal to the Press and Legislators of the Civilized World. Showing Monetization of Silver to be a Need of Mankind* (Virginia City: n.p., 1876).

3. *New Orleans Democrat,* October 16, 30, November 8, December 20, 1877; August 17, 1878.

4. *Chicago Times,* April 23, 1874; Topeka *Commonwealth,* August 2, 1877; Cincinnati *Commercial,* October 3, 1878; Cincinnati *Gazette,* February 16, 1878; George L. Anderson, "Western Attitudes Toward National Banks, 1873–74," *Mississippi Valley Historical Review,* XXIII (September 1936), 211–16.

Notes to Chapter 18

1. Sherman to Grant, Washington, February 11, 1873, draft in Sherman papers, Library of Congress.

2. *Commercial and Financial Chronicle*, January 11, 18, October 20, 1873, January 7, March 7, 1874; *Banker's Magazine*, November 1873, 418–22, January 1874, 513; *Iron Age*, October 2, November 27, 1873, April 30, 1874; *Workingman's Advocate*, September 27, November 1, 1873.

3. *House Journal*, 43:1, *passim; Senate Journal*, 43:1, pp. 981–82.

4. *House Journal*, 43:1, pp. 648–49, 801–02; *Senate Journal*, 43:1, pp. 433–34, 464; *Congressional Record*, 43:1, pp. 2350–70, 2393–95, 2495–2508, 2548–99, 2703–08, 2803–10, 2829–35, 2886, 2917–21, 2964-76, 3002, 3077–78.

5. *SED* 44, 43:1; *Senate Journal*, 43:1, p. 505.

6. *Congressional Record*, 43:1, pp. 3839, 3882–97; 5189; *HMD* 293, 43:1; *House Journal*, 43:1, p. 1286; *Commercial and Financial Chronicle*, October 10, 1874; *Banker's Magazine*, May 1874, 917; *Industrial Age*, April 25, 1874; *Iron Age*, April 16, June 25, 1874; *Workingman's Advocate*, May 2, 1874; *New York Times*, April 22, 23, 1874; *Indianapolis Sentinel*, April 23, 1874; *Chicago Times*, April 9, 23, 1874; *Topeka Commonwealth*, April 11, 17, 1874; *San Francisco Daily Bulletin*, April 3, 11, 15, 1874.

7. As Professor Unger has clearly shown; Irwin Unger, "The Business Community and the Origins of the 1875 Resumption Act," *Business History Review*, XXXV (Summer 1961), 253–55, and *The Greenback Era,* chapter viii.

8. *Senate Journal*, 43:2, pp. 58, 67–68, 85, 115–16; *Congressional Record*, 43:2, pp. 161, 186–208, 317–18; *McPherson's Hand-Book of Politics*, 1876, pp. 125–27; Spaulding, *History of Legal Tender Paper*, pp. 20–22.

9. *Commercial and Financial Chronicle*, December 26, 1874; *Banker's Magazine*, February 1875, 569; National Board of Trade, *Proceedings*, 1875, pp. 15–16; *Railway World*, January 9, 30, November 13, 1875; *Workingman's Advocate*, March 20, May 29, 1875; *Industrial Age*, January 2, 1875; New York *World*, January 2, 7, 1875; *New York Times*, January 8, 1875; *Chicago Times*, January 15, 16, 1875; Cincinnati *Gazette*, January 8, 1875; *Indianapolis Sentinel*, January 8, 1875; *San Francisco Daily Bulletin*, January 8, 1875.

Notes to Chapter 19

1. *Senate Journal*, 44:1, pp. 108, 217, 432, 566, 575, 606, 784; George L. Anderson, "The Proposed Resumption of Silver Payments in 1873," *Pacific Historical Review*, VIII (September 1939), 304–15; *SED* 11, 44:1; Neil Carothers, *Fractional Money*, pp. 248–57; Sherman to Secretary of the Treasury B. H. Bristow, Washington, February 23, 1876, NA RG 56, to ST, box 82; Sherman to C. L. Conant, telegram, Washington, April 6, 1876, *ibid.;* Sherman to Samuel B. Ruggles, Washington, March 6, 1876, in Sherman papers, Library of Congress; *SMD* 35, 44:1; *Congressional Record*, 44:1, pp. 3684–86 (June 8, 1876).

2. *Congressional Record*, 44:1, pp. 1811, 2917, 3555–56, 4704, 4733, 4865–68, 5080, 5216–45, 5323, appendix pp. 283–88; *House Journal*, 44:1, pp. 1392–93 and *passim; McPherson's Hand-Book of Politics*, 1876, pp. 170–83, 234–35.

3. *House Journal*, 44:2, pp. 71–72, 109–10; *Senate Journal*, pp. 96, 162, 254, 290; *Congressional Record*, 44:2, pp. 162–72, 647 (December 13, 1876, and January 16, 1877); Sherman to McCulloch, Senate Chamber, December 21, 1876, in McCulloch papers, Library of Congress.

4. "Report and Accompanying Documents of the United States Monetary Commission, organized under Joint Resolution of August 15, 1876," *Senate Report* 703, 44:2 (2 vols.; 1877, 1879), *passim;* British Parliamentary Papers, "Copy of Extracts of Papers received from the Government of India," 1877, lxiii, p. 18.

5. J. A. Dacus, *Annals of the Great Strikes in the United States* (St. Louis: Scammell & Company, 1877), pp. 100–01, 114–15; James Dabney McCabe, *The History of the Great Riots* (Philadelphia: National Publishing Company, 1877), p. 118; *Chicago Times*, July 23, 1877; *Indianapolis Sentinel*, July 23, 1877.

Notes to Chapter 20

1. *Congressional Record*, 45:1, pp. 203–04, 241–42, 255, 257–62, 266–68, 581, 628–33 (October 31 through November 23, 1877); *House Journal*, 45:1, pp. 143–44 (November 5, 1877); *McPherson's Hand-Book of Politics*, 1878, pp. 143–74.

2. Sherman, *Recollections*, pp. 571–77; discussion of resumption by Hugh McCulloch, William D. Kelley, David A. Wells, Joseph Ropes, Thomas Ewing, and John Sherman in *North American Review*, November-December 1877, 397–426.

3. National Board of Trade, *Proceedings*, 1877, pp. 94, 155–59, 175–

76, 189–217; Linderman, *Money and Legal Tender*, pp. 100–03; *HED* 80, 45:2; *HMD* 44, 45:2; Sherman, *Recollections*, pp. 604–05; *Commercial and Financial Chronicle*, December 15, 1877; *Railway World*, October 27, 1877; *HMD* 26, 45:2; *Senate Journal*, 45:2, petitions, *passim*.

4. Leland L. Sage, *William Boyd Allison* (Iowa City: State Historical Society of Iowa, 1956), pp. 152–57, believes Allison made his amendments on his own initiative but that they adequately suited Secretary Sherman. Also, *Congressional Record*, 45:2, pp. 47, 88–93, 549–61, 607–18, 627–28, 666–70, 726–28, 757–63, 789, 820–22, 843–54, 983–89, 1052–1112, 1238–85; *McPherson's Hand-Book of Politics, 1878*, pp. 127–35; *Senate Journal*, 45:2, pp. 31, 209, 231, 252; *House Journal*, 45:2, pp. 458, 485; T. Harry Williams, ed., *Hayes, the Diary of a President, 1875–1881* (New York: David McKay Company, Inc., 1964), pp. 115-16; *HED* 59, 45:2; *Commercial and Financial Chronicle*, February 23, 1878; *Banker's Magazine*, February 1878, 661; New York *World*, February 17, 1878; New Orleans *Democrat*, March 1, 1878; *Indianapolis Sentinel*, February 22, 1878; Topeka *Commonwealth*, February 19, 1878; *New-Yorker Staats-Zeitung*, February 11, 1878; *The Nation*, February 28, 1878.

5. Sectionally the vote on Voorhees' amendment was as follows (including announced pairs): Northeast 3–16; Midwest 9–10; South 17–6; Far West 2–2. Of the eleven absentees (those for whom a decision might have been too difficult to make or announce), five were from the Northeast and four from the Far West, including both Oregon Senators. The party breakdown: in favor, 22 Democrats, 8 Republicans, one Independent; opposed, 9 Democrats, 25 Republicans. Contrary to the usual trend of their party or section: in favor, 3 Northeastern Democrats (Maryland, West Virginia, Pennsylvania), 3 Midwestern Republicans (Illinois and both Kansans), 3 Southern Republicans (Mississippi, Alabama, Florida); opposed, 7 Northeastern Democrats (2 from Connecticut, 2 from Delaware, 2 from New Jersey, one New Yorker) and two Southern Democrats (South Carolina, Florida).

Chicago Times, February 4, 27, 1878; *Cincinnati Commercial*, February 20, 1878; (London) *Times*, February 15, 1878; *House Journal*, 45:2, p. 1406 and *passim*; Senate Journal, 45:2, pp. 1001–02 and *passim*; *HMD* 62, 45:2, *passim*; Bolles, *Financial History*, p. 297; *McPherson's Hand-Book of Politics, 1878*, pp. 147–52; *Congressional Record*, 45:2, pp. 2689, 3080–87, 3189–93, 3470, 3491–99, 3561–65, 4536–49, 4620, 4785–86.

Notes to Chapter 21

1. *Commercial and Financial Chronicle*, May 4, 1878; K. Baekeder, *Paris and its Environs* (Leipsic: Karl Baedeker, 1878), p. 6 and maps; *Galignani's New Paris Guide for 1878* (Paris: The Galignani Library, 1878), pp. 291, 293, and maps; *The Illustrated Catalogue of the Paris International Exhibition* (London: Virtue & Co., 1878), p. x.

2. *Senate Report* 39, 44:1; *House Report* 918, 45:2, p. 14; Russell, *International Monetary Conference*, pp. 203–04; *Banker's Magazine*, May 1878, 850.

3. British Parliamentary Papers, 1878–79, lv, p. 24; *ibid.*, 1877, lxiii, pp. 3, 4, 18; Walter Bagehot, *Some Articles on the Depreciation of Silver*, pp. iv–v, 96; Treasury Official to Sir Julian Pauncefote (at Foreign Office), Treasury, Whitehall, March 28, 1878, in Public Record Office (London), FO 5/1653; Louis Mallet to Under-Secretary of State of Foreign Office, India Office, London, May 16, 1878, in *ibid.*

4. Gebhardt, *op. cit.*, pp. 403–04, 407; Walther Lotz, *Die Ideen der deutschen Handelspolitik*, pp. 119–22, 154; Sartorius von Waltershausen, *Deutsche Wirtschaftsgeschichte*, p. 298; Graham, "Cobden's Influence on Bismarck," 440–41; Hartwig, *Bamberger*, p. 58; Lambi, *Free Trade and Protection in Germany*, pp. 91–92.

5. Esquirou de Parieu, "L'Unification monétaire devant l'Exposition Universelle de 1878," *Journal des Economistes*, I (4th series; February 1878), 179; Esquirou de Parieu, "La question de l'uniformité monétaire en 1878," *Correspondant*, LXXV (new series; May 25, 1878), 720–26; Victor Bonnet, "La Reprise de l'Etalon d'Argent aux Etats-Unis et le Projet de Conférence Internationale," Revue des Deux Mondes, XXVII (3d series; June 1, 1878), 679–80, 688; Henri Cernuschi, *The Bland Bill: Its grounds Its Alleged Dishonesty, Its Imperfections, Its Future* (Paris: Published by the Author, 1878), pp. 9–10, 17; George Walker, "Bi-Metallism in Europe," *Banker's Magazine*, May 1878, 854–55; Francis A. Walker, *Money in its Relations to Trade and Industry*, p. 171; Francis A. Walker, "The Monetary Conferences of 1867 and 1878, and the Future of Silver," *loc. cit.*, 47–52; London *Economist*, December 1, 1877, p. 1425; France, Ministère des Finances, *Recueil des Lois de Finances*, 1878, p. 7; Say, *Les Finances de la France sous la Troisième République*, ii: 107; *Annales du Sénat et de la Chambre des Députés*, 1878, i: 14, 61–63, 374 (January 12, 24, 28, 31, 1878).

6. The American Commissioners were Reuben E. Fenton, a former Republican Governor and Senator from New York, then on the outs with the New York Republican organization, and no financial expert;

William S. Groesbeck, the free-silverite Congressman from Ohio who had been a member of the U.S. Monetary Commission of 1876; and Francis A. Walker, the international bimetallist, then Superintendent of the U.S. Census and a Professor of Political Economy at Yale. The Secretary was S. Dana Horton, with Walker the other leader of theoretical international bimetallism in the United States.

Richard Assheton Cross, M.P. (Parliamentary Private Secretary to Prime Minister Lord Salisbury) to John Welsh (of the U.S. Legation, London), June 11, 1878, in Public Record Office, London, FO 5/1653; Senator William B. Allison to Samuel B. Ruggles, Washington, November 23, 1877, in Ruggles papers, New York Public Library; *SMD* 109, 44:1; *House Journal*, 45:2, p. 1281; *New York Times*, July 23, 1878; *Commercial and Financial Chronicle*, June 15, August 17, 1878; *Nation*, June 20, 1878; Topeka *Commonwealth*, April 25, July 6, 1878.

7. Ernest Seyd to Francis A. Walker, London, August 16, 23, 27, 29, 1878, in Walker papers, Library of Congress; Seyd, *The Wealth and Commerce of Nations and the Question of Silver, with Special Reference to the Indian Valuation and the Indian Monetary Conference at Paris* (London: Eden Fisher & Co., 1878), especially p. 54.

8. *SED* 58, 45:3, pp. vii, 1–169 (Procès-verbaux of the International Monetary Conference); Cernuschi, *La Diplomatie Monétaire en 1878* (Paris: Librairie de Guillaumin et Cie, 1878), pp. 15–20, 28, 32–33, 39, 48–49, 80; Joh. Phil. Schneider, *Die Pariser Münz-Conferenzen von 1878* (Bremen: Verlag von G. Rauchfuss, 1879), pp. 36–44, 73–74, 84–87. Feer-Herzog had been a rigorous and vocal monometallist for years, and had represented Switzerland at the Latin Union Conference of 1865 and the International Monetary Conference of 1867. Göschen was a Member of Parliament, a former Cabinet minister, and a monetary theorist of some reputation.

9. Feer-Herzog and C. Lardy, *La Conférence Monétaire Americaine, tenue à Paris du 10 au 29 âout 1878. Rapport au Conseil Fédéral Suisse* (Berne: Imprimerie de K.-J. Wyss, 1878), pp. 18–20, 60–67; "Report of the Commissioners appointed to represent Her Majesty's Government at the Monetary Conference held at Paris in August 1878," British Parliamentary Papers, 1878–79, xxi (C. 2196), pp. 105–15; *SED* 58, 45:3, pp. 203–16, 741–57; *Commercial and Financial Chronicle*, September 7, 1878.

10. *HMD* 29, 45:3; *Indianapolis Sentinel*, October 30, 1878; Sidney Fine, *Laissez Faire and the General-Welfare State*, pp. 307–08; Lee Benson, *Merchants, Farmers, and Railroads*, pp. 102–04, 138.

11. Albert S. Bolles, *Financial History*, pp. 298–300; John Jay Knox,

United States Notes, p. 141; Cincinnati *Commercial,* December 17, 18, 1878; Topeka *Commonwealth,* December 1878, *passim;* Railway World, December 21, 1878; (Pittsburgh) *National Labor Tribune,* December 21, 1878; *Commercial and Financial Chronicle,* January 4, 1879.

12. *House Journal,* 45:3, *passim; ibid.,* 46:1, p. 396 and *passim; HMD* 11, 46:1; *Banker's Magazine,* November 1878, 349, December 1878, 456, 459, June 1879, 988; *Railway World,* December 6, 1879; W. A. Shaw, *The History of the Currency 1252 to 1894* (London: Clement Wilson, 1896), iii: 280–81; Horace White, *Money and Banking,* p. 77.

Notes to Chapter 22

1. See for example, its appearance in the statements of President Herbert Hoover in Albert U. Romasco, *The Poverty of Abundance* (New York: Oxford University Press, 1965), chapter 2.

2. Schumpeter, *Business Cycles,* i: 44, 544–48; Rendigs Fels, *American Business Cycles, 1865–1897* (Chapel Hill: The University of North Carolina Press, 1959), p. 89; Kindahl, "The Economic of Specie Resumption," pp. 59–60; F. D. Graham, "International Trade Under Depreciated Paper. The United States, 1862–79," *Quarterly Journal of Economics,* XXXVI (February 1922), 248, 272–73; Mitchell, *Gold, Prices and Wages Under the Greenback Standard,* pp. 250, 252, 257–63, 273–76; George Boutwell to Edward Atkinson, Washington, July 6, 1868, in Atkinson papers, Massachusetts Historical Society.

3. Samuel Rezneck, "Distress, Relief, and Discontent in the United States During the Depression of 1873–78," *Journal of Political Economy,* LVIII (December 1950), 501–07.

4. *HED* 5, 46:2, p. 396; William D. Kelley, *Speeches,* p. 193; *Congressional Record,* 53:1, pp. 217–23 (August 8, 1893); Henry McNeil to Francis A. Walker, London, November 7, 1896, in Walker papers, Library of Congress; Horace White, *Money and Banking,* pp. 19–23; New York Daily Commercial Bulletin, *The Money Agitation* (n.p., 1879); Willard Fisher, " 'Coin' and His Critics," *Quarterly Journal of Economics,* X (January 1896), 207–08; J. Laurence Laughlin, *The History of Bimetallism in the United States* (2d ed.; New York: D. Appleton and Company, 1896), pp. xi–xii, 5–7. The hard-money bias of financial historians and theorists into the 1930's was remarked upon very ably by Bray Hammond, "The North's Empty Purse, 1861–1862," *American Historical Review,* LXVII (October 1961), 15.

5. Gustav Cassell, *The Downfall of the Gold Standard* (Oxford: At the Clarendon Press, 1936), pp. 7, 14, 91.

Index

INDEX

Conference of 1867, proposed at, 84
adopted by, 87
Prussia, received in, 119–24
Ruggles argues for, 136–37

San Francisco Mint, 135, 159
San Francisco Chamber of Commerce, 217
Sargent, Aaron, 156
Saulsbury, Eli, 247
Savannah Cotton Exchange, 248
Say, Leon, 62, 182, 197, 253–56
Say's Law, 26; *see also* supply and demand
"science," as rhetorical term, 23–25, 186
Schenck, Robert, 95, 110
Schumpeter, Joseph, 266
Scribner's Monthly, 217
seignorage, proposed for pound sterling, 112–13
Seven Weeks' War, 13
seventies as a watershed, 5
Seward, F. W., 82
Seward, William H., 73, 101
appoints American Commissioner General for Paris Exposition of 1867, 72
asked about American participation in Latin Monetary Union, 76
informed of Ruggles' work at 1867 Monetary Conference, 89
invited to name American representative to 1867 Monetary Conference, 81
Seyd, Ernest, 189, 196, 198
American coinage, 1871–72 views on, 153–54
as conspirator, 163–66

French monetary commission of 1868, testimony before, 117
gold-silver situation in 1876, explains, 179
Hooper contacts concerning U.S. coinage bill, 153–55
on international bimetallism, 194
International Monetary Conference of 1878, gloomy about, 255
on social effects of bimetallism, 192–93
Seyd, Ernest, Jr., 166
Sharkey, Robert P., 5, 30
Sherman, John, 75, 81–82, 92, 129, 148, 246–47, 252, 254, 266, 271
bimetallism, cautiously supports, 198
biographical sketch, 77–78
Bland bill, reports to Senate in 1877, 235
Boutwell, concurs in policies of, 141
bullionist ideologue, as, 37
Coinage Act of 1873, does not press in 1870, 138
reports to Senate in 1871, 145–47
denies in 1871 that it makes major changes, 146
urges it to protect public credit, 146–47
presents to Senate in late 1872 and early 1873, 157–60
later defends role in, 162
compromise, seeker for in 1874, 221–22
Grant destroys his efforts for, 225